FORERUNNERS OF DRAKE

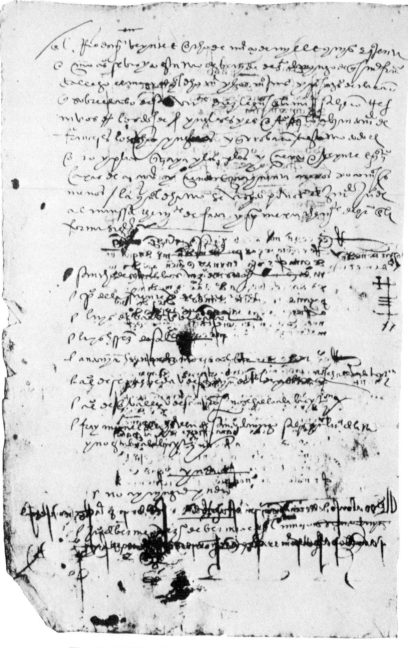

The first folio of the report on the inspection
of the *San Salvador* on 28 March, 1545

Archivo General de Indias, Contratación,
Legajo 2439, Ramo 6, No. 2.

FORERUNNERS
OF DRAKE

A Study of English trade with Spain
in the early Tudor period

GORDON
CONNELL-SMITH

PUBLISHED FOR THE ROYAL EMPIRE SOCIETY

GREENWOOD PRESS, PUBLISHERS
WESTPORT, CONNECTICUT

Library of Congress Cataloging in Publication Data

Connell-Smith, Gordon.
    Forerunners of Drake.

    Reprint of the 1954 ed. published for the Royal
Empire Society by Longmans, Green, London, New York,
which was issued as no. 21 of Royal Empire Society
imperial studies.
    Bibliography: p.
    Includes index.
    1. Great Britain--Commerce--Spain. 2. Spain--
Commerce--Great Britain. I. Title. II. Series:
Royal Commonwealth Society. Imperial studies ; no. 21.
HF3508.S7C6 1975   382'.0942'046   75-7237
ISBN 0-8371-8100-3

First published 1954 for The Royal Empire Society
by Longmans, Green and Co., London

Reprinted with the permission of The Royal Commonwealth
Society and Dr. Gordon Connell-Smith

Reprinted in 1975 by Greenwood Press,
a division of Williamhouse-Regency Inc.

Library of Congress Catalog Card Number 75-7237

ISBN 0-8371-8100-3

Printed in the United States of America

PREFACE

THIS book is concerned with merchants and their trade to Spain and the Spanish Indies in the early Tudor period—a section of the English community which, by its contact with Spain and her overseas dominions and its later resort to privateering and piracy against that same country, paved the way for the famous Elizabethan merchant seamen. I have called these men 'Forerunners of Drake', and I include in this description the early trader fully as much as the later privateer.

In substance this book is my doctoral thesis ('Anglo-Spanish trade in the early Tudor period', accepted by the University of London, 1950), revised and with some important additional material. The last three chapters formed the basis of my essay 'Forerunners of Drake', which was awarded the Julian Corbett Prize for Modern Naval History at the Institute of Historical Research, 1949. I must emphasize to my Spanish readers that this book deals primarily with English merchants and only in passing with Spaniards. One of its main purposes is to draw the attention of English historians to rich sources of material to be found in the Spanish archives, which my own researches have merely tapped.

During the preparation of this book I have received much valuable assistance and encouragement, which I acknowledge with deep gratitude. At the Institute of Historical Research, Professor J. G. Edwards, the Director, has taken a helpful interest in my researches and shown me innumerable kindnesses over a long period. Mr. A. Taylor Milne, the Secretary and Librarian, has also done everything possible to further my work. At Birbeck College I am much indebted to Professor R. R. Darlington. My biggest academic debt, however, is to Dr. Alwyn Ruddock, who supervised my researches and whose seminar on overseas trade in the Tudor period I attended during the preparation of my thesis. Her unrivalled knowledge of the important early records of the High Court of Admiralty was particularly valuable and I owe a great deal to her critical encouragement of my efforts.

My thanks are also due to the officials of the Public Record

Office, to Mr. S. R. Donaldson at the Civic Centre, Southampton, and to Mr. J. E. Willmott, the Archivist at the Drapers' Hall where I studied the ledger of Thomas Howell and made extracts from it through the courtesy of the Court of Assistants of the Drapers' Company. I have received much kindness in the Spanish archives from Sres. D. José de la Peña and D. Diego Bermúdez Camacho at the Archivo General de Indias at Seville; Sr. D. José Cervera at the Archivo de Protocolos de Sevilla; Sr. D. Juan Puebla at the Archivo de Protocolos de Cádiz; and the officials at the Archivo Histórico Nacional at Madrid. I was very fortunate in receiving expert assistance in the photographing of documents in Seville from Dr. Adele Kibre. My studies in the Spanish archives were made possible by grants from the Central Research Fund of the University of London. Sr. D. Abdón M. Salazar provided me with some useful information about Luis Vives and his acquaintance with Spanish merchants in Bruges and London and also made valuable suggestions on a number of points coming within his own field of research. I would like also to thank Mr. Denis Costello who helped me to prepare the maps and Mr. Vernon Southward who gave me much of his valuable time in reading the proofs and made a number of important suggestions and corrections. In the proof stages of the book I must pay tribute to the kindly patience of the editor of the Imperial Studies Series, Professor Vincent Harlow, and Miss G. L. Buhler, Secretary of the Imperial Studies Committee.

Finally, I owe a very special debt of gratitude to my mother and sister who suffered with so little complaint the writing of this book. To them, then, I dedicate 'Forerunners of Drake'.

GORDON CONNELL-SMITH

INSTITUTE OF HISTORICAL RESEARCH,
LONDON

CONTENTS

APPENDICES

PLATES

MAPS

LIST OF ABBREVIATIONS

Add.	*Addenda.*
Add. MS.	Additional Manuscript.
A.P.C.	*Acts of the Privy Council.*
B.M.	British Museum.
Cal. Pat. Rolls.	*Calendar of Patent Rolls.*
H.C.A.	High Court of Admiralty
K.R.	King's Remembrancer (of the Exchequer).
Letters and Papers	*Letters and Papers of the Reign of Henry VIII.*
P.C.C.	Prerogative Court of Canterbury.
P.R.O.	Public Record Office.
Spanish Calendar	*Calendar of State Papers, Spain.*
Stat.	Statute of the Realm.

INTRODUCTION

THIS study of English trade with Spain in the early Tudor period has a two-fold purpose. It attempts to give an account of the general character of the trade and its significance in the economies of England and Spain and at the same time to assess its importance in the history of Anglo-Spanish relations in the Tudor period. The commercial rivalry between England and Spain has long been recognised as a determining factor of the war in Elizabeth's reign and this book attempts to throw new light upon the significance of the earlier period in its development. Although it thus looks forward to the Age of Elizabeth, the study forms a complete story in itself. The period covered begins with the development of a flourishing commerce encouraged by the suppression of lawlessness at sea and the establishment of an alliance between England and Spain and ends with widespread privateering and piracy once again crippling peaceful trade and with unmistakable signs of the eventual end of the Anglo-Spanish alliance. The vicissitudes of the trade from the negotiation of the Treaty of Medina del Campo to the 'Reneger Incident', which virtually marks its break-down as a commercial agreement, provide the main theme of the book.

Much information about commercial relations between England and Spain in the early Tudor period is contained in the diplomatic correspondence of the reigns of Henry VII and Henry VIII. Calendared documents from the collections in the Public Record Office and British Museum have already been used to give some indication of the nature and importance of the trade in general accounts of English overseas commerce in this period by historians such as Georg Schanz[1] and Dr. J. A. Williamson[2]. These sources, inevitably inadequate, have led to a number of errors. Schanz's account of the important commercial struggle between Henry VII and the Catholic Kings, for example, has been corrected by reference to the particulars of customs.[3] Williamson's account of the ill-treatment of the English merchants by the Spanish Inquisition must be modified in the light

---

[1] *Englische Handelspolitik gegen Ende des Mittelalters.*
[2] *Maritime Enterprise, 1485–1558,* etc.   [3] *Vide infra,* p. 49.

of other evidence[1], while the significance of the formation of the Andalusia Company and its difficulties could only be assessed in the light of a detailed history of the trade. This study also reveals the complexity of the trade and the business technique of those taking part in it from new and little used sources in England and Spain.

One of the most important discoveries from the Spanish sources concerns the trade of Englishmen to the New World in this period which, since it was conducted from Spain itself, may be regarded as a branch of Anglo-Spanish trade.[2] Very little has so far been discovered about this trade, although it is known that a small number of Englishmen did take part in it. Richard Hakluyt mentions one, a certain Thomas Tison, of whom he says:

This Thomas Tison (so farre as I can conjecture) may seeme to have bene some secret factour for M. Thorne and other English marchants in those remote partes; whereby it is probable that some of our marchants had a kinde of trade to the West Indies even in those ancient times and before also: neither doe I see any reason why the Spaniards should debarre us from it at this present.[3]

Hakluyt, it is clear, believed that the trade carried on was a surreptitious affair, and it is evident that his informants of his own generation knew very little about it. He cites other Englishmen as well established in commecre with the Indies in Mary's reign, but tells us that they were married in Spain.[4] From these and other references in Hakluyt's 'Voyages' J. A. Williamson concluded that the ban against Englishmen in the New World was not complete. Certain Englishmen, he believed, were permitted by Charles V to penetrate into the New World, but these merchants had been so long resident in Spain, that, he affirmed, 'Save for the legal formality they were to most intents and purposes naturalised Spaniards. Only to that extent was Spain prepared to be liberal to Englishmen.'[5] The same author expressed his surprise that Englishmen acquiesced in this state of affairs, for there existed throughout the early Tudor period commercial treaties between England and Spain under whose terms, he believed, English merchants should have been

---

[1] *Vide infra*, pp. 100–101.
[2] Direct trade to the Canaries has not been included in this study.
[3] *The Principal Navigations*, x, p. 6.
[4] ibid., ix, pp. 338 *seq.*   [5] *The Age of Drake*, p. 50.

allowed to trade in both Spain and her colonies alike. 'It is certainly puzzling', he said, 'that the English Government is not found urging the favourable interpretation of the treaties or making any reference to them, for it is out of the question that their existence can have been overlooked.'[1] Sir Julian Corbett was of the same opinion. Both these historians have assumed that the Spanish monarchs refused to apply the terms of the treaties between England and Spain to their American colonies and that while the Anglo-Spanish friendship lasted no attempt was made by the English merchants as a whole to push their way into the Spanish possessions in the New World.[2]

It is true that little evidence of the activities of English merchants in the Indies has been found in English archives. Spanish archives, however, yield much more information on this point and documents in Seville throw entirely new light on the problem. They show that the Spaniards did not, in effect, ignore or refuse to apply the terms of the treaties between England and Spain to their New World colonies, but that in the reign of Henry VIII an open and flourishing trade to the Indies was carried on by English merchants in Spain who were far from being 'to most intents and purposes naturalised Spaniards'.

The Treaty of Medina del Campo stated that Englishmen should be free to trade in the dominions of the Spanish monarchs on the same footing as the latter's own subjects.[3] In Spain, however, from the earliest days, the American trade was closely controlled in the interests of the monarchy,[4] and there was nothing in the treaty to suggest that Englishmen should be exempted from the plethora of regulations governing the Spaniards themselves trading to the Indies. Under no treaty could the English claim direct and unregulated trade with the New World, for Spanish subjects themselves did not enjoy this privilege. Such a concession would, of course, have been quite contrary to the spirit of the time and to the Spanish conception

---

[1] Williamson, *Sir John Hawkins*, p. 88. In a more recent book, *Hawkins of Plymouth*, p. 9, Dr. Williamson still regards the Englishmen trading to the Indies from Seville in this period as especially favoured by the Emperor (the Catholic Kings are not mentioned in this connection) and the treaties as not being implemented (ibid., pp. 57 *seq.*).

[2] Corbett, *Drake and the Tudor Navy*, vol. i, p. 80. Williamson, *Sir John Hawkins*, p. 88; *The Age of Drake*, p. 13.

[3] *Vide infra*, p. 38.

[4] E. Schäfer, *El Consejo Real y Supremo de las Indias*, Tomo i, pp. 9 *seq.*

of Empire.[1] Subject, however, to the regulations of the *Casa de la Contratación* restricting all trade with the Indies to the privileged Spanish ports, English merchants were able to trade freely and openly in the New World.

Early in the reign of Henry VIII a growing number of wealthy English merchants were living in Seville on the friendliest terms with the Spaniards, employing factors, English as well as Spanish, in all parts of the Spanish dominions and conducting their business side by side with the natural subjects of the Spanish king. Far from being to most intents and purposes naturalised Spaniards, there were among them some of the most patriotic elements of the realm.[2] They were the first Englishmen to suffer for their loyalty to Henry's religious changes and when their trade was crippled as a result, they were among the first to challenge the Spaniards on the high seas.[3] Before the Reformation in England eventually led to its prohibition, however, they enjoyed a perfectly legal participation in the wealth of the Spanish Indies. Ample evidence of this is contained in the notarial documents now preserved in the *Archivo de Protocolos de Sevilla* and elsewhere in Spain.

The registers of the notaries of the Andalusian ports provide the most fruitful source of material for a study of the activities of the English merchants in Spain during this period. These registers, originally the private property of the notaries themselves, were appropriated by the Spanish government in the last century and placed together to form *archivos comunes de protocolos*. At Cadiz, where the documents are badly stored and difficult of access, the records prior to 1545 have been destroyed, a result, local officials claim, of the sack of the city in Elizabeth's reign. At San Lucar de Barrameda, so important in the history of the Andalusia Company, the papers in the *Archivo de Proto-*

---

[1] cf. E. J. Hamilton, 'The Role of Monopoly in the Overseas Expansion and Colonial Trade of Europe before 1800', in *The American Economic Review*, vol. xxxviii, no. 2 (May 1948), p. 40.

[2] It must be remembered that the question of being a good Catholic (with its implication of disloyalty to Henry VIII), which Dr. Williamson states was a necessary qualification for being allowed to trade to the Indies (*Hawkins of Plymouth*, p. 9), did not arise until a third of the sixteenth century had passed. The Catholic Englishman trading to the Indies from Seville in Philip II's reign may fitly be called disloyal to Elizabeth, but the Plymouth merchant of the earlier period had as little chance of being allowed direct trade to the Indies as his Protestant descendant (ibid., p. 67).

[3] *Vide infra*, pp. 198–199.

colos were apparently destroyed by fire in 1933.[1] It is fortunate
that there is preserved in Calle Feria in Seville a large collection
of registers of the public notaries of the city dating from the end
of the fifteenth century. These documents, well kept and easily
accessible to the student, make possible a more accurate picture
of English trade to the New World in the early Tudor period.
Charter parties, powers of attorney, obligations, ownership of
vessels plying the trade and purchase and sale of commodities
are among the papers drawn up by the public scriveners. Details
of the day to day business of the English merchants are given,
showing their relations with the Spaniards and with each other.
It is of particular interest that these documents not merely
destroy that conception of the trade which originated with
Hakluyt but disprove the actual case he mentioned. Thomas
Tison, far from being Thorne's secret factor as the great chroni-
cler of the Elizabethan voyages suggested, was one of the official
agents of English merchants in San Domingo, and his transactions are recorded in the registers of Francisco de Castellanos.[2]

The most useful English source for the technique of the Anglo-
Spanish trade in the early Tudor period is furnished by the
little used earlier records of the High Court of Admiralty.[3]
Among these files have been found charter parties and other
notarial documents drawn up in Spanish ports, bills of exchange
and detailed accounts of their transactions and adventures in
Spain by many English merchants engaged in the trade. They
contain in particular a great deal of information about the employment of factors in Spain and the powers entrusted to them
in handling their employers' business. Several detailed descrip-
tions of voyages between England and Andalusia, including all
the necessary preparations, are also to be found in these papers.
The depositions of numerous witnesses provide much informa-

---

[1] P. Barbadillo Delgado, *Historia de la Ciudad de Sanlúcar de Barrameda*,
pp. 65–66.

[2] Archivo de Protocolos de Sevilla, *Oficio* V, 1525, *Libro* I, f. 349; ibid., 1526,
Libro IV, ff. 218v, 234v etc. It has not so far been possible to trace Tison's
passage to the Indies. He is known to have been in Seville in February 1525
and in San Domingo in November 1526. The records of passages to the New
World between these two dates are far from complete. cf. *Catálogo de Pasajeros
a Indias durante los Siglos XVI, XVII y XVIII*, ed. Don Cristóbal Bermúdez
Plata, vol. i (1509–1534).

[3] cf. Alwyn A. Ruddock, 'The Earliest Records of the High Court of Admiralty (1515–1558)', in *Bulletin of the Institute of Historical Research*, vol.
xxii, no. 66 (November, 1949), p. 139.

tion about the affairs of the English merchants in Andalusia and northern Spain to supplement evidence found in the Spanish notarial records. Biographical details about some of the leading English merchants trading to Spain are also found in these depositions. The records of the High Court of Admiralty have been used extensively to illustrate the character of the Anglo-Spanish trade and to provide further information about the Andalusia Company and its members. They have also proved invaluable in illustrating the widespread English attacks upon Spanish shipping following the 'Reneger Incident' and the beginning of a new hostility towards the Spaniards on the part of the English seamen. Transcriptions of several documents in these records are included as an appendix to this volume.[1]

Further details of the technique of the trade are contained in the ledger of Thomas Howell, now preserved in the Drapers' Hall.[2] Howell was a prosperous member of the Worshipful Company of the Drapers of London in the sixteenth century, and the ledger contains an account of his property and commercial transactions from 1517 until 1528. The Drapers claim that this book is the earliest known English example of the system of double entry accounts.[3] The Rev. A. H. Johnson, who wrote a history of the company over thirty years ago, included an abstract of the ledger as an appendix to the second volume of his work.[4] Johnson's extracts provide ample evidence of the value of this document to economic historians and particularly to students of English overseas trade and cloth industry in the sixteenth century, but so far they have aroused little interest in the ledger as an historical source.[5] Thomas Howell's book is invaluable, however, for a study of Anglo-Spanish trade in the early Tudor period since he spent almost thirty years on and off in Seville and resided in the Andalusian port during

[1] *Vide infra*, Appendix B.
[2] See my article, 'The Ledger of Thomas Howell' in *The Economic History Review*, Second Series, vol. iii, no. 3, 1951, pp. 363 *seq*.
[3] This is of particular interest because Howell compiled his ledger for the most part in Spain, which has been claimed as the birthplace of double-entry. Italian examples of this type of book-keeping, however, ante-date Howell's ledger by nearly two centuries. cf. B. S. Yamey, 'Scientific Bookkeeping and the Rise of Capitalism', in *The Economic History Review*, Second Series, vol. i, nos. 2 & 3 (1949), p. 101.
[4] *The History of the Worshipful Company of the Drapers of London*, vol. 2, pp. 251 *seq*.
[5] I understand that a transcription of Howell's ledger is now being prepared with a view to editing this valuable document.

most of the period in which he compiled it. Such an account of his trade by a prosperous sixteenth-century English merchant is almost unique[1] and furnishes a far more detailed picture of this branch of English commerce than it is possible to draw from surviving particulars of customs. Thomas Howell's ledger is a record of his transactions and above all of his dealings with his agents. It is not a profit and loss account. Indeed, as is usual at this period, there is 'scant evidence of any attempts at a precise calculation of profits and capital'.[2] An accurate analysis of Howell's profits is therefore not possible.

The particulars of customs are the only possible source from which statistical data for the Anglo-Spanish trade in this period could be obtained. Yet, although these contain the names, quantities and values of commodities, the names and nationalities[3] of the merchants, dates of shipment and the names of the ships and their masters,[4] their limitations are so fundamental that no statistical survey could be made from them. Speaking of the particulars of customs as a possible source for a general survey of English overseas trade Prof. H. L. Gray declared:

. . . the results would be fragmentary. Relatively few of the port books survive, and many of those which do are injured or extend over periods briefer than a year. It would probably be impossible to reconstruct from them the trade of all English ports for any single year of the fourteenth, the fifteenth, or the sixteenth century, to say nothing of a series of years.[5]

Even were these records complete, it would be impossible to extract from them accurate figures for any one branch of English overseas commerce. With very few exceptions the accounts do not specify the ports of destination and provenance of the shipments detailed, and while experience may enable the student to identify in some cases both merchants and commodities peculiar to a branch of trade, this will be mere approximation.

---

[1] Since this book was written another ledger, kept by John Smith of Bristol and covering the years 1538–1549, has come to light. I myself have not yet seen this ledger, but Dr. Alwyn Ruddock, who has examined it, has very kindly allowed me to make use of her notes.

[2] Yamey, op. cit., p. 110.

[3] Usually only whether 'native' or 'alien' in this period.

[4] More often the masters only.

[5] *Studies in English Trade in the Fifteenth Century* (ed. E. Power and M. M. Postan), p. 321.

B

No branch of English overseas commerce presents more difficulties to the statistician or reveals more clearly the limitations of the particulars of customs than Anglo-Spanish trade in the early Tudor period. An attempt to extract it from these records has confirmed the complexity of this commerce. There is no sign of any organisation comparable with the Flanders Galleys or the Gascon wine fleets. Vessels of all sizes brought Spanish commodities into countless English ports from a variety of routes. Anglo-Spanish trade in this period cannot be separated for statistical purposes from English trade with the Low Countries, the Levant or Portugal. Even the trade with northern Spain cannot always be distinguished with confidence from that with south-western France. The development of closer commercial and political relations between Spain and the Low Countries led to an increasing flow of Anglo-Spanish trade in a triangular movement between the three countries, particularly affecting London and Southampton. Levant traders from the capital and the Hampshire port, often lading their merchandise in Spanish vessels, made shipments to Spain by this route, on which Cadiz was an important port of call. Even the Spanish trade of Bristol, which was conducted chiefly direct with Spain, cannot be separated from the Portuguese trade of the port, for most English ships sailing to Andalusia also called in at Lisbon. During the whole of this period five 'particular' accounts of Bristol—three for the reign of Henry VII and two for the reign of Henry VIII—alone of all these records specify the countries, and sometimes the ports, of destination and provenance. Taking these entries at their face value, an analysis of the Spanish trade of Bristol in these years has been attempted and is included as an appendix.[1] An attempt has been made in the text to give some indication, from the particulars of customs, of the Spanish trade of other leading English ports during the same period.

It is evident from the customs accounts and from other sources that the volume of Anglo-Spanish trade in the reigns of Henry VII and Henry VIII was relatively small compared with that of the other main branches of English overseas commerce. Spain was only one of the chief secondary markets for English cloths. But its significance in the history of Tudor England,

[1] *Vide infra*, Appendix A.

because of its intimate link with the religious and political changes of the time, was quite out of proportion to its size. It can indeed be said that without a study of this trade it is impossible to appreciate the later development of Anglo-Spanish maritime and commercial rivalry. An attempt has therefore been made to show the intimate link between Anglo-Spanish commercial and diplomatic relations throughout the period and to stress the significance of this contact between Englishmen and Spaniards in the transition from the political alliance to the eventual rivalry between the two countries.

The commercial struggle of Henry VII's reign has been recounted in detail, not only because of its bearing upon Anglo-Spanish commercial relations during the whole of the period, but for the picture it gives of Henry's commercial and financial policies. The methods of the English king can nowhere be better seen than in the negotiations for the Spanish alliance. It is of interest that an examination of the diplomatic correspondence between England and Spain from the point of view of the commercial agreements by no means confirms the general judgement of political historians upon the Anglo-Spanish treaty of 1489. The Treaty of Medina del Campo has been declared a one-sided agreement in consideration of the terms upon which Henry and the Catholic Kings agreed to wage war against France. If the clause concerned is taken at its face value, this is certainly the case and it fits in well with the 'cap in hand' attitude suitable to Henry's status among the European powers.[1] But can it be supposed that Henry ever intended to make a serious attempt to regain the French territories? On the contrary, there is every indication that he had not the slightest intention of wasting his resources upon continental schemes. He wished to make a show of war, not so much to impress the Spaniards as his own people, from whom he proceeded to raise large sums of money for the purpose. That being the case, the very impossibility of the terms was an advantage, for it would furnish an excuse for backing out of the war, which he did. Nor is Henry's alleged eagerness to accept the Spanish alliance at all cost borne out by any haste to ratify the treaty, for he de-

[1] There has been a tendency to exaggerate the strength of Ferdinand and Isabella at this stage, but, as Prof. C. H. Williams has pointed out, 'the full development of Spanish power had not really begun'. *The Making of the Tudor Despotism*, p. 45.

layed doing so until September 1490. Henry has been described as the only English monarch to make war pay. He certainly made a financial bargain in the Treaty of Medina del Campo, for not only did he obtain large sums from his own subjects on account of the French war it arranged, but the *parvenu* king forced the subjects of his new ally to pay considerably higher customs duties than before and no appeals from the Spanish monarchs could make him lower them again.[1]

The history of the trade during the reign of Henry VIII is a history of the efforts of the English merchants to retain and develop it in the face of increasing difficulties. The formation of the Andalusia Company to meet these difficulties has been studied in detail for the first time and an attempt has been made to assess the extent of the persecution of the English merchants by the Spanish Inquisition. The policy of the Holy Office in Spain in dealing with Englishmen accused of heresy in the years following the Reformation in England is shown from documents among its records in the *Archivo Histórico Nacional*. The accounts of the merchants themselves have been examined and these throw a great deal of light upon their attitude towards Henry's religious changes. The deposition of Thomas Pery is of particular interest. Among the English merchants trading to Spain (almost the only section of the English nation to be affected in this way) bitter hostility towards the Spaniards and the Roman church was already taking root in this period. These men, whose livelihood and at times even their lives were threatened by the Spanish Inquisition, would be ready to take their revenge when an occasion presented itself. Their opportunity came in the last French war of Henry VIII's reign. The defection of the Emperor in making a separate peace with France in 1544 gave the English seamen an excuse for indiscriminate attacks upon Spanish shipping. These became more frequent and much bolder after the 'Reneger Incident' and the arrest of English property in Andalusia in 1545.

The career of Robert Reneger, an ambitious Southampton merchant who became established in the trade to Spain when its most prosperous days were over, furnishes a fitting ending to a study of English trade with Spain in the early Tudor period. His plunder of a Spanish treasure ship from the Indies

[1] *Vide infra*, pp. 39 *seq.*

is at once the climax of the widespread privateering and piracy against Spanish merchantmen in the last years of Henry VIII's reign and the fore-runner of the feats of the Elizabethan sea-dogs. It struck a heavy blow at the old commercial agreements and the first in the Anglo-Spanish maritime struggle which, in spite of renewed friendship under Mary, was now becoming inevitable.

The official Spanish account of this incident is contained in documents now in the Public Record Office.[1] It is fortunate that these papers have been preserved in England, since the originals, of which they are attested copies, no longer exist in Spain. The register of Alonso de Cazalla, public notary of Seville, who issued all the available notarial documents concerned with Reneger's exploit, is missing for the first half of the year 1545. There are many entries in his later registers kept in the *Archivo de Protocolos de Sevilla*, however, which throw interesting light upon the settlement of the affair. The *Archivo General de Indias* has also yielded valuable information without which no true account of Reneger's exploit would have been possible. Information contained in the ship's register of the *San Salvador* and certain letters among the records of the *Casa de la Contratación* have corrected a number of false impressions of vital aspects of the incident conveyed by the diplomatic correspondence. The latter, which, because of the errors of the Imperial diplomats, has misled historians who have so far referred to the 'Reneger Incident', bears full testimony to its importance in Anglo-Spanish relations in the sixteenth century. The correspondence shows clearly that the diplomatic struggle over his seizure of the treasure marks the beginning of a new attitude towards Spain which was to find its full expression in Elizabeth's reign. There must already have been a growing conviction among more far-seeing Englishmen of the incompatibility of the interests of England and Spain which events in Mary's reign were soon to confirm.

Among English seamen these new sentiments were already becoming common by the end of Henry VIII's reign. Corbett said that the English seamen in Elizabeth's time were fully

---

[1] Published by the present writer in 'Roberto Reneger, Precursor de Drake' in *Anuario de Estudios Americanos*, Tomo vii, 1950, pp. 87 *seq*.

aware of Spanish weakness at sea.[1] It could hardly have been otherwise, for their fathers had already revealed it in the earlier period. The feats of the earlier generation of English seamen can be seen from the diplomatic correspondence and the records of the Privy Council. There is ample evidence in these sources of the number and scope of English depredations upon Spanish merchant shipping and the inability of the Spaniards to retaliate effectively. More vivid, however, are the depositions of English and Spanish mariners to be found in the files of the High Court of Admiralty. These records have yielded the most valuable evidence, not only of the activities of these earlier pirates and privateers, but also the new attitude of contempt for Spanish maritime power which was so marked among them.

Robert Reneger's exploit and its consequences make him an outstanding figure in this study, but he is only one of the many interesting personalities who were attracted by the Anglo-Spanish trade in the early Tudor period. The names of such important merchants as Robert and Nicholas Thorne of Bristol, Roger Barlow the geographer, Thomas Howell and other leading figures of the Drapers' Hall, William Ostriche and the pilot Henry Patmer occur frequently in this account. The contact between these leading representatives of the rising English merchant class and the trade and colonies of the foremost maritime power of the day must surely have provided much of the stimulus behind the overseas expansion of the Elizabethan Age.

---

[1] *Drake and the Tudor Navy*, vol. 1, p. 129. In spite of her overall strength Spain lacked a naval force organised specifically for the defence of the ocean routes and the coasts of her dominions and capable of swift retaliation against attacks at different points. cf. D. Manuel Fernández Alvarez, 'Orígenes de la rivalidad naval hispano-inglesa en el siglo XVI' in *Revista de Indias*. Año viii. Núms. 28–29, 1947, p. 313. 'Para defender las rutas oceánicas y los vastos dominios de ultramar, de los asaltos de sus contrarios, "no poseía la Corona Española una Armada, o sea un conjunto de naves, organizado para defender las costas, para atacar en caso preciso a los enemigos, que fuese representante del poder de la nación equivalente sobre el mar a los ejércitos permanentes" The quotation is from F. Castro y Bravo, *Las naos españolas en la carrera de las Indias*, pp. 43 *seq.*

CHAPTER I

THE CHARACTER OF THE TRADE

Two main factors contributed to the development of Anglo-Spanish trade as an important branch of English overseas commerce in the early Tudor period—the political alliance with Spain and the economic policy of the Catholic Kings. The former produced conditions favourable to the development of peaceful commerce after many years of extreme lawlessness at sea; the latter, by increasing wool exports to the Low Countries, ensured that Spain would soon become one of the chief secondary markets for English cloths. From early in their reign Ferdinand and Isabella encouraged the aggressive promotion of wool exports by the Mesta leaders, a policy which, according to Julius Klein, 'became the keynote of the commercial programme of those royal devotees of mercantilism'.[1] The most important markets for Spanish wool were in the Low Countries, where the decrease in the available quantity of English wool and the closer political ties with Spain produced increasingly advantageous conditions for the Spaniards. According to J. Finot[2] the period from 1480 to 1500 brought the greatest prosperity to the commerce between Spain and Flanders, and this is reflected in Spanish trade with England. From the Spanish point of view the latter was a branch of their trade with the Low Countries. It was largely in the hands of the big merchant families in Bruges and Antwerp who generally kept factors in London, although many wealthy Spanish merchants were also residing in the English capital at the time of Henry VII's accession.

The close links between the economies of both Spain and England with the Low Countries are of fundamental importance in a consideration of the character of English trade with Spain in this period. The Spanish wool trade was organised under the newly formed *consulado* of Burgos and the wool *flotas* sailed from the northern coast ports to Flanders. A study of the Spanish

[1] Julius Klein, *The Mesta*, p. 37.
[2] *Relations commerciales et maritimes entre la Flandre et l'Espagne au Moyen Age*, p. 224.

merchants in Bruges during the early Tudor period reveals that the vast majority were from Burgos and the northern provinces [1] and J. A. Goris noted the same thing in his study of foreign merchants in Antwerp.[2] A study of Anglo-Spanish trade in this period reveals that the majority of Spanish merchants taking part were likewise from northern Spain. At the same time an increasing proportion of the trade passed in a triangular movement between the three countries. After the accession of Charles V to the Spanish throne commercial relations between England and Spain were even more intimately connected with those with the Low Countries, although by this time Spanish trade with the latter was already declining.[3]

The importation of foreign cloths into Spain was a necessary corollary to the promotion of wool exports. An edict of the Cortes of Castile of 1462 had made concessions to the native cloth industry, ensuring that not more than two thirds of the annual clip should be exported.[4] The Catholic Kings had considered it expedient to confirm this edict, but throughout their reign the interests of the cloth industry were subordinated to those of the wool trade. Thus the importation of foreign cloths was encouraged at first and it was not until after the death of Isabella that Ferdinand made some attempt to encourage the native woollen cloth industry. In 1511 the 'ordinances of Seville' were elaborated into a code of 118 paragraphs 'specifying details on wool-washing, widths and weights of cloth, adulteration, dyeing, inspection, and the distribution of the cloth in successive stages of completion among various crafts'.[5] Foreign cloths not complying with the technical requirements of native cloths were prohibited.[6] This prohibition was not always enforced, however, although spasmodic support of the Spanish cloth industry during Charles V's reign led to the denunciation from time to time of English cloths as *paños falsos*.[7] Charles attemp-

---

[1] *Vide* L. Gilliodts-van Severen, *Cartulaire de l'ancien Consulat d'Espagne à Bruges;* D. Carmelo de Echegaray. *Indices de documentos referentes a la Historia Vasca que se contienen en los Archivos de Brujas, passim.*
[2] J. A. Goris, *Etude sur les Colonies Marchandes Méridionales (Portugais, Espagnols, Italiens) à Anvers de 1488 à 1567,* p. 57.
[3] Finot, op. cit., pp. 225 *seq.*
[4] Klein, op. cit., pp. 36–7.
[5] ibid., p. 38, n. 1.
[6] José Larraz, *La Epoca del Mercantilismo en Castilla,* p. 38.
[7] *Vide infra,* pp. 77, 128.

ted to encourage the manufacture of native cloth by limiting the annual export of wool to half the clip, but provoked such opposition from the Mesta and the merchant guild of Burgos that the old proportion was restored.[1] Thus for the greater part of the early Tudor period the Spanish woollen cloth industry was not sufficient to meet either home needs or the increasing demands of the Indies. As Prof. Carande has described the situation:

El favor que gozó la lana como exportación predilecta durante el reinado de los Reyes Católicos, el dispensado por Carlos a la industria de sus tierras nativas, más los compromisos impuestos en sus operaciones de crédito, contribuyeron a debilitar el crecimiento y entorpecer el perfeccionamiento de la industria textil en los reinos peninsulares.[2]

English cloths therefore found a ready market both in Spain and the Spanish Indies during this period.

As cloth was by far the biggest English export to Spain the encouragement of the Mesta by the Spanish monarchs was a great factor in determining the volume and importance of Anglo-Spanish trade. An analysis of the available particulars of customs of Bristol shows that in the first years of Henry VII's reign cloth exports to Spain already amounted to half the total shipped from the Gloucester port. Early in Henry VIII's reign they rose to more than 75 per cent of the total. These accounts show that cloths without grain (*panni sine grano*) predominated, though kerseys, Welsh 'straits', Welsh cloths and other less expensive varieties were exported to Spain from Bristol in smaller quantities. The ledger of Thomas Howell, a prosperous London draper living in Seville in Henry VIII's reign, provides much more detail than the customs accounts. Scarlets, Violets, 'Friars Colour', Kentish Russetts, Light Tawneys and Long Fine Blues are but a handful of the numerous varieties Howell exported to Spain. The London draper bought large quantities of unfinished cloth and had them barbed, folded, pressed, sheared

---

[1] Klein, op. cit., p. 36.

[2] 'The favour wool enjoyed as the leading export in the reign of the Catholic Kings, the concession of Charles to the industry of his native country, above all the restrictions placed upon its credit operations, contributed to weaken the growth and prevent the development of the textile industry in the peninsular kingdoms.' Ramon Carande, *Carlos V y sus Banqueros, La Vida Económica de España en una Fase de su Hegemonía, 1516–1556*, p. 111.

and dyed before being sent out, for Howell handled cloth at all stages of production. His accounts furnish ample evidence of the importance of Anglo-Spanish trade in this period as well as a wealth of information about the cloth industry.

The decline of Spanish agriculture resulting from the economic policy of the Spanish monarchs created an almost constant demand for English wheat and other foodstuffs during this period. Wheat, beans and flitches of bacon were frequent exports to Spain in addition to hake, herrings and other fish. Apart from normal demand in Spain there were a number of occasions when Charles V requested victuals for his troops in Fuenterrabia and San Sebastian, which for a number of reasons had in any case to be provisioned by sea.[1] Wheat and other cereals were clearly the most important English export to Spain after cloth. The dearth in Spain brought about a great increase in the price of wheat, especially in the 1530's[2] and the export of cereals from England became a most profitable business enterprise. It was often necessary to obtain licences for this purpose because of the needs of the home market, but less scrupulous merchants made secret shipments[3] or exported considerably more than their licences permitted.[4] Leather, in the form of tanned hides, tanned calfskins and other skins, lead, tin, pewter and carved alabaster were among other English exports to Spain.

English imports from Spain were much more varied than these exports. They included many luxuries from the south but were largely necessities. The ledger of Thomas Howell illustrates the complementary nature of the trade as far as the cloth industry was concerned, for his imports were mainly dyestuffs, mordants and the indispensable Seville oil. The latter was of vital importance to the English clothiers. A contemporary writer wistfully declared that 'England havyng the fynest woll, if it had wolle oyles, that Godd hath gevyn to Spayn and other contreys, than wolde England sette nought be Spayn'.[5] But England needed Spanish oil and during the break with Spain in 1528 it was affirmed that unless some could be obtained many clothiers in the Midlands would be forced to stop work.[6]

---

[1] *Letters and Papers of Henry VIII*, iv (1), nos. 735 etc.
[2] Carande, op. cit., p. 83.
[3] *Letters and Papers*, xv, no. 426.   [4] *Vide infra*, p. 137.
[5] *Tudor Economic Documents* (ed. Tawney and Power), vol. 3, p. 99.
[6] *Letters and Papers*, iv (2), no. 4239.

Howell's ledger shows that he paid for the cloths he exported to Spain partly in oil and dyestuffs. An analysis of the particulars of customs of Bristol indicates that alum,[1] orchil, woad (most often a re-export from southern France), resin and oil were among its chief imports after wine. Scarlet grain was also imported from Spain in smaller quantities, though more came from Portugal. Soap in different forms, including the white Castile soap and smigmates (black and white), was another important commodity from Andalusia. Spanish wines, of which many different types were produced in the basin of the Guadalquivir, had found a ready market in England ever since the loss of Gascony, although the latter still supplied considerably more wine than Spain. In Bristol some 25 per cent of the total wine imported came from Spain,[2] though in time of war with France it rose in one year to more than 75 per cent.[3] Fruits, including oranges, prunes, dates and figs, sugar, honey, marmalade, almonds, liquorice, saffron, vinegar and cinnamon were prominent among the delicacies from the south. Spanish skins and leather goods were shipped to England in considerable quantities and expensive velvets and silks for the wealthier classes. More necessary was salt for the fishing industry from the low sand dunes of south western Spain.

The most essential import from the northern Spanish ports was iron. Spanish iron was in increasing demand in England during the early Tudor period, especially in Henry VIII's reign when a more bellicose foreign policy required a plentiful supply of arms. It was also preferred to German iron for agricultural purposes on account of its flexibility.[4] Ordnance was often made in the Biscay foundries and shipped to England, the Spanish monarchs waiving the laws forbidding the exportation of arms[5] in favour of their ally. A certain Thomas Batcock was commissioned by the English government on several occasions to have guns manufactured at Fuenterrabia.[6] The customs accounts usually mention only iron or iron 'yendes', but in many cases it

[1] Although most of this alum was probably a re-export there were alum deposits in Castile. cf. Sir Charles Singer, *The Earliest Chemical Industry*, p. 81.
[2] In the accounts analysed.
[3] *Vide infra*, p. 61.
[4] J. B. Williamson, *The Foreign Commerce of England under the Tudors*, p. 23.
[5] Larraz, op. cit., p. 37.
[6] *Letters and Papers*, ii (2), no. 4108; ibid., *Add.* i (1), nos. 220 etc.

came in the form of ordnance and other manufactured iron goods. This may be seen in a letter written by a merchant's factor from Renteria to his master in Bristol on 4 August 1537. William Spratt was informed that he had been sent two guns in the *Mary Bryd* and a cable in the *Trinity* on 27 July. A third gun had been shipped in the *Saviour* of Renteria. The factor, Hugh Tipton, said he would have sent more, but the price, 30 ducats apiece, had been too dear.[1] The arrival of these three ships can be traced in the particulars of customs of Bristol. It is of great interest that not one of the guns nor the cable is specified; in each case the customer has entered a certain quantity of iron.[2] Smaller goods like nails and wool combs are named in the particulars of customs, but otherwise it is impossible to tell from these records what form the iron took which was imported into England from Spain in this period. There are also payments to Spanish merchants for ordnance, handguns and other weapons recorded in the appropriate receipts of the treasury[3] and bow-staves were also imported.[4] Spanish horses were highly prized at this time and Henry VIII frequently sought them. On one occasion the English king sent a member of his Household on a memorable journey to purchase some on his behalf.[5]

The Spanish ports frequented by English merchants in the early Tudor period may be divided conveniently into two groups, both geographically and by the commodities obtained from each—the northern Spanish ports and the Andalusian. The north coast of Spain contained a large number of ports and havens whose merchants and ships visited England and where English merchants traded. San Sebastian, Bilbao, Fuenterrabia ('Fontraby'), Pasajes ('Passage'), Portugalete, Laredo, Santander, Bermeo ('Vermewe'), Corunna ('The Groyne') and El Ferrol were the chief of these. A document entitled 'a note of all the hauens in the realme of Spaine, harbers keies creek*es* roodes and ffisher townes a longe the coste of Spaine . . .', probably compiled some time in Elizabeth's reign, gives details of the capacity of most of these ports[6]—though with what accuracy

---

[1] *Letters and Papers*, xii (2), no. 443.
[2] P.R.O., K.R. Customs, 199/3.
[3] *Letters and Papers*, i (2), nos. 1968 etc.
[4] P.R.O., K.R. Customs, 20/9, 199/1 etc.
[5] *Vide infra*, pp. 118 seq.
[6] B.M., Lansdowne MS. 171, f. 262.

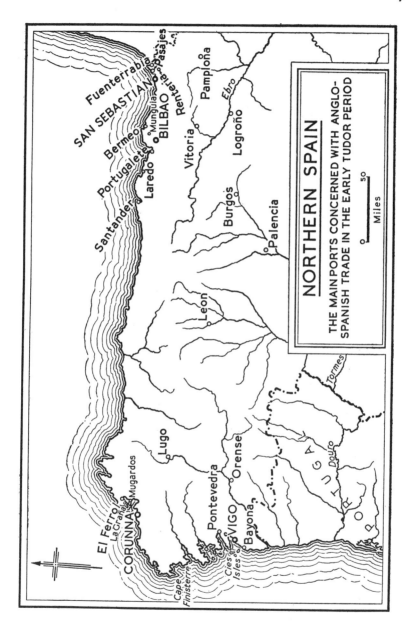

NORTHERN SPAIN

THE MAIN PORTS CONCERNED WITH ANGLO-SPANISH TRADE IN THE EARLY TUDOR PERIOD

is conjectural. There is ample evidence that a number of English merchants resided in some of the north Spanish ports. Bilbao, chief centre for the wool *flotas*, attracted many Englishmen, including Nicholas Wilford, a substantial merchant with whom the English ambassador negotiated for the payment of sums due to Wolsey from Spain in 1527,[1] Thomas Traves and John Shaa. At least two English merchants, Thomas Holland and Roger Jefferson, were married in Bilbao,[2] and John Joyce was buried there.[3] In Renteria ('The Rendry'), a small port between San Sebastian and the French frontier, lived Thomas Batcock, perhaps the best established Englishman in those parts, who was many times employed on diplomatic and commercial matters by the English government.[4] Batcock, too, may have been married in Spain, for he declared on one occasion that none of his children could write English[5] and he had a relation in the service of a member of Charles V's council.[6] English merchants almost certainly resided in San Sebastian, where several received sentences from the Inquisition for upholding Henry VIII's Supremacy.[7] Corunna and El Ferrol were usual ports of call for ships proceeding to the south and Englishmen lived[8] and died[9] there also.

English merchants were clearly better established in Andalusia than in the northern provinces. This is to be expected since the Biscayans and merchants of Burgos took a much more active part in the trade to England and the Low Countries than the Andalusians. The English were most advantageously placed in San Lucar de Barrameda, the little port at the mouth of the Guadalquivir under the suzerainty of the Dukes of Medina Sidonia. For many years before the beginning of the Tudor period the dukes had encouraged English merchants to trade in their town and granted them special privileges. The Andalusia Company had its headquarters there and an English church was built on land provided by one of the dukes for the purpose.

[1] *Letters and Papers*, iv (2), no. 3040.
[2] P.R.O., High Court of Admiralty, Examinations, 92, undated. Deposition of Christopher Vavasor.
[3] Somerset House, Prerogative Court of Canterbury Wills, F. I. Dyngeley.
[4] *Letters and Papers*, ii (2), nos. 4108, 4165, etc.
[5] ibid., ix, no. 33.
[6] ibid., xii (1), no. 873.
[7] ibid., xii (2), no. 716.
[8] *Vide infra*, p. 13.
[9] Somerset House, P.C.C. Wills, 24 Blamyr.

The earlier Bristol customs accounts confirm the popularity of San Lucar among English merchants trading to Andalusia. Seville, the first port of Castile and centre of the trade to the New World, attracted some of the wealthier English merchants. Robert Thorne, Roger Barlow and other leading Englishmen in those parts resided in Seville and sent their shipments to the Indies in the same manner as Spaniards.[1] Cadiz, the chief Andalusian port of call for Levant traders of all nations, attracted many English merchants, and if these wished to send goods to the New World they could always give powers of attorney to merchants of Seville, English or Spanish, to handle their cargoes. Port St. Mary, Port Royal, Huelva, Jerez de la Frontera, Lepe, Moguer, Palos and Trigueros were also frequented by English merchants. So were Ayamonte, where the unfortunate Thomas Pery resided,[2] Malaga and Gibraltar.

London, Southampton and Bristol were the most important English ports concerned with the Anglo-Spanish trade. London's trade to Spain, at first dominated by the Spaniards, was greater in volume than that of the other two ports and came largely in ships returning from the Levant and the Low Countries. Southampton's Spanish trade, inconsiderable before the Treaty of Medina del Campo, was greatly increased by the alliance with Spain and the closer ties between the latter and the Low Countries. Many of the leading London merchants, English, Spanish and Italian, traded through Southampton, which they used as an outport in this period.[3] Besides the London capitalists, who dominated the Levant trade, there was a group of local burgesses trading directly between England and Spain. Anglo-Spanish trade played a much bigger part in the fortunes of Bristol, where it was already an important branch of overseas commerce when the Tudor period opens. The trade of Bristol with Spain differed from that of London and Southampton in two important aspects. It was almost entirely in the hands of local merchants and was in the main conducted along the direct routes to the Spanish ports. The geographical position of Bristol was not favourable to trading with the Low Countries and the

---

[1] *Vide infra*, pp. 71 *seq.*

[2] *Vide infra*, pp. 111 *seq.*

[3] cf. Alwyn A. Ruddock, 'London Capitalists and the Decline of Southampton in the early Tudor Period', in *The Economic History Review*, Second Series, vol. ii, no. 2 (1949), p. 141.

port had little direct trade to the Levant.[1] A study of the commerce of Bristol with Spain, for these considerations and because of the greater detail provided in the particulars of customs of the port, gives a much clearer picture of Anglo-Spanish trade in the early Tudor period than is possible for London or Southampton. The connection of Bristol with Spain was of great importance in fostering the interest of her merchants in voyages of discovery. Robert and Nicholas Thorne were Bristol men and Roger Barlow, the early Tudor geographer, had Bristol connections. George Monox, one of the most prominent London drapers in Henry VIII's reign, had migrated to the capital from his native Bristol after trading from the latter to Spain in his younger days.[2] Thomas Howell was almost certainly a Bristol man; so was William Ostriche, governor of the Andalusia Company during the persecution of the English merchants in the late 1530's.[3]

Of great significance, too, was the interest of other West Country ports in the Anglo-Spanish trade. West Country piracy, 'the school of English seamen' in the fifteenth century,[4] died down under the stronger rule of the Tudors, and ships like the *Anne* of Fowey were able to ply a peaceful trade to Andalusia even when the master's name was Hawley.[5] Fowey, Ilfracombe, Truro, Barnstaple and other lesser creeks were visited by Spanish ships and sent their own vessels to Spain. Exeter, Dartmouth and Plymouth had a considerable Spanish trade, partly by way of the Low Countries but also some directly with Spain. In Plymouth, William Hawkins and members of the Horsewell family are among the English merchants trading to Spain in Henry VIII's reign; so are members of the Grisling family.[6] Hawkins himself visited Andalusia. He was master of the *Jesus* of Plymouth, for instance, when she returned to the Devonshire port with wine, oil, fruit, soap, sugar and almonds on 9 January 1526.[7] William Hurst, John Winter and John Maynard were among the leading Exeter merchants trading to Spain

---

[1] Nicholas Thorne traded to the Levant through Southampton. Southampton Municipal MSS., Brokage Book, 1542–43.
[2] P.R.O., K.R. Customs, 20/5, 20/7, 20/9, etc.
[3] *Vide infra*, p. 119.
[4] C. L. Kingsford, *Prejudice and Promise in XVth Century England*, p. 78.
[5] John Hawley was a notorious West Country pirate in the fifteenth century.
[6] cf. J. A. Williamson, *Sir John Hawkins*, pp. 20 *seq.*
[7] P.R.O., K.R. Customs, 116/6.

in the same period. When the trade was crippled at the end of Henry VIII's reign West Countrymen played a leading part in the privateering and piracy which replaced once more the peaceful trading of the earlier Tudor period.

There are few particulars of customs available for the port of Chester at this time, but there are other indications that Chester merchants traded to Spain. The arrest of a Spanish ship in Chester[1] and complaints of Chester merchants of an arrest in Spain[2] are but two recorded incidents. One of the most flagrant acts of piracy in the last French war of Henry VIII's reign was committed by West Countrymen upon a Spanish ship proceeding to Chester.[3] It is of interest that in a search among the (at present) unsorted bundles of notarial documents at Bilbao the only reference to Anglo-Spanish trade found by the present writer was the charter party of a Spanish vessel, the *Santa María de Guadalupe*, for a voyage to Chester in 1519. Ships of Hull also visited Spain[4] and shipments of Spanish goods found their way into a great many other ports and creeks of the coasts of England.

It is by no means clear how the Spanish trade was conducted from all these ports, for it was a most complex business, but there were four main routes. Ships plying between England and the Levant carried a certain proportion into London and Southampton, for they called in at Cadiz and sometimes San Lucar de Barrameda on their way from the Mediterranean as well as at Corunna and other northern Spanish ports. A larger proportion of Anglo-Spanish commerce came *via* the Low Countries, especially in the case of London, Southampton and other ports of southern and eastern England. Even the West Country ports received a part of their Spanish goods by this route. Bristol alone of the bigger ports conducted almost all of its Spanish trade direct with Spain. There were two direct routes to Spain from England. The shorter, to the north Spanish ports, could be covered in less than a week from Plymouth. Juan Martínez de Recalde, the great Biscayan admiral, spoke of a voyage from England to Bilbao which had taken nine days, however[5], and two Bristol ships, shown by a factor's letter to have left a north

---

[1] *Letters and Papers*, xx (1), no. 746.
[2] ibid., xx (2), no. 290.   [3] *Vide infra*, p. 165.
[4] *Letters and Papers*, xiii (2), no. 429.
[5] *Calendar of State Papers, Spain, 1545–46*, no. 467.

Spanish port on 27 July 1537[1] are recorded in the particulars of customs as having arrived at Bristol on 7 August.[2] Very early in the Tudor period the route from Bristol was considered a good one for the despatch of diplomatic correspondence. De Puebla, the Spanish ambassador to Henry VII, considered the voyage from Bilbao too long and bad and that Fuenterrabia and San Sebastian were the best ports from which to send letters to England.[3] On the other hand, when it came to sending Princess Katherine to England, Queen Isabella declared the shortest passage from Spain was from Corunna and that she should embark from that port.[4]

The voyage to Andalusia took much longer and there were several ports of call *en route*. Goods were sold and exchanged in the northern ports and it is evident from Thomas Howell's ledger that communication between English merchants in northern and southern Spain was maintained through the ships passing between England and Andalusia. Howell's factor in Renteria (Thomas Batcock) sent both money and goods to him in this way.[5] A large proportion of English vessels plying the Spanish trade called in at Lisbon, too, a fact which makes an analysis of the trade very difficult.[6] An interesting account of a voyage from London to Andalusia is provided by the evidence in a case brought before the Admiralty Court by a certain Richard Field against the owners of the *Erasmus* of Erith in 1537. The suit concerned the loss of nearly 200 ducats by Field's factor, Robert Harvey, on the way out. Field was one of a number of merchants freighting the *Erasmus* for a voyage to Spain in the autumn of 1536. The ship's cargo consisted of cloth and leather, Field's shipment being two packs of cloth containing 24 northern straits 'of colors', 33 white kerseys and 'a remenawnte of xij yardes of whyte kersey/ and xliiij northern dossens'.[7] In accordance with usual custom merchants could accompany their goods or send factors with them. Richard Abbis,[8] Thomas Spenser, Anthony Cornell and Philip Kever

---

[1] *Letters and Papers*, xii (2), no. 443. [2] P.R.O., K.R. Customs, 199/3.
[3] *Spanish Calendar, 1485–1509*, no. 221, p. 192. [4] ibid., no. 296.
[5] Ledger of Thomas Howell, ff. 15, 78, 79.
[6] *Vide supra*, Introduction, p. xviii.
[7] P.R.O., H.C.A., Examinations, 2, 3 July 1537.
[8] A prominent London merchant whose letters from Spain throw interesting light upon the activities of the Inquisition against the English merchants in Spain. *Vide infra*, p. 107.

were among those who sailed in the *Erasmus*. Field did not
accompany his cloths, but sent Robert Harvey, a young
Plymouth lad, to 'lerne the ffashyon and maner of those parties/
in the cowrse of marchaundise'.[1] According to the ship's purser,
Field stated, when settling his servant's board for the voyage,
that he was sending Harvey out to Spain under Thomas Pery.[2]
The latter declared in evidence that Field had 'consignyd his
said clothes / by the same byll of ladyng to be delyverd at
Groyne Loysheborne or Aymowntey,[3] to this deponent[4] and in
his absens to Robert Harvy'.[5] When the *Erasmus* put into Rye,
however, Pery left the ship and Harvey was placed in sole
charge of Field's packs of cloth.

Freed from the supervision of Pery, Harvey apparently gave
himself up to riotous living. Several of the merchants present on
the voyage declared in evidence that the young factor was constantly drunk and at various ports of call spent money lavishly
upon entertainment. The ship's fare was not to the liking of
Master Robert and every time he went ashore he brought back
wine and 'somtyme a henne or two / and somtyme a cocke'.[6]
Most of those who criticised Harvey in the Admiralty Court
admitted borrowing sums from him and some doubtless helped
him spend his money. The first ports of call after leaving
England were El Ferrol and Corunna where the *Erasmus*
arrived on 1 November. The merchants also went ashore at
Mugardos and La Graña near El Ferrol. Harvey conducted a
little business for Field at El Ferrol, and at Corunna sold
northern dozens, straits and kerseys to the value of 210 ducats.
Anthony Cornell stated that he was present in the house of a
certain Robert, an Englishman, at Corunna when Harvey made
a settlement with the customer. According to Cornell, Harvey
paid the official 10½ ducats at the rate of 5 in the 100. This is of
interest for two reasons. In the first place Corunna was one of
the northern ports where the *diezmo*, or tenth, was levied upon
imports and exports.[7] Secondly, it appears that Harvey was
able to take his gold out of the Spanish port quite easily, although
the export of bullion was forbidden.

[1] P.R.O., H.C.A., Examinations, 2, 13 October 1537.
[2] ibid., 9 May 1537.   [3] i.e. Corunna, Lisbon or Ayamonte.
[4] i.e. Pery.   [5] P.R.O., H.C.A., Examinations, 2, 3 July 1537.
[6] ibid., 2, 5 May 1537.
[7] Larraz, op. cit., p. 39.

The *Erasmus* tarried in the Galician ports for at least a month before setting out for the next stage of her voyage. Harvey placed his money in bags and put them in the care of the ship's steward. Later he transferred them to his chest which was placed in the purser's cabin. This was by no means a safe place, for there was no lock upon the door and all members of the crew had access to it. The young factor meanwhile continued his rake's progress, if the evidence is to be believed, until the ship reached Lisbon. At the Portuguese capital, where they arrived a few days before Christmas, Harvey went ashore and while he was there his ducats were stolen. The discovery of the theft was not made until the following night when Harvey suddenly wanted money to buy fish for the entertainment of some Devon men from another English ship in port. The master of the *Erasmus* called all the mariners before him on Christmas morning and questioned them on oath. He also searched their chests and those of the merchants—with no success. Upon arrival at San Lucar de Barrameda the matter was reported to James Fitzjames, 'Judge of the Englis nacyon', and evidence was heard before the consul and his deputy, Edward Lewis.[1] As a result two mariners were imprisoned, but later released. The fate of Harvey's ducats is not known. The young factor's indiscretion did not end his career as a merchant, however, for in the *Archivo de Protocolos de Sevilla* there is evidence of his transactions in Andalusia some years later.[2] He may even be the Robert Harvey mentioned in diplomatic correspondence from Spain in Elizabeth's reign.[3]

Throughout the early Tudor period Spanish ships carried a good proportion of the trade between England and Spain. At the accession of Henry VII they carried by far the greatest part of it. Even at Bristol, where local merchants made almost all the shipments, many more Spanish ships carried them than English.[4] The great majority of these ships, like many of the Spanish merchants taking part in the trade to England, were from the northern ports. Vessels of all sizes—caravels, crayers, balingers, barks and so on—both English and Spanish, seem to

---

[1] P.R.O., H.C.A., Examinations, 2, 3 July 1537.
[2] Archivo de Protocolos de Sevilla, *Oficio* XV, 1545, *Libro* II, ff. 139v, 140, etc.
[3] *Calendar of State Papers, Foreign Series, Elizabeth, 1564–65, passim.*
[4] *Vide infra*, p. 34.

have plied the Anglo-Spanish trade and it is quite impossible to
think of a typical ship or determine an 'average capacity'.
Nicholas Thorne, in a petition to Henry VIII, declared that his
ship the *Saviour*, of 250 tons, was too large for the Spanish trade
(although she was frequently employed in it) and that he had
hired her out for voyages to the Levant.[1] The *George* of London,
which made voyages to Spain and the Levant, was described
in the Admiralty Court as being of 280 tons.[2] Licences issued to
Spanish merchants to trade to England in Henry VII's reign
often mention the tonnage of their ships. The *Holy Ghost* of
Antonio de la Sola is described as of 180 tons;[3] and the *María*
of Fuenterrabia of 'John Sancius of Venesse' as of 250 tons.[4] The
accuracy of these figures, like those in the lists of the ships
serving with the King's Fleet, is dubious; at best they are a
rough guide, sometimes a deliberate falsification. Some of the
small shipments brought in by unspecified vessels[5] seem hardly
to constitute an economic proposition, but what proportion of
the ship's cargo they represented or whether they had been taken
off a larger ship can seldom be learned from the material to
hand. Even if more data were available it is doubtful if the
answer would be different. The ships were undoubtedly as varied
as the size of the cargoes and the different sources of the Spanish
commodities suggest. Clearly the Spanish trade coming *via* the
Low Countries and along the Levant route was carried in bigger
ships and the smallest vessels probably sailed between northern
Spain and ports of the West Country. It cannot be established
from the available evidence that these ships sailed either in
fleets (except for convoys in time of war) or even at any particular times, although much of the produce of Andalusia was
seasonal.

If little is known about the ships we have a great deal of
information concerning the merchants who freighted them.
Spaniards, nearly all from northern Spain, dominated the
Spanish trade of London at the beginning of the Tudor period
and had a large share of the traffic in Gascon wine and Toulouse

---

[1] *Letters and Papers, Add.* i (1), no. 812.
[2] P.R.O., H.C.A., Examinations, 4, 10 July 1539.
[3] *Spanish Calendar, 1485–1509*, no. 8.
[4] *Materials for a History of the Reign of Henry VII*, (ed. W. Campbell),
vol. 1, p. 251.
[5] In many cases only the name of the master is given.

woad.[1] At this time there were a number of very wealthy Spanish merchants residing in the English capital and some of them also traded through Southampton in the same manner as the native London capitalists.[2] The majority of these were members or representatives of the leading Spanish merchant houses of Burgos and Bruges, with branches at Rouen, Bordeaux and other commercial centres of Europe. Such were Diego de Castro, who, according to Roger Machado, arranged the lodging of Richard Nanfan and Dr. Savage in Burgos on their way to conclude the marriage treaty between Henry VII and the Catholic Kings;[3] Diego de Soria, prime mover in the foundation of the *consulado* of Burgos in 1494[4] and frequently employed in diplomatic affairs;[5] and Pedro de Salamanca, one of the consuls of the Spanish nation at Bruges.[6] It would appear that for the greater part of this period the Spanish merchants were subject to their consuls in the Low Countries where the Castilians and the Biscayans had their separate 'nations'. At Henry VII's accession there is reference to a 'procuratour and attourney' of the Biscayans[7] but no evidence that he resided in England, while later on the Spanish ambassador, himself perhaps something of a merchant and apparently heartily disliked by his compatriots, was *de facto* consul over the subjects of Ferdinand and Isabella in England.[8] Closer political ties between Spain and both England and the Low Countries brought an increase in the number of Spanish merchants in England in the years following the Treaty of Medina del Campo, but their number dwindled in the new century until Chapuys, the Imperial ambassador, declared in December 1540 that there were only six of his master's subjects residing as merchants in London.[9] The decline of Spanish trade with the Low Countries drew an increasing number of wealthy Spaniards away from England, especially since the aggressive commercial policy of Henry VII had undermined their favoured position there. The difficulties following the English Reformation and the decline of the trade

---

[1] *Vide infra*, pp. 33, 37, 40.   [2] *Vide infra*, p. 33.
[3] *Memorials of King Henry the Seventh* (ed. J. Gairdner), p. 335.
[4] Gilliodts-van Severen, op. cit., pp. 125 etc.
[5] *Vide Spanish Calendar, 1485–1509*, nos. 98, 117.
[6] Gilliodts-van Severen, op. cit., p. 220.
[7] *Vide infra*, p. 32.
[8] *Vide infra*, p. 47.
[9] *Spanish Calendar, 1538–42*, no. 144, p. 301.

in the last years of Henry VIII's reign also contributed to the diminishing participation of the Spaniards in the Anglo-Spanish trade.

A number of leading Spanish merchants prominent in the Anglo-Spanish trade took out denization papers in the 1530's when the Spaniards in London were apprehensive for their future.[1] Among them were Alvaro de Medina,[2] Juan de Orduña[3] and Alvaro de Astudillo,[4] shown by the particulars of customs of the capital to have been among the biggest traders to Spain in these years.[5] Alvaro de Astudillo, who made arrangements for John Mason's credit in Spain during his projected visit in 1540,[6] traded through other English ports[7] and both he and Juan de Orduña also purchased licences to import Toulouse woad.[8] It is of interest that Juan de Orduña was mortally wounded in London by Juan de Carrión, servant of Alvaro de Astudillo.[9] A copy of his will is preserved in Somerset House.[10] A letter from the Council to the lord mayor of London in January 1541 ordered him to forbear levying a subsidy upon Alvaro de Astudillo, Antonio Jamis, Antonio de Mazuelos and Felipe de Aranda.[11] The last named three may also have taken out papers of denization. Antonio Guarras, the probable author of the *Spanish Chronicle*,[12] who later fulfilled the function of Spanish ambassador for a time in Elizabeth's reign, was another of the few prominent Spaniards still residing in London at the end of Henry VIII's reign.

Living among the Spanish merchants in London during the reign of Henry VIII and himself almost certainly taking part in trade was the famous Spanish humanist, Juan Luis Vives.

---

[1] *Vide infra*, p. 102.
[2] *Letters and Papers*, v, no. 364.
[3] ibid., vi, no. 929.
[4] ibid., v, no. 766. These three merchants appear in the references as Alvarez de Medina, John de Herdunna and Alvarus de Astodillo. Throughout the book I have given correct Spanish names where I have been able to establish them. Many have been distorted beyond recognition by the English writers and these I have left as they appear in the documents. In some cases I have put doubtful and possible originals in footnotes.
[5] P.R.O., K.R. Customs, 82/8, etc.
[6] *Letters and Papers*, xvi, no. 493. *Vide infra*, p. 126.
[7] P.R.O., K.R. Customs, 36/7, etc.
[8] *Letters and Papers*, v, nos. 978, 1065.
[9] ibid., xiv (2), no. 435.
[10] Somerset House, P.C.C. Wills, 31 Dyngeley.
[11] *Proceedings and Ordinances of the Privy Council*, vol. vii, p. 109.
[12] According to Martin Hume. cf. *Spanish Calendar, 1545–46*, p. 117, fn.

Vives had married the daughter of Bernardo Valdaura, a Valencian merchant established in Bruges, one of whose letters to De Puebla, the Spanish ambassador in England, is among the diplomatic correspondence calendared by Bergenroth.[1] Vives traded in Bruges and acted as arbitrator in mercantile cases. In 1525 he received licences from Henry VIII to import Gascon wine and Toulouse woad and to export corn.[2] He shared lodgings in London with Alvaro de Castro, a member of the prominent Burgos merchant family, for whom he began to write his dissertation upon matrimony. Diego de Astudillo and Diego Ortega de Burgos, two fellow merchants in England, translated some of Vives' works.[3]

Although London attracted the great majority of Spanish merchants in England in the early Tudor period some resided in other parts of the country, occasionally, perhaps, as agents of the others. Fernando de Ibarra, for example, had been married and settled in Chester for fifteen years when he was imprisoned by the mayor in 1535 for selling certain cloths in the open market in contravention of the city charters. According to the local authorities Fernando rode about the country buying up cloth for foreign merchants which used to be bought by merchants of Chester.[4] More often in all probability the Spaniards employed Englishmen to purchase cloths for them. Diego de Astudillo, for example, had a factor named George Aytonale at Norwich.[5] Several leading Spanish merchants in England, including Pedro de Miranda and Alonso de Cisneros, performed services for Henry VII in the garrisons of Calais and Berwick.[6] Others were concerned in supplying ordnance and arms to Henry VIII.[7]

A more detailed study has been made of the English merchants in Spain. Documents in the *Archivos de Protocolos de Sevilla y Cádiz* provide ample evidence of the business enterprise of the English in Andalusia in this period. The important status of Robert Thorne, who, according to the English ambassador, was held in high esteem in Spain,[8] is clearly to be

---

[1] *Spanish Calendar, 1485–1509*, no. 225.
[2] *Letters and Papers*, iv (1), nos. 1293, 1298.
[3] I am indebted for much of my information about Vives to Sñr. Don Abdón M. Salazar.
[4] *Letters and Papers*, ix, no. 794.   [5] ibid., xvii, no. 670.
[6] *Spanish Calendar, 1485–1509*, nos. 84, 88, 230.
[7] *Letters and Papers*, i (1), nos. 1420, 1463; ibid., i (2), nos, 1968, etc.
[8] ibid., iv (1), no. 2095, p. 940.

seen from the number and content of the documents he had attested before Francisco de Castellanos, one of the leading notaries of Seville. One of these shows that Thorne and Thomas Malliard, a leading London merchant,[1] were partners of a Seville banker and an Italian in a soap factory doing business in Seville, Cadiz, and Ayamonte.[2] Among English merchants owing money to Malliard on account of transactions in soap it is of interest to find William Ostriche, already in 1523 trading in San Lucar de Barrameda.[3] Robert Thorne gave powers of attorney to numerous Spaniards to attend to his business in other parts of Andalusia. Thorne also acted on behalf of Paul Withypoll, his old master,[4] but later delegated his power to act on Withypoll's behalf to Thomas Tison.[5] Much of the business of Roger Barlow, a close friend of Thorne's, is also recorded in the papers of the same notary and there is ample evidence of their trade— and that of other English merchants—to the Indies.[6] Leading London merchants whose affairs are mentioned in these papers include Richard Reynolds, Francis Bawdwyn, Andrew Woodcock and Thomas Howell.

In the notarial records of Cadiz the name of John Sweeting, sometime deputy governor of the Andalusia Company, occurs as frequently as that of Robert Thorne in Seville. It also occurs in the Seville records. Reference is made to a John Sweeting of Cadiz, then deceased, in a document in which Robert Thorne, as his executor, is shown engaged in settling his affairs.[7] Perhaps this Sweeting was the father of the later deputy governor. The latter had a younger brother, signing himself 'John Sweeting the Younger', living in Seville whom he employed to handle his cargoes from the Indies.[8] There is an interesting notarial document referring to the theft of 300 ducats belonging to the Cadiz Sweeting during a stay at his brother's house in Seville. Hugh Tipton, later governor of the Andalusia Company and benefactor of some of John Hawkins' men taken prisoner at San Juan de Ulua,[9] was another guest in the house. Tipton lost a

---

[1] *Vide infra*, pp. 20, 67, etc.
[2] Archivo de Protocolos de Sevilla, *Oficio* V, 1523, *Libro* III, f. 93.
[3] ibid., f. 120v.   [4] Somerset House, P.C.C. Wills, 18 Thower.
[5] *Vide infra*, Appendix C, p. 229.
[6] *Vide infra*, pp. 71, *seq.*
[7] Archivo de Protocolos de Sevilla, *Oficio* V, 1523, *Libro* III, f. 81v.
[8] ibid., *Oficio* XV, 1545, *Libro* II, f. 68v.
[9] *Calendar of State Papers, Foreign Series, Elizabeth, 1569–71*, no. 711.

silver cup which was subsequently recovered at Jerez and Sweeting gave powers of attorney to two Spaniards to recover his property in the same place.[1] Another document of special interest is a power of attorney given by George Masters of San Lucar de Barrameda to his wife Juana de Perreta.[2] Spanish wives of English merchants seem to have carried on business for their husbands in the same way as English women. There is even record in Seville of an Englishman's Spanish mother-in-law acting on his behalf.[3] The list of Spanish merchants despoiled by Robert Reneger in 1545 also contains the names of several women.[4]

A more detailed picture of an English merchant's Spanish trade is contained in the ledger of Thomas Howell.[5] Howell, who lived in the district of Santa María in Seville, had agents in England, northern Spain, Andalusia and Hispaniola. He was thus concerned in all three branches of Anglo-Spanish trade, the Biscayan and Andalusian in Spain itself and the New World through the privileged port of Seville. The merchants employed by him as factors in Spain are themselves interesting figures in the history of the trade during the early Tudor period, while many of the leading English merchants in those parts are shown by the ledger to have had business dealings with Howell. Thomas Malliard, Howell's factor in Seville, was one of the first Englishmen to take part in the trade to the Indies, and records of his business are contained in the registers of the public notaries of the city in the early years of Henry VIII's reign.[6] Soap and oil were the chief commodities Malliard bought for Howell with the proceeds from the sale of his cloth. It appears that on at least one occasion he tried to defraud the draper. On 13 May 1521 Malliard charged Howell 1200 *maravedís* per quintal for white soap which he had laden on the ship of a certain Walter Tomson. But, Howell admonished him, 'yt cost yow but 960 *maravedís* the kyntall as be yor ownne boke dothe apere and as I cann prove off the marchaunt ye bowght yt off'.[7] Reference is made in the same month to the purchase of 100 ducats' worth of soap in

---

[1] Archivo de Protocolos de Cádiz, *Oficio* XIX, 1547, f. 270.
[2] ibid., f. 306.
[3] Archivo de Protocolos de Sevilla, *Oficio* XV, 1540, ff. 439v, 453 v.
[4] *Vide infra*, Appendix D, p. 241.
[5] *Vide supra*, Introduction, p. xvi.
[6] *Vide infra*, p. 71.
[7] Ledger of Thomas Howell, f. 13v.

Seville which had been sold subsequently in London at 20s. 'the hundred', showing a profit of 18 ducats or just over £4.[1] If the cost had been 240 *maravedís* per quintal less than Malliard had stated, however, Howell's eventual profit was over £8 10s. It is of interest that, although he most often records his transactions in ducats or *maravedís*, Howell converts them into sterling in his columns his rates for conversion being 375 *maravedís* to the ducat and 1,000 to 12 shillings sterling. The ducat he reckoned to be worth approximately 4s. 6d. and the silver *real* 5d.

Thomas Bedforth handled similar cargoes on Howell's behalf at Cadiz. From his account we gain details of the purchase and lading of oil. Four tuns 'clere abord' the vessel taking them to England cost Howell 42,290 *maravedís* or about £25 7s. 6d.[2] Twelve tuns of oil bought for 138,996 *maravedís* (£83 8s.) cost 12,000 *maravedís* (£7 4s.) to get aboard ship.[3] Freight charges, English customs duties and services on their arrival in England would be paid for by Howell's agent there. According to the ledger Howell usually sold oil in England at £12 or more per tun.[4] The draper also employed a Spanish broker, Alonso de la Lonja of Seville, to conduct his business in Andalusia. The following entry in his ledger, also concerned with oil, is of interest:

Alonso de la Longe / coredor / de la loja de Sevilla[5] owzt to geve a cashe / for dobill ducattes of gold I delyverd yow in Sevill at my departyng from Sevill / as it apereth be yow recado / fowre thowsand sevyn honderd *and* fyfte ducattes sengill in / iijmᵗccclxxv / dubill ducattes *wech* amou*nt* starlyng after vs the ducatt / mᵗclxxxvij li xs / the for said ducattes be my comysho*n* to be bestowid in oyllis and to be put in iij almazens [6] in Calle de Cozenos in Sevill of the wech almazens I have paid for the rent / for ij yere wech cost me litill more or les / c ducattes / so it amou*nt* al starlyng / 1192 : 10. / – li. mᵗclxxxxij s x d -.[7]

This large sum gives a good indication of the prosperity of the

---

[1] Howell's ledger, f. 13v.
[2] ibid., f. 14.
[3] ibid.
[4] ibid., ff. 2v, etc.
[5] A broker of the Seville Exchange. At this time the *Casa Lonja* had not been built and the merchants probably used the Cathedral. cf. C. H. Haring, *Trade and Navigation between Spain and the Indies*, p. 325.
[6] Warehouses.
[7] Howell's ledger, f. 65v.

London merchant and of the importance of Seville oil in the Anglo-Spanish trade.

In northern Spain Howell's business was conducted by Thomas Batcock. Iron was by far the most important commodity Batcock shipped to England on Howell's behalf. His account reveals that he bought it at prices ranging from approximately £3 10s. to £4 10s. per ton 'clere abord' ship[1] and that it was sold in England at prices up to £6 per ton.[2] Batcock also purchased woad in smaller quantities, usually, like iron, 'in trocke of cloth'.[3] He maintained communication with Howell by the English ships calling in at the Biscayan ports on their way to Andalusia and sent goods and money by this route.[4]

Robert Lesse, another London draper, was Howell's factor in England. Lesse took possession of the cargoes from Andalusia and Biscay arriving in London and shipped the cloths he bought for Howell from the capital. Sometimes there would be a dispute over the amount of goods or their condition on arrival in port. An entry on 21 January 1525 illustrates the responsibility of the ship's purser, on behalf of the owner, for the goods on his ship until their safe delivery to the consignees:

The same day for a flaskett / that Robert Lisse made the porser pay for wech was lost / for the xv ton in the Crist above wretty*n* owzt to be / xxj li vij s vj d but for this flaskett was batted[5] xxxvj s - li i s xvj d-.[6]

There was an intimate connection between the goods Lesse received from Andalusia and those he shipped out there, for the clothiers and cloth finishers with whom Howell dealt were paid partly in alum, woad, grain and other Spanish commodities necessary to the home industry. The complementary nature of Howell's Andalusian trade is one of its main features, for he seems to have dealt very little in wine, fruits and other produce of southern Spain. His trade with Biscay was almost exclusively in iron, for Spanish iron was in great demand as long as Henry VIII was determined to take an active part in the Hapsburg-Valois struggle. The commerce with Spain, as illustrated by

[1] Howell's ledger, ff. 77v–82.
[2] ibid., f. 82v.
[3] This makes an analysis of prices and profits very difficult indeed.
[4] Howell's ledger, ff. 15, 78, 79.
[5] i.e. rebated.
[6] Howell's ledger, f. 53v.

Howell's ledger, was thus in necessities and not a luxury trade.

Howell's wife, Joanna, seems to have been in England during the greater part of the period covered by the ledger and Lesse paid to her from time to time the money he obtained from the sale of her husband's goods. The most common entry on the credit side of Lesse's account is a payment to 'my wyfe be taylle'. Lesse employed brokers at Howell's expense to make the sales, as the other agents did, and the main responsibility of the factors was shipping and unlading Howell's goods and keeping records of transactions made on his behalf.

Howell's relationship with the men conducting his business is of great importance. He describes them all as 'my factor', a term which might seem to imply that he had the exclusive use of their services, but this was certainly not so. Lesse, Malliard, Batcock and Bedforth were all merchants on their own account. Their relationship with Howell was known in Spain as a *compañia*, a term loosely applied at this time to a wide variety of business partnerships.[1] Howell's factors were, in effect, commission agents; indeed, the ledger tells us that their 'provishon', as Howell called it, was usually $2\frac{1}{2}$ per cent.[2] The employment of commission agents seems to have been a common practice of the merchants conducting business with Spain in the early Tudor period, although there is record of prosperous English merchants sending their sons[3] and even promising young men of little experience[4] to Spain as factors. It was obviously more advantageous to employ established merchants with experience of Spanish business methods and good connections in Spain to handle merchandise on a commission basis. A number of cases in the High Court of Admiralty concerned with this very question show that many of the English in Spain handled the goods of other merchants as well as their own.[5] The notarial records in Spain bear out the statements made in the English sources. An aggravation of the difficulties caused to the English merchants by the activities of the Spanish Inquisition in the late 1530's was the confiscation of all goods in the possession of any one of

[1] cf. André Sayous, 'Partnerships in the Trade between Spain and America and also in the Spanish Colonies in the Sixteenth Century', in *Journal of Economic and Business History*, vol. i, no. 2 (Feb. 1929), p. 282.
[2] Howell's ledger, ff. 78, 79, etc.
[3] *Vide infra*, p. 25.
[4] *Vide supra*, p. 13.
[5] e.g. the case of *Austin and others v Castelyn*. *Vide infra*, p. 25.

them arrested on a charge of heresy.[1] Many more merchants were thus affected than those remaining in Spain during that difficult period.

Another important branch of Howell's trade in Spain was with the Indies. In common with most of the wealthy English merchants in Seville Howell traded to the New World in accordance with the privileges granted to Englishmen by the treaties between England and Spain. The *Archivo de Protocolos de Sevilla,* in which there are numerous references to Howell's transactions,[2] contains a great deal of evidence of this trade, but in his ledger is to be found the only record of an Englishman sending goods to America in this period so far discovered in an English source. An entry on 20 August 1527 reads:

The saide day for a recaudo of John de Morsyns my factor in to the Indias into Isla de San Domyngo for sartene stofe that I sent with hym as be the recaudo playnly dothe apere to the some of 200/ ducattes amount – 1 li.[3]

'John de Morsyns' was doubtless a commission agent and the terms of the *compañia* similar to many others drawn up for English merchants by the notaries of Seville.[4] The 'sartene stofe' probably consisted chiefly of cloths which had a prominent place among the exports of the English merchants in Seville to the New World. Howell had another Spanish agent, Pedro del Campo of Medina del Campo, who conducted his business at the great fairs. Howell stated in his will that Pedro owed him more than 9,000,000 *maravedis* for various transactions and bequeathed him 500 ducats. The draper's will also gives us information about his residence in Seville. He rented a house from a certain Juan Pérez de las Cuentas with the consent of someone whom he called 'My Lady Donna Maria'. The lease had not expired at his death.[5] There is evidence of English merchants in Spain residing in their own establishments, but whether they rented them or bought them is not known. Thomas Pery alone of the leading merchants is known to have dwelt with a Spanish host.[6]

---

[1] P.R.O., State Papers, Henry VIII, vol. 161, ff. 76–78.
[2] Archivo de Protocolos de Sevilla, *Oficio* V, 1525, *Libro* I, ff. 390, 607, 617v, etc.
[3] Howell's ledger, f. 65v.   [4] *Vide infra,* pp. 72 *seq.*
[5] Somerset House, P.C.C. Wills, 24 Alen.
[6] *Vide infra,* p. 112.

Details of other aspects of the business methods of the English merchants in Spain are contained in the evidence given before the Admiralty Court in the case of *Austin and others v Castelyn*. The suit concerns the repayment of money borrowed by James Castelyn on behalf of his brother William, a prominent London merchant, to fit out the latter's ship, the *George*, for a voyage between Spain and England. An original copy of the charter party for the voyage (in Spanish) was produced in the Admiralty Court[1] and also an English translation.[2] It was drawn up in the form of a notarial instrument in the 'howse of awdience publique' at Cadiz on 5 January 1538 by Luis Vivián, public notary of the city. The chief signatories were James Castelyn, the ship's captain, and Philip Barnes, son and factor in Spain of George Barnes, citizen and haberdasher of London. Barnes, as 'cape merchant' or chief merchant freighting the *George*, was to lade two hundred butts of wine at Port St. Mary within eighteen days of the agreement. Then the ship was to proceed to the bay of Cadiz to complete her lading with the remainder of Barnes' goods. If at the time of her departure from Port St. Mary the weather was too bad for lading at Cadiz it should be completed at the more sheltered harbour of Port Royal. Within six weeks from 6 January 1538 Castelyn was bound to set sail for London 'wher owght to be her ryght dyscharge of the sayd shippe' where the cargo should be delivered to the merchants named in the bills of lading.

Castelyn was to receive six ducats of gold and one English shilling for every ton freighted by Barnes and these charges were to be paid within eight days of the delivery of the merchandise. Castelyn was also to receive two and a half *reals* per ton average charges as soon as he had signed the bills of lading. He agreed to provide thirty-two hands to man the ship, four gunners and a competent pilot, and promised the ship should be equipped in every way for such a voyage. For his part, Barnes agreed to Castelyn's terms of lading and payment and bound himself to pay the full freight charges even if he failed to lade the ship to capacity. Each agreed to pay the other two hundred ducats by way of compensation if he broke the agreement, Castelyn pledging the ship, her fittings and the freight charges as his surety and

[1] P.R.O., H.C.A., Libels, etc., 6, ff. 19–21v. *Vide infra*, Appendix B, p. 215.
[2] ibid., ff. 17–18v. *Vide infra*, Appendix B, p. 219.

Barnes the cargo. At the foot of the charter party other merchants, including John Sweeting, recorded their agreement to
lade merchandise totalling eighty-six tons in the *George*. This
was in accordance with the customary practice whereby one
merchant, known as the 'cape merchant', would undertake to
freight the full capacity of a ship but occupy only a part of the
cargo space with his own goods and let out the remainder to
other merchants.

Shortly after the charter party had been signed James
Castelyn found it necessary to raise money among the English
merchants dwelling in Andalusia. Thomas Pery lent some of his
own money; John Sweeting and six others lent him money or
goods belonging to merchants in England for whom they were
conducting business in those parts. Some of these may have
been full time factors like Philip Barnes, but others, like John
Sweeting, were merchants in their own right handling other
merchants' goods on a commission basis. In all these transactions James Castelyn was acting as the attorney of his brother
William and bound the latter, his ship and possessions as security
for the repayment of these sums. He raised the money by bills
of exchange, and both the powers of factors to deliver and receive money by exchange and the obligations undertaken in
those bills were debated at length in the High Court of Admiralty. The records of this case thus provide a great deal of
information about business procedure in the Anglo-Spanish
trade.

Several witnesses of long experience of the trade to Spain,
the Levant and other foreign parts gave evidence. Thomas Pery
declared that any captain, master or purser could bind the owner,
his ship, fittings and freight charges and any factor his master
and goods for any money they took up by exchange or otherwise 'withe owte specyall power gevon vnto any such capytayne
master / purser / or factor / by ther owners or masters'.[1] All the
other witnesses agreed, however, that such representatives of
shipowners or merchants should have special powers delegated
to them if they were to issue bills of exchange binding upon
their masters. In effect, as a certain Richard Grey asserted, no
merchant of experience would deliver money by exchange or

---

[1] P.R.O., H.C.A., Examinations, 92, undated. The above quotation is
underlined in the original.

receive any obligations from a ship's captain or merchant's factor unless these had the necessary power to issue such bills and obligations.[1] When the owner of a ship did not sail with her on a voyage it was customary for him to appoint as his attorney either the captain, master or purser, or perhaps all three together or severally. Then, in the event of the ship sustaining loss of equipment or requiring victuals or should money be needed for some other purpose, his attorney could (if his powers were sufficient) raise money by exchange, binding the ship and her owner for repayment. Merchants' factors proceeding to conduct their masters' business in foreign countries were granted like powers. In this particular case James Castelyn had received the necessary authority to raise money by exchange and the merchants' factors to deliver it. Many similar powers are contained in the notarial records of Seville and Cadiz.

In all the obligations James Castelyn acknowledges that he has received in Spain a certain sum of money in ducats towards the fitting out of his ship and promises to repay the same amount in English money upon the safe arrival of the *George* in London. The merchants delivering the money were also bearing the risks of the voyage and would be repaid only on the safe arrival of the ship at its port of 'right discharge', viz London.[2] In return for 'bearing the adventure' they were to receive a high rate of interest on their money. As one witness said, 'the same marchauntes shuld receave more money then they delyverd to James Castelyn incase they do recover the somes demawnded / for he saythe that trate of marchauntes is to receave xx duckettes in the hundryd more then they delyver / from Cadiz to London / because they bere thadventure of the money delyverd'.[3] Thomas Chamber, for instance, declared he delivered 100 ducats (£25) to Castelyn to be paid £31 5s. by exchange according to the bill.[4] So it was in all the bills, whether money or goods were delivered.

The *George* did not reach London, however, She was clearly unseaworthy from the beginning and after a hazardous voyage as far as Cape Finisterre it was agreed to make for the Azores. As she was unable to continue to London, Castelyn was forced

[1] P.R.O., H.C.A., Examinations, 4, 19 June 1539.
[2] ibid., Libels, etc., 6, f. 28.
[3] ibid., Examinations, 3, 8 February 1538.
[4] ibid., 14 February 1538. *Vide infra*, Appendix B, p. 222.

to allow the merchants to discharge their goods at Ponta Delgada and accept half the freight charges for the full voyage in order to pay the mariners. From Castelyn's point of view it would have been preferable that the ship and cargo became a total loss, but some of the merchants who had freighted her were on board and forced a 'right discharge' in the Azores. In his obligations Castelyn had specified that even if the *George* should change her course and not go to London his creditors should be paid as agreed. The question of 'right discharge' was of particular importance when long sea-voyages were relatively precarious undertakings. A bill of assurance, dated 16 May 1523, unfortunately incomplete, gives a good indication of the hazards of the Anglo-Spanish trade:

The saide marchauntes assurers doo assure make warantyse and warantith all the saide goodis and marchaundises laden in the saide ship from alle maner of daungiers of the see of the ffyre wynde tempest reprysayle detaynyng / or witholdyng of eny kyng or kynges/ lorde or lordys/ capytayn / or capytaynes or eny of their subiectes or of any other person or persons beyng enymyes or pyrattes what estate or degree so ever they be of also the sayd assurers assuren and warraunten all the sayd goodes *and* marchaundysys for all *and* all manner falshedes untruthes or mysordres of the mayster owner or marynars and of all other maner of chaunces mysfortunes pyracis and daungiers whatsoever that shall happen or may falle vnto the saide ship goodis and marchaundises in any maner of wyse and therunto the saide assurers by thise presentes byndith theim to take the hole aventure of all the saide goodis and marchaundises vntill suche tyme the saide goodis and marchaundises shalbe arryved and sau elye discharged uppon the land in Portegalet Bilbo Alleredo or in oon of theym.[1]

It is greatly to be regretted that the terms upon which the 'marchauntes assurers' issued this comprehensive policy have not survived.

Further details of voyages to Spain are revealed in other cases before the Admiralty Court in the latter years of Henry VIII's reign. That of *Dolphin v Parker* tells of the storage of Malaga raisins arriving in Bristol 'unmerchantable'.[2] A suit concerning Nicholas Thorne's ship, the *Saviour*, shows the re-

---

[1] P.R.O., State Papers, Henry VIII, vol. 27, f. 281.
[2] P.R.O., H.C.A., Examinations, 2, 3, *passim*.

sponsibility of the purser for delivering merchants' goods at the port of discharge. Robert Hunt, a tallow chandler, sued Thomas Dale, purser of the *Saviour*, for failure to deliver his ten barrels of tunny fish transported from San Lucar de Barrameda to London. The plaintiff declared he had not received the letter informing him of the despatch of the fish and so had failed to collect it from the quayside. According to Hunt it was customary for the merchant or factor lading goods aboard ship to send:

by the saied shippe / as by the purser of the same, takyng chardge of suche goodes and marchaundis*es*, *lette*res directed to the parson to whome suche goodes be consigned *with* superscription vppon the same *lette*res, declaryng the name of the parson vnto whome suche *lette*res be directed / and specifieng what goodes and marchavndis*es* the consignaunte hathe in the saied shippe / and . . . by vse and custome, the master and purser of such shippe, do enter in the custome house at tharryvall of ev*er*y shippe, the name of the same shippe, w*ith* the nomber of tonnes of all the goodes ladon therein / accordyng to his booke of ladyng, and . . . suche *lette*res be often tymes delyv*er*yd to marchauntes in Lumberte Streate, and yf the m*ar*chaunte and o*w*ner of goodes be not there, then the purser, ys bounde by the saied custome to delyv*er* the saied *lette*res / at the m*ar*chauntes house, to whome they be directed . . . but at some tymes the ship comithe w*ith*oute *lette*res and the m*ar*chaunte certified by *lette*res sente by lande or by other shippes / and yet nev*er*thelesse, allthough there come no suche *lette*res at all, the purser ys bounde to delyv*er* every m*ar*chaunte his good*es* accordyng to his booke and bill*es* of ladyng, made betwene the marchaunte lader and the purser.[1]

Another question raised in this case was the price of tunny fish. Thomas Pery, a witness in so many of these suits, declared it was worth at least 23s. 4d. a barrel. He himself would gladly give that sum for it, since his wife sold tunny on his behalf at 28s. a barrel.[2] Henry Gardiner, a London fishmonger, said he sold tunny at 4d. the pound, which gave him a return of 33s. 4d. for a barrel.[3] Other Admiralty cases give some evidence of prices of the commodities in this trade. Seville oil, quoted at £24–£26 per tun in Edward VI's reign,[4] shows the great rise in price since Howell sold it for £12 per tun a generation earlier.[5] The sale of

[1] P.R.O., H.C.A., Examinations, 92, 22 November 1543.
[2] ibid., 28 May 1543.   [3] ibid., 14 June 1543.
[4] ibid., 6, *passim.* Case of *Wigmore v Worland.*
[5] *Vide supra,* p. 21.

wheat to Spaniards at 16s. a quarter around the year 1547[1] likewise illustrates the great increase in the price of wheat in Spain.[2] Such information is insufficient, however, from which to compile a list of prices or profits made in the Anglo-Spanish trade. Even Howell's ledger is inadequate for that purpose.[3]

Of the importance of the trade there is ample evidence. The wills of merchants such as the Thornes and Howell show the profits that were made from it, and the persistence of the English merchants in the face of increasing difficulties fully confirms the value of the trade to them. These difficulties were political and religious rather than economic, for, as a study of the character of the Anglo-Spanish trade reveals, the economic interests of England and Spain were to no small degree complementary. Yet the opening of the Tudor period which brought a political alliance with Spain witnessed a commercial struggle between Henry VII and the Catholic Kings lasting for the greater part of Henry's reign and becoming a determining factor in the eventual domination of the trade by the English merchants under his successor.

[1] P.R.O., H.C.A., Examinations, 5, 25 October 1547.
[2] cf. Carande, op. cit., p. 83.
[3] *Vide supra*, Introduction, p. xvii. The prices of many of the commodities of the Anglo-Spanish trade are, of course, known from the extensive researches of J. E. T. Rogers, *A History of Agriculture and Prices in England*, and E. J. Hamilton's *American Treasure and the Price Revolution in Spain*.

CHAPTER II

DIPLOMACY AND TRADE
IN THE REIGN OF HENRY VII

AT the accession of Henry VII Anglo-Spanish trade possessed
two features of great importance for its subsequent development in the early Tudor period. It still suffered from the lawlessness at sea engendered by the Hundred Years' War and it
was largely in the hands of Spaniards. The two were not un-
related, for Edward IV had granted concessions to the Spanish
merchants in an effort to stimulate peaceful commerce between
England and Spain. An alliance with Castile had been one of the
main objects of Edward's foreign policy, and his treaty of 1466
with Henry IV included an agreement that Spanish merchants
in England should be treated on the same footing as English
subjects. Following this treaty Spaniards paid no more customs
duties than Englishmen and became the most favoured aliens
after the Hansards. In 1482 commercial ties between England
and Spain were further strengthened by a treaty of mercantile
intercourse for ten years with the maritime province of Guipuscoa.[1] In spite of Edward's efforts, however, the trade continued
to suffer from depredations at sea, in which men of the West
Country played a notorious part.[2] Time and again the English
king granted Spanish merchants exemption from payment of
customs duties as compensation for damage inflicted upon them
by his subjects. In December 1474 Edward declared himself
bound to the men of Guipuscoa in the sum of 5,000 crowns for
losses sustained by them before Christmas, 1472 and 6,000
crowns from that date until 28 May 1474.[3] Up to the end of his
reign it was necessary to appoint frequent commissions for the
investigation of complaints by Spanish merchants that they had
been despoiled by Englishmen.[4] These conditions persisted
through Richard III's reign and some years elapsed before the
Spaniards ceased to consider it necessary to take out letters of

---

[1] Rymer's *Foedera* (Hague ed.), vol. v, pt. iii, p. 117.
[2] cf. Kingsford, *Prejudice and Promise in XVth Century England*, p. 78.
[3] *Cal. Pat. Rolls, 1467–77*, pp. 480, 599.
[4] ibid., pp. 317, 354, 377, etc.; ibid., *1476–85*, p. 347.

protection from Henry VII to safeguard themselves and their merchandise from the attentions of his subjects.

Nevertheless, Edward IV's concessions and the improved political situation had caused a marked increase in Anglo-Spanish trade during his reign and in the number of Spanish merchants taking part in it. At the accession of Henry VII the Spaniards controlled a very large proportion of the trade, particularly in London, where they shipped most of their goods. A number of wealthy Spanish merchants had taken up residence in the capital in the two previous reigns. Among them were Diego de Castro, at whose request Henry issued a number of safe-conducts in the first months of his reign,[1] Diego de Cadagua, Martín Maluenda, Pedro de Salamanca and other prominent Spaniards granted compensation by the Yorkist kings.[2] Also prominent in the trade from London was Juan Sánchez de Aris of the province of Guipuscoa who early in the new reign received £40 compensation for some of his merchandise despoiled by Englishmen.[3] De Aris, receiving further payment from the Treasurer in July 1486, is described as 'procuratour and attourney of and for the cuntrey of Biskey, subgiettes unto oure cousin the king of Spaigne'.[4]

Particulars of customs of the port of London are not available for the first year of Henry VII's reign, but the dominant position of the Spanish merchants in the Anglo-Spanish trade from the capital at the beginning of the Tudor period may clearly be seen from a controlment of the subsidy of tunnage and poundage for the year 1487–88. As this is the last account of London in the reign where the Spaniards are designated by nationality[5] a more accurate assessment of their trade is possible than in any subsequent year. Unfortunately, since Spanish merchants did not at this time pay a subsidy on cloth, the largest export to Spain, it is not possible even for this year to determine the full extent of their exports. Nevertheless, a number of interesting features of the trade can be seen from a study of this account. Nearly fifty ships brought in goods from Spain or goods shipped

---

[1] *Materials for a History of the Reign of Henry VII*, (ed. Campbell), vol. 1, pp. 156, 158.
[2] *Cal. Pat. Rolls, 1476–1485*, p. 531.
[3] Campbell, op. cit., vol. 1, p. 227.
[4] ibid., p. 520.
[5] P.R.O., K.R. Customs, 78/7. After the Treaty of Medina del Campo they are classified as aliens.

by Spaniards from other ports during the year.[1] More came from northern Spain than from Andalusia and some by way of the Low Countries. Only a fifth of these vessels were English and the proportion of shipments made by English merchants in them was even less. According to the account, Juan Sánchez de Aris, in partnership with his son and Juan de Olivares of Bilbao, imported the largest amount of Spanish merchandise into London in this year. A considerable number of other leading Spanish merchants, including Diego de Castro, Martín Maluenda and Pedro de Miranda, imported goods on their behalf.[2] Nearly all these Spaniards were from the northern provinces and the greater part of their trade was in the commodities of those parts, with iron the most important. Spanish merchants also imported large quantities of Toulouse woad in ships of their fellow countrymen.

It is significant that the English ships, on the other hand, returned from Spain laden with wine, oil, fruit and other produce of Andalusia. Spanish shipping was more numerous at this time than English and in the northern provinces, whose merchants were more actively engaged in trade with northern Europe[3] than the Andalusians, the English merchants were at a disadvantage. In Andalusia for many years they had been more favourably treated, finding influential patrons in the Dukes of Medina Sidonia, whose town of San Lucar de Barrameda became their headquarters. Among leading Englishmen trading to Andalusia from London in the year 1487–88 were Richard Odiham, John Bond, John Chicheley, Thomas Spens and Stephen Jennings. A number of London merchants, English and Spanish, are shown from the particulars of customs of Southampton to have brought goods from Spain into the Hampshire port during the same year, including John Bond, John Chicheley, Diego de Castro and Juan Pardo.[4] Direct trade between Southampton and Spain was very small at the accession of Henry VII, however, and most Spanish goods came into the port by way of the Low Countries and some from the Flanders

---

[1] This account, like the great majority, does not specify the ports from which the ships arrived. *Vide supra*, Introduction, p. xvii.

[2] So the account tells us. It may well be, however, that these merchants were taking advantage of a licence granted to Juan Sánchez de Aris and his partners.

[3] *Vide supra*, pp. 2, 14.

[4] P.R.O., K. R. Customs, 142/10.

Galleys. Particulars of customs of Exeter in this reign prior to 1489 are too mutilated to yield any useful information, but a Plymouth customs account for part of the year 1487–88 shows that customs and subsidies paid by Spanish merchants amounted to approximately one seventh of the total customs revenue of the port during that period.[1]

A more detailed picture of Anglo-Spanish trade at the beginning of the Tudor period may be seen in the particulars of customs of Bristol for the year 1485–86.[2] But Bristol cannot be considered as illustrating the general characteristics of the trade at Henry's accession since its commerce with Spain was already on a firmer footing than that of any other port of the realm and its overseas trade generally more free of alien domination. The position of the Spaniards is nevertheless emphasised by the amount of Biscayan shipping carrying the Spanish trade of the port. Eight of the twelve vessels bringing in commodities from Spain in this year and no fewer than seventeen of the twenty-three ships sailing from Bristol to Spain were Spanish. The four English ships brought in goods from Huelva and Seville and, as in the case of London, the majority of English vessels setting out for Spain were bound for Andalusian ports. Otherwise the picture is quite different. Englishmen shipped 96 per cent of the cloths without grain exported from Bristol to Spain in the year 1485–86, 95 per cent of the wine imported and 86 per cent of all other commodities of the trade.

Commerce with Spain was already an important branch of Bristol's overseas trade at the accession of Henry VII. In the first year of the reign 1,977 cloths without grain, 54 per cent of the total exported from the port, were shipped to Spain. 253 tuns of wine came from Spain, 21 per cent of the total imported. Other imports during the same year were valued for customs purposes at £1,577 10s. 10d. and exports other than cloths without grain and tanned hides (7 dickers) at £236 11s. 8d. representing together 19 per cent of the corresponding total for the port. Woad heads the list of these imports with a customs valuation of £582 2s. 6d. Iron (£498 15s.), oil (£277), fruit (£132), sugar (£46) and salt (£25 16s. 8d.) follow next in importance; while wax, vinegar and soap were also imported in small quantities.

---

[1] P.R.O., K.R. Customs. 115/3.
[2] ibid., 20/5. *Vide infra*, Appendix A, p. 208.

Exports other than cloths without grain include tanned hides and calfskins, Welsh cloths and 'straits', beans and alabaster. Most of this trade was in the hands of the merchant families of Bristol itself, such as the Vaughans and Brownes, and other prominent local men such as John Esterfield, John Drewes and the elder Thorne, although at least one London merchant, Richard Odiham, traded through the Gloucester port during this year. The name of George Monox, a Bristol burgess who was twice elected lord mayor of London,[1] occurs frequently in this account. A number of Bristol women are also shown to have taken part in the Spanish trade, including Alice Brown, Isabel Lyncoll and Elizabeth Gowith.

These details of the trade of the leading English ports with Spain in the first years of the Tudor period indicate the characteristics of Anglo-Spanish commerce at the close of an era. The new period beginning with the unification of Spain under Ferdinand and Isabella and the accession of Henry VII in England was to display very different characteristics. Both English and Spanish sovereigns pursued more positive economic policies along mercantilist lines, and, although their commercial interests were at first to no small degree complementary,[2] those policies were bound eventually to lead to conflict. Commercial relations between England and Spain in the reign of Henry VII were closely linked with diplomatic relations between the two countries, and the correspondence of De Puebla, the Spanish ambassador, shows how much attention was paid by both parties to commercial matters. The Catholic Kings, however, were always willing to make a trading concession to gain a political point, whereas Henry relentlessly pursued an aggressive commercial policy designed to reduce the position already gained by the Spanish merchants in the Anglo-Spanish trade and to augment his treasury at their expense. It is clear, too, that Henry was much better informed about commercial questions affecting the two countries than Ferdinand and Isabella.

The overthrow of the Yorkists, from whom they had received their privileges, must have filled the Spanish merchants in England with some misgiving about their own future, and many hurried to purchase licences from the new king to carry on their

---

[1] A. H. Johnson, *The History of the Worshipful Company of the Drapers of London*, vol. 2, p. 21.   [2] *Vide supra*, pp. 1–5.

trade.[1] It is of interest that Don Pedro de Ayala, one of the Spanish envoys in England, suggested in 1500 that Henry bore many of the Spaniards no goodwill, partly because of their dealings with Richard III and partly on account of Perkin Warbeck.[2] The concealment of the pretender by Biscayan seamen did not take place until 1497,[3] however, and by 1500 Henry's feelings towards Spain had already markedly cooled. At all events Henry VII confirmed the privileges of the Spanish merchants a few months after his accession. On 6 December 1485 he informed the Treasurer and the Barons of the Exchequer that:

subgiettes of our cousin the kyng of Castell and Leon . . . from the first day of our reygne furthwardys shall pay no more custumes subsidies and othir dueties for theire goodes and marchaundises to be by theym brought into this oure realme and to be ladde oute of the same but as denizyns and our naturall subgiettes pay or ought to pay acordyng to the lygue and entrecours which was taken and concluded betwene . . . kyng Edward the iiijᵗʰ . . . and our seide cosin.[4]

The privileges thus confirmed were extensive. At Henry's accession Spaniards paid 1s. 2d. custom on every cloth without grain instead of the 2s. 9d. paid by other aliens (except the Hansards). Moreover, being on the same footing as Englishmen, they did not pay the subsidy of 1s. in the £ upon cloths, amounting to a further 2s. on every cloth without grain exported. The difference in the custom upon more expensive cloths was even greater. The Spaniards were also free of the petty custom of 3d. in the £ levied in addition to the *ad valorem* subsidy of 1s. in the £ upon all exports and imports subject to the latter. On every last of tanned hides they paid custom of 13s. 4d., subsidy of £3 6s. 8d. and 'Calais penny' of 8d. instead of £1, £3 13s. 4d. and 1s. 4d.

Henry VII's confirmation of their privileges enabled the Spaniards to continue in their favoured position for the moment, but it is evident that the English king intended to revoke them as soon as an opportunity arose. National and personal interests alike made such a course desirable. The domination of the trade

---

[1] *Spanish Calendar, 1485–1509*, nos. 1, 3, 4, 6, etc.
[2] ibid., no. 260.
[3] ibid., no. 221, p. 186.
[4] P.R.O., K.R. Memoranda Rolls, 262, Easter Term, m. 2.

by Spanish shipping was particularly harmful in view of the condition of the Navy at Henry's accession. At the same time the king's revenue would greatly benefit from an increase in the duties paid by the Spanish merchants, while further sums could be obtained from the sale of licences permitting them to contravene any additional measures passed against them. The identification of national with personal interests was an important feature of Tudor policy and Henry soon embarked upon an aggressive campaign on behalf of his subjects trading to Spain designed to fill his own pocket. A modest beginning was made in his first Parliament when an act to remedy the decay of the Navy forbade the use of foreign vessels to import the wines of Guienne and Gascony.[1] A considerable number of Spanish merchants had been taking part in this branch of English trade, including Diego de Castro, Fernando de Carrión and Pedro de Miranda.[2] Now, all Spaniards wishing to continue using their own ships to import these wines had to obtain licences and it is recorded that certain English merchants also purchased licences enabling them to freight Spanish vessels for the same purpose.[3]

Spanish merchants also continued to purchase safe-conducts for themselves and their goods even after the confirmation of their privileges, for conditions were still unsettled. In July 1488 Henry complained to Ferdinand and Isabella that Spanish letters of marque had been issued against his subjects. Some months previously, he said, a Spanish vessel freighted with goods at Bristol had been seized by the governor of Guipuscoa at the behest of some Spanish merchants possessing letters of marque against English subjects. The English king claimed this was an infringement of the last treaty of Edward IV's reign.[4] In the same month De Puebla reported that the English complained constantly of the activities of Spanish privateers and said he believed, from his own experience, that their complaints were justified. He had himself seen two English ships seized by Spaniards at Corunna in the presence of forty other Spanish vessels, none of which stirred to oppose the capture.[5] At this very time negotiations were proceeding for a military alliance be-

[1] Stat. 1 Hen. VII, c. 8.
[2] *Spanish Calendar, 1485–1509*, no. 1.
[3] Campbell, op. cit., vol. 2, pp. 518, 525, etc.
[4] *Spanish Calendar, 1485–1509*, no. 17.
[5] ibid., no. 21, p. 12.

tween England and Spain and measures for improving commercial relations between the two countries were included in the new treaty. It is of interest that Henry suggested at this stage that the Spanish merchants in London should provide security for the prompt payment of Katherine's marriage portion, since it indicates the wealth of the Spaniards in the English capital at that time.[1] The proposal was rejected by Ferdinand and Isabella, however, as both impracticable and dishonest[2], and payment was eventually made through Italian bankers.[3]

The Treaty of Medina del Campo[4] contained four commercial clauses. Clause 1 stated that the subjects of each of the contracting parties should be allowed to travel, stay and carry on commerce in the dominions of the other contracting party without general or special passport and should be treated on the same footing as the citizens of the country in which they were temporarily residing. It was also declared that customs duties would be reduced to rates current in time of peace thirty years previously. By clause 13 all letters of marque and reprisal were to be revoked. Any Spanish or English vessel sailing from a Spanish or English port was to give security for good behaviour at sea to the amount of double the value of the vessel, its equipment and provisions. If during its voyage it caused damage to Spanish or English vessels the injured party should be indemnified from this security. Should justice be denied, the king of the injured party was twice to demand redress from the sovereign of the party which had inflicted the injury before issuing letters of marque and reprisal. Clause 14 stipulated that the treaty was not to be dissolved through infractions of its terms by individual subjects of either of the contracting parties; and Clause 15 that letters of marque and reprisal might be issued if redress could not be obtained for a subject of either of the two countries who had been injured by a subject of the other, after it had been demanded by the government of the injured party. The treaty was to be proclaimed in all the towns and sea-ports of England and Spain within six months after its signature.

Such were the relevant terms of the treaty which formed the

---

[1] Katherine's marriage portion was to be 200,000 *escudos*, each *escudo* valued at 4s. 2d. sterling. *Spanish Calendar, 1485–1509*, no. 34, p. 23.
[2] ibid., no. 22, p. 13.
[3] *Documentos Inéditos para la Historia de España*, (ed. M. F. Navarrete, etc.), Tomo i, pp. 356 *seq.*   [4] *Spanish Calendar, 1485–1509*, no. 34.

basis of Anglo-Spanish commercial relations throughout the early Tudor period. Many political historians have declared that Medina del Campo was a one-sided agreement, owing to Henry's comparatively weak position. This is a questionable judgement which subsequent events do not seem to justify.[1] Henry's attitude, as revealed in the diplomatic correspondence, certainly betrays no consciousness of inferiority and he undoubtedly gained the advantage in the commercial clauses. It was not long before the Spanish merchants found they were worse off than before the treaty. In May 1489 Ferdinand complained that certain Spanish merchants in England had been forced to pay higher duties on goods which they had imported into the country than they had paid previously. The English customs officials had declared they were not subjects of the crown of Castile. Ferdinand protested that under the terms of the treaty all his subjects without distinction should be treated equally with Englishmen.[2] Far worse was soon to be discovered. The Spaniards believed that all imposts had been increased during the period of the civil wars in England and a reversion to the duties current thirty years earlier would be to their advantage. In fact, it enabled Henry to cancel the privileges granted them by Edward IV and make them pay the same duties as other less favoured aliens. The Spanish monarchs protested bitterly that they had been mistaken about the English customs duties and vainly requested Henry to interpret the clause of the treaty in accordance with their intention, which was to lower, not raise the imposts on Spanish commerce.[3] In the following year, during the negotiations for a new marriage treaty, the Spanish commissioners were instructed to take the greatest care to amend this clause,[4] and Ferdinand and Isabella continued to demand the removal of the additional duties imposed under pretext of the treaty, which they said was in any case null and void as Henry had not yet signed it.[5]

[1] *Vide supra*, Introduction, p. xix. Henry's financial gains from the increased customs duties paid by the Spanish merchants must have been considerable because of the importance he clearly attached to maintaining them. It is evident that the Catholic Kings paid much less attention to commercial questions affecting the two countries than Henry VII did—and took the French war much more seriously.

[2] *Spanish Calendar, 1485–1509*, no. 37.

[3] ibid., no. 41, p. 29.

[4] ibid., no. 60.

[5] ibid., no. 91. Henry ratified the treaty on 20 September 1490. ibid., no. 55.

Meanwhile Henry dealt another blow at the Spanish merchants by extending his navigation act to include the traffic in Toulouse woad and adding a regulation that his subjects should freight foreign ships only when no English were available in port.[1] This was much more serious for the Spaniards than his first act, for they took an even more prominent part in this branch of English commerce than in the wine trade with Guienne and Gascony. A very large share of the importation of woad into London was in their hands.[2] It is not surprising that Ferdinand and Isabella denounced the new act as infringing existing treaties.[3] Early in 1495 De Puebla was ordered to ask Henry not to deprive the Spaniards of the privileges they had hitherto enjoyed,[4] but the English king denied they had ever been granted the concessions which they were claiming. He refused to acknowledge that Edward IV's last treaty had conferred them.[5] Despite Henry's unfavourable answer, however, Ferdinand and Isabella continued to press the matter. De Puebla was told he should have requested Henry to allow the Spaniards to retain all privileges they could prove they possessed by right and had in fact enjoyed until the English king revoked them in consequence of the Treaty of Medina del Campo. The Spanish monarchs claimed they wanted the affair of the merchants settled satisfactorily so that no subject of dispute might remain after the conclusion of the marriage, affirming their own wish to treat the English merchants in Spain just like their natural subjects.[6]

By the end of the year Henry had expressed his readiness to reach a satisfactory agreement[7] but only after the marriage alliance had been concluded. In the meantime he advanced the same reasons for continuing to impose the higher duties. The Spanish monarchs insisted that the settlement of the commercial dispute should be made at the same time as the alliance, for, they declared, it would not do for them to have such differences afterwards and perhaps be forced to retaliate upon the English merchants in Spain. In truth they were anxious to avoid a repetition of their last experience. At the same time they offered Henry that, should he declare war on France and consider the higher duties necessary to help meet the expenses of the cam-

---

[1] Stat. 4 Hen. VII, c. 10.   [2] *Vide supra*, p. 33.
[3] *Spanish Calendar, 1485–1509*, no. 91.   [4] ibid., no. 93.
[5] ibid., no. 94.   [6] ibid., no. 107.   [7] ibid., no. 113, p. 74.

paign, they should be paid for the duration of hostilities. They must be removed when peace was restored, however, and Henry should give security that this would be done.[1] The gesture was wasted, for the English king felt no need of making either the political or commercial concession which the Spaniards demanded. Henry VII's position was growing steadily more secure and his need of Spanish friendship less urgent. The English commissioners negotiating the new treaty resisted all Spanish demands on behalf of their merchants trading to England.[2]

Meanwhile, in spite of its unfortunate result for the Spanish merchants, the alliance had caused a great increase in Anglo-Spanish trade. This may best be seen in the first available particulars of customs of Bristol following the Treaty of Medina del Campo—those for the year 1492-93.[3] Most marked is the increase in the value of imports from Spain which rose from £1,577 10s. 10d. in the year 1485–86 (representing with exports[4] valued at £236 11s. 8d., 19 per cent of the relevant total for the port) to £6,495 11s. (representing, with exports[5] valued at £284 17s. 1d., 54 per cent). The number of cloths without grain exported to Spain increased from 1,977 to 3,283 (54 per cent to 58 per cent of the total exported from Bristol) and wine imported from 253 tuns to 746 (21 per cent to 29 per cent of the total imported). Woad again heads the list of imports other than wine with a customs valuation of £3,042 3s. 1d. Iron (£1,641 6s.), oil (£1,282), pepper (£110 12s.) and wax (£105) were the next largest imports. Almonds, fruits, salt, sugar, resin and honey were chief among the commodities imported in smaller quantities. Englishmen shipped 99 per cent of the cloths without grain from Bristol to Spain in the year 1492–93, 88 per cent of the wine from Spain and 98 per cent of all other commodities between the two countries. The same Bristol merchants dominated the trade in this year, and in October, 1492 almost all the other leading merchants of the port imported woad and iron from northern Spain as 'factors, deputies and attorneys' of Henry Vaughan and John Esterfield.[6] Martín de Geldo, master of *Le Mawdelyn de Rendre* which brought these shipments into Bristol,

---

[1] *Spanish Calendar, 1485–1509*, no. 121, p. 85.
[2] ibid., no. 136, p. 102.
[3] P.R.O., K.R. Customs, 20/9. *Vide infra*, Appendix A, p. 209.
[4] Other than cloths without grain and tanned hides.
[5] ibid.   [6] *Vide supra*, p. 33, n.2.

is styled 'alien' in this account. In the first year of the reign, when he plied the trade with the same ship, he appeared as 'Spaniard, native'. It is a significant illustration of Henry's policy against the Spanish merchants that Martín de Geldo not only paid alien rates of custom on his goods but deemed it advisable to purchase a licence to trade to England with his ship after Medina del Campo.[1]

Spanish shipping still predominated in this year though not to such a marked degree as before. Eleven of the twenty-six vessels which brought in commodities from Spain were English and so were eight of the twenty-three exporting goods to Spain. Trade with the north Spanish ports was still greater than with Andalusia and it is interesting to note that as many English ships visited the northern ports as Spanish—encouraged, perhaps, by the decrease of piracy in those waters. In the early Bristol accounts the names of the Andalusian ports are sometimes given and San Lucar de Barrameda is specified in the case of eight of the eleven ships coming from southern Spain in this year. It must not be forgotten, however, that many of these ships called at more than one Andalusian port and probably also visited Lisbon and a north Spanish port on their way to England.

The increase of the trade is also seen from the particulars of customs of London. An account of the collectors of the subsidy of tunnage and poundage for the year 1490–91[2] shows Spaniards still dominating the trade of the capital with Spain. One very prominent Spanish merchant was Alonso de Cisneros, later employed by Henry VII in connection with the garrisons at Berwick[3] and Calais.[4] Spaniards also imported large quantities of woad, often using English ships for the purpose. The recent extension of Henry's navigation act made it necessary for those freighting their own ships to purchase licences. The extent of the export of cloths by Spaniards is indicated by this account since they now paid the subsidy on cloth, and a great many shipments to Spain were made by them. A considerable increase in the activity of the English merchants in the trade is shown in the details of imports into London during the year

[1] *Spanish Calendar, 1485–1509*, no. 39.
[2] P.R.O., K.R. Customs, 78/12.
[3] *Spanish Calendar, 1485–1509*, no. 84.
[4] ibid., no. 230.

1494–95.[1] Here, too, the effect of the second navigation act is more noticeable, for nearly twenty English ships brought in woad for Spanish merchants. Again the tendency was for most English ships to go to southern Spain. Richard Wotton made two voyages to Andalusia with the *Rossimus* during this year, returning laden with fruit, soap, wine, oil and sugar. John Chicheley, William Scalder, John Bond, George Hunt and William Nightingale were among the English merchants shipping these commodities with Wotton. Several years previously some of these merchants had found it necessary to purchase licences to send their cloths to Spain in Spanish vessels,[2] and in the year 1494–95 Spanish ships continued to carry a large proportion of the goods of English merchants from both Andalusia and the northern provinces. Large quantities of iron were imported into London during this year, mostly by Spaniards in Spanish ships. At least one English ship also brought in iron from northern Spain, including a large shipment for Richard Odiham and a smaller one for William Nightingale.

The Spanish alliance, and even more the new ties between Spain and the Low Countries, brought particular benefit to Southampton, so well placed for the trade routes between them. So beneficial was the influx of Spanish vessels into the Hampshire port that for a time this increase helped to compensate for the decline of the Italian shipping in Southampton and there was no appreciable drop in the customs revenues of the town.[3] Particulars of customs for Southampton in the year 1491–92[4] show that a considerable proportion of the Spanish commodities coming into the port were from ships calling in from the Low Countries and some from the Flanders Galleys. Several English ships seem to have visited Andalusia during this year, however, and Spanish ships brought in quantities of wine and fruit. Although it is badly kept and difficult to analyse, the local port book for the year 1494–95 is more revealing.[5] The Hampshire port is seen as a collecting centre for the ships returning to Spain from the Low Countries. There is now a group of Southampton

[1] P.R.O., K.R. Customs, 79/5.
[2] *Spanish Calendar, 1485–1509*, no. 69.
[3] Ruddock, 'London Capitalists and the Decline of Southampton in the early Tudor Period', in *The Economic History Review*, Second Series, vol. ii, no. 2 (1949), p. 147.
[4] P.R.O., K.R. Customs, 142/11.
[5] Southampton Municipal MSS., Local Port Book, 1494–95.

merchants regularly engaged in the Anglo-Spanish trade, including Nicholas Cowart, William Justice, Robert Young and John Favor. A number of leading Spanish merchants still traded through Southampton, notably Alonso Compludo, Juan de Castro, Francisco Arbieto and Pedro de Salamanca. Richard Wotton (soon to become a burgess of Southampton)[1] called in with the *Rossimus* on his way to London, and Richard Odiham, John Bridges and other leading London merchants imported Spanish goods into Southampton. It is also of interest that a Southampton ship brought in iron for John Raleigh of Exeter during the year.

Raleigh was one of a number of Exeter merchants shown by the particulars of customs of the Devonshire port to be trading to Spain at this time.[2] Others included William Taylor, Thomas Mongay, Richard Unday and John Simon. The earliest account is for the year 1491–92[3] from which the trade does not seem to have been large but was mostly in the hands of Englishmen and a high proportion carried in the ships of the Devon ports. Spanish ships visited Exeter, however, and also Barnstaple and Dartmouth. Iron was the chief Spanish import and the commodities of northern Spain were more numerous than those of Andalusia. More goods were imported from southern Spain in the year 1498–99 when there was a marked increase in the volume of the trade as a whole.[4] The particulars of customs of Plymouth for the previous year indicate that, as in the case of Exeter, English merchants and ships were dominating the Spanish trade of the port.[5]

Henry VII's refusal to take part in further hostilities against France after the Treaty of Etaples had an effect upon Anglo-Spanish commercial relations foreshadowing the more serious difficulties of Henry VIII's reign. Ferdinand and Isabella appreciated the use of English ports for re-victualling Spanish ships active against the French[6] but did not relish the profit the English made from their neutrality. Franco-Spanish trade suffered severely from the war, but England, at peace with both countries, was able to conduct a brisk carrying trade between

---

[1] Southampton Municipal MSS., Book of Oaths and Ordinances, f. 1.
[2] P.R.O., K.R. Customs, 201/1, 41/15, etc.
[3] ibid., 201/1.
[4] ibid., 201/2.
[5] ibid., 115/7.   [6] *Spanish Calendar, 1485–1509*, no. 137, p. 105.

them. The Spaniards saw clearly that while this profitable form of commerce was open to his subjects Henry would be in no mind to make the concessions which they had been demanding ever since the Treaty of Medina del Campo. They therefore ordered that all vessels leaving Spanish ports, regardless of nationality, should provide security that they would not carry merchandise to France.[1] The Spaniards were particularly concerned about the export of iron there by foreigners, and as many Englishmen were engaged in this traffic Henry was begged to prohibit it.[2] Queen Isabella expressed her willingness to exempt the English merchants from the obligation of finding security in Spain, however, if Henry specifically promised they would not trade between Spain and France. Indeed, the queen wrote that she had already given orders for the release of a number of English captains who had laden their ships with iron at Laredo and were unable to find the necessary securities. They had been permitted to depart after promising on oath not to carry their merchandise to France.[3] This gesture of goodwill was doubtless intended to influence the larger issue on which De Puebla was still labouring.

The Spanish ambassador reported in the summer of 1496 that he had discussed the question of the merchants with Henry VII as much as all other matters put together but had found the king adamant. De Puebla declared he had done his utmost to secure a favourable settlement, but he had been reliably informed that even if a duty of one ducat were imposed upon every English cloth in Spain it was unlikely that Henry would give way. The only remedy he could suggest lay in securing the person of Perkin Warbeck. Then, he believed, the affair of the merchants could speedily be settled.[4] In subsequent conversations Henry continued to deny that the privileges the Spaniards claimed had been conceded by Edward IV and demanded to be shown the original grant, which he promised to implement were it produced. De Puebla asserted that the English were so badly informed that if the Bible were read to them they would think it was the Koran![5] If he really believed English obstinacy in

---

[1] *Spanish Calendar, 1485-1509*, no. 137. p. 106.
[2] ibid., no. 139.
[3] ibid., no. 153.
[4] ibid., no. 143, p. 112. It is ironical that Warbeck crossed from Ireland to Cornwall in a Biscayan ship. ibid., no. 221, p. 186.
[5] ibid., no. 144.

this matter was founded upon ignorance, which is indeed very doubtful, self-deception could hardly have been carried to greater lengths than in this judgement of the first of many Spanish ambassadors to be outwitted by the Tudors.

In the following September Queen Isabella told De Puebla that unless Henry could be persuaded to remove the extra duties it must be stipulated in a separate legal instrument that the treaty would not be infringed if English merchants in Spain were made to pay customs duties equivalent to those paid by Spaniards in England.[1] She declared that the new treaty must not be delayed on account of this difference, however—a sign of her increased anxiety for the marriage alliance and an example of Spanish subordination of commercial to political interests.[2] Early in the next year (1497) Henry seems to have promised not merely to remove all the extra duties from Spanish commerce but even to grant exceptional privileges to her merchants. Ferdinand and Isabella declared the advantage of these liberal measures would soon be clear to the English king. The Spanish people, believing they had been treated unjustly in England, were by no means favourably disposed towards him, but as a result of better treatment he would gain their firm support.[3] The Spanish monarchs were also gratified at this time by Henry's punishment of French pirates who had maltreated their subjects.[4]

In July 1497 Henry promised to order without delay that Spaniards wrecked off the English coast should receive better

---

[1] It has not been possible to determine the customs duties paid by English merchants in Spain in this period. Larraz, op. cit., p. 39, gives it as a general rule that in the northern provinces the main impost was the *diezmo* or tenth, while in Andalusia there was a duty of $2\frac{1}{2}$ per cent on exports and 5 per cent on imports. In addition there was the *alcabala* or sales tax of 10 per cent. But Carande, *Carlos V y Sus Banqueros, La Hacienda Real de Castilla*, pp. 292 *seq.*, shows the difficulty of determining the Spanish customs from the available evidence. English and Spanish sources show a wide discrepancy from the figures given by Larraz. Robert Harvey, for instance, paid 5 per cent custom on his cloths at Corunna (*vide supra* p. 13) and Thomas Howell paid the *alcabala* at $3\frac{1}{2}$ per cent (the ledger, f. 14). Documents in the *Archivo de Protocolos de Sevilla* show Englishmen in Seville paying *diezmos*. One important aspect of this struggle over the customs duties in Henry VII's reign is quite clear, however. The English king had a greater personal interest in the question because the royal revenues were augmented by the increased duties paid by the Spanish merchants, whereas the Castilian seaport customs duties had been alienated from the control of the royal exchequer since 1469 (Klein, *The Mesta*, p. 46).
[2] *Spanish Calendar, 1485–1509*, no. 158.
[3] ibid., no. 175, p. 139.
[4] ibid., p. 141.

treatment, but in the meantime he had not kept his other promises. On the contrary, he complained of the excessive amount of time De Puebla spent in discussing the duties paid by the Spanish merchants and said he could not believe the ambassador had been instructed to do so. All his other business together did not occupy as much time as this minor subject alone, the king complained, and Henry could only imagine he did it to refute allegations that he was neglecting the merchants' interests.[1] Just at this time ill reports of De Puebla had caused Ferdinand and Isabella to despatch two special envoys to England with instructions to investigate his conduct. Their report was extremely unfavourable. The Spanish merchants, they said, intensely disliked the ambassador. They alleged that he could easily have induced Henry to abolish the extra duties imposed upon them had he wished, but instead De Puebla seemed to look after the English king's interests instead of theirs. They declared there was not a Spanish captain or even a single sailor who was not obliged to pay a fee to the ambassador if he wanted any favour in England. De Puebla had sold two royal licences for importing wine and woad in Spanish vessels for 200 crowns and charged a prominent Spanish merchant 100 gold crowns for securing him a pardon for perjury. As a consequence of De Puebla's conduct the Spaniards were less esteemed and worse treated in England than any other foreigners.[2] This was part of an indictment of the ambassador which has been generally accepted until recent years. As Professor Mattingly has pointed out in his defence of De Puebla, however, the acceptance of fees for the services he rendered was more general than otherwise.[3] There is ample evidence, too, of De Puebla's strenuous efforts to secure their privileges for the Spanish merchants.

Henry continued to express surprise at the persistent request for the lowering of the duties. Surely, he said, it was evident that they were not paid by the Spaniards who imported the goods but by the English who consumed them. The Spaniards, having paid higher duties on their merchandise, sold them dearer, thus receiving more money to buy English cloth and other commodities. Needless to say, this plausible exposition of one

[1] *Spanish Calendar, 1485–1509*, no. 182.
[2] ibid., nos. 204, 206.
[3] G. Mattingly, 'The Reputation of Doctor De Puebla', in *The English Historical Review*, vol. lv, no. 217 (January, 1940), pp. 33–34.

of the disadvantages of protection made little impression upon the Spaniards. Henry went on to say that since the merchants of other countries importing large quantities of goods into England paid the same duties without complaint, he saw no reason why the Spaniards should not do so. He now admitted that Edward IV had made special concessions to the king of Castile, but declared it had been for exceptional considerations no longer relevant. Yet he would willingly grant similar or even greater privileges to Spanish subjects, were he not afraid of the scandal such an act of favouritism would create in England and abroad. He promised, nevertheless, in celebration of the happy arrival of Princess Katherine in England, to lower the duties paid by the Spaniards to rates considerably less than those imposed upon merchants of other nations.[1] Perhaps Henry realised the inconsistency of this generous promise, for it was never implemented.

In the diplomatic correspondence of these years are a number of references to English interest in projects of discovery. On 28 March 1496, in reply to a letter of De Puebla informing them of John Cabot's negotiations with Henry VII, Ferdinand and Isabella instructed the ambassador to do his best to dissuade the English king from encouraging such enterprises. The Spanish monarchs suggested that the French king had instigated the whole business in an effort to distract Henry's attention. The latter should not allow himself to be deceived, for these voyages were uncertain ventures and in any case could not be undertaken without prejudice to Ferdinand and Isabella and the king of Portugal. The efforts of the ambassador proved unsuccessful, however, and Ayala reported two years later on the progress of Cabot's expedition. He stated, too, that the men of Bristol had for the last seven years been sending ships in search of Brazil and the seven cities.[2] Bristol men, including the elder Robert Thorne and Hugh Elliott among many trading to Spain, maintained their interest in the 'new found land' for some years to come.[3]

A new treaty was signed on 10 July 1499. Its commercial clauses were similar to those of Medina del Campo with an addi-

---

[1] *Spanish Calendar, 1485–1509*, no. 182.
[2] ibid., nos. 128, 210.
[3] *Vide* J. A. Williamson, *Maritime Enterprise, 1485–1558*, Chap. v.

tional article dealing with shipwreck and salvage. No reference was made to the duties.[1] It is curious that this important question is not mentioned again in the diplomatic correspondence, and in the absence of evidence to the contrary it might be supposed that it had been settled in the Spaniards' favour. This assumption was in fact made by Georg Schanz.[2] Moreover, De Puebla had written in the previous August that he was making no further reports about the duties as Henry had already given the necessary promises over his seal and signature.[3] Reference to the particulars of customs of the English ports in this period, however, shows that the Spaniards continued to pay the increased imposts. The marriage arrangements were now occupying the greater attention of the Spanish monarchs and the merchants' grievances were pushed for a time into the background. Moreover, trade with England was already coming to be of decreasing importance to the Spaniards as prospects in the New World became more glittering. Since the marriage would bring more Spaniards to England De Puebla urged that he should be given power of civil and criminal jurisdiction over his fellow countrymen.[4] If he was granted this power in spite of the allegations against him, his appointment must have been a further blow to the Spanish merchants in their struggle against Henry's imposts.[5]

Although a more cordial atmosphere was created by the marriage, commercial disputes continued, now concerned chiefly with the navigation acts of the two countries. Early in 1501 Henry complained that the Spanish monarchs had prohibited all foreign vessels lading merchandise in their ports.[6] In fact they had put into force the *pragmática* of 21 July 1494 *para estímulo de la navegación nacional*[7] which prohibited the use of foreign ships when Spanish were available in port. This was one of a number of mercantilist measures of the Catholic Kings en-

---

[1] *Spanish Calendar, 1485–1509*, no. 244.

[2] *Englische Handelspolitik gegen Ende des Mittelalters*, vol. 1, p. 274. Schanz cites in support of his contention the list of customs duties on p. 193 of the 1811 edition of *The Customs of London, otherwise called Arnold's Chronicle*, which shows the Spaniards paying similar rates to English subjects. Schanz's theory that this list, which is undated, was post 1499 is disproved by the particulars of customs. cf. N. S. B. Gras, *The Early English Customs System*, p. 690.

[3] *Spanish Calendar, 1485-1509*, no. 221, p. 189.

[4] ibid., no. 268, p. 228.

[5] ibid., nos. 274, 276.   [6] ibid., no. 293.

[7] Referred to in Larraz, *La Epoca del Mercantilismo en Castilla*, p. 40.

forced with varying strictness against the English merchants throughout the period. The enforcement of this *pragmática* was a severe blow to the larger number of English ships now visiting Andalusia and it was fortunate that Henry shortly gained a diplomatic advantage which made Ferdinand and Isabella more willing to grant commercial concessions. This arose from the death of Arthur in April 1502. The Spanish monarchs were eager for a new marriage between Katherine and Prince Henry[1] although ostensibly demanding the return of the Princess and the repayment of the first instalment of her marriage portion.[2] A special envoy, Hernán Duque de Estrada, was instructed to tell Henry that, in addition to other advantages he would gain from assenting to the betrothal, letters patent would be issued enabling goods to be shipped in English vessels from Spanish ports in the same manner as those of Spanish subjects.[3]

The promised concession was a timely one, for commercial relations between the two countries had been steadily deteriorating for several years. Henry complained that Spanish captains exporting cloth from English ports in Spanish vessels were detained in the ports of Spain while others completed their cargoes and sailed away.[4] He also protested against acts of piracy committed daily by Spanish captains in English ports and waters on his subjects as well as foreigners.[5] He had already remonstrated against the capture of a French ship in Winchelsea harbour by Spaniards two months earlier (July 1503).[6] These infringements of the treaties were perhaps, as Schanz suggests, by way of revenge for the extra customs duties.[7] They were certainly a sign of the aggravated commercial relations between the two countries. In the meantime the Spanish monarchs and Henry were disputing the matter of Katherine's marriage portion while, in fact, both parties were intent upon the new match. Finally Henry, who had appeared the more reluctant throughout the negotiations,[8] agreed to conclude a treaty for a marriage between Katherine and Prince Henry. In consideration of this treaty Isabella sent Henry a document authorising the ships of

---

[1] *Spanish Calendar, 1485–1509*, no. 318.   [2] ibid., no. 317.
[3] ibid., no. 360, p. 299.
[4] ibid., no. 367.   [5] ibid., no. 377.   [6] ibid., no. 366.
[7] op. cit., vol. 1, p. 275.
[8] Henry could afford to be, since he had in his power both the person of Katherine and the first instalment of her marriage portion.

his subjects to traffic in the Spanish kingdoms under the same conditions as the ships of her own subjects.[1] This document does not seem to have entirely satisfied the wary English king, however, for shortly afterwards Ferdinand and Isabella instructed Hernán Duque to tell him it was customary for such matters to be written on paper in the Castilian tongue. Henry had wanted it on parchment with a leaden seal.[2]

In November 1504 the Spanish monarchs announced that they had issued letters patent prohibiting the export of goods from their ports in foreign vessels while there were any Spanish ships available in which they could be carried. In consideration of the new marriage agreement, however, English subjects in Spain were to be treated like Spaniards. They were therefore permitted to export, in Spanish or English vessels, all kinds of merchandise to England as they used to do before the issue of the letters patent, excepting only those goods which even their own subjects were forbidden to export.[3] This order was to be published in all cities, towns and sea-ports.[4] In the following March, for the same consideration, Henry declared that similar concessions were granted to all subjects of his brother the king of Aragon and Regent of Castile.[5]

These promises failed to improve commercial relations, however, for it was not long before Ferdinand's concession proved worthless. In the summer of 1505, while the Spanish ambassador was in attendance upon Henry at Richmond, eight hundred Englishmen came back from Seville complaining that they had been totally ruined. They had taken cloth and other merchandise to the Spanish port on the understanding that in accordance with the royal proclamation they would be allowed to export all kinds of goods from Spain. But the Spaniards had not permitted them to export anything, and, being obliged to return without freight, they had suffered great losses. De Puebla, reporting this incident to Ferdinand, depicts Henry in a most violent rage and the ambassador undoubtedly had a stormy interview. His excuse, that the English official sent by Henry to Spain on this business was at fault for not forwarding the

---

[1] *Spanish Calendar, 1485–1509*, no. 380, p. 318.
[2] ibid., no. 394, p. 326.
[3] A list of prohibited goods is given by Larraz, op. cit., p. 37.
[4] *Spanish Calendar, 1485–1509*, no. 405.
[5] ibid., no. 424. Queen Isabella died on 26 November 1504.

proclamation to the governor of Andalusia, failed to placate the king. It is not surprising. De Puebla begged Ferdinand to give instructions that the English should be treated in accordance with the last agreements, for he had heard that the council of of Castile, 'still possessed by the devil', had again issued an order prohibiting English, Flemish and other nations from lading their ships in Andalusia.[1]

A further unpleasant interview for De Puebla followed a few days later when he was visited by members of the Privy Council accompanied by the merchants who had been forbidden to freight their ships at Seville. The latter claimed that their losses amounted to at least 20,000 ducats. Other merchants returning from Spain only a short time previously said the royal proclamation had been published in Seville, but immediately afterwards an order of the council of Castile had been sent to the governor of Andalusia not to permit them to freight their ships. There was a judicial process pending in the Court of Admiralty concerning the whole affair. De Puebla besought Ferdinand to protect the interests of the English merchants in Andalusia and to write a gracious letter of excuse to Henry. The ambassador said he went in fear of being stoned by English sailors if reparations were not made.[2]

But Ferdinand was in no position to comply with De Puebla's urgent request. His authority in Castile was insufficient for him to attempt the enforcement of the proclamation against the opposition of a council hostile to the privileges of the English merchants in Spain and determined to curtail them. There were influential people in Castile wishing to stop Anglo-Spanish trade altogether, alleging that it only drained gold from the country and brought nothing in return but English cloth.[3] Just at this time, after the death of Isabella, the council was more powerful and the position of the English merchants in Spain precarious in consequence. Even in San Lucar de Barrameda the influence of hostile elements was felt, and it eventually became necessary for the English merchants to petition the Duke of Medina Sidonia for the confirmation of their privileges.[4] Isabella's death was, in fact, followed by a swift deterioration in

---

[1] *Spanish Calendar, 1485–1509*, no. 438.
[2] ibid., no. 442.
[3] *Letters and Papers*, i (1), no. 6.
[4] *Vide infra*, p. 82.

relations between England and Spain. The last years of Henry VII saw an increasing animosity between the English king and Ferdinand and the steady dwindling of Spanish interests in England as Henry devoted his efforts to stirring up trouble for his former ally.

Spanish commercial interests in England were already tending to decline by the end of Henry VII's reign for economic reasons quite independent of his measures against them. The trade between Spain and the Low Countries, with which Anglo-Spanish trade was so closely linked, was already past its peak. The decline of Bruges, the attraction of the New World and the general decadence of Spanish agriculture, commerce and industry are considered to have been the main contributory factors.[1] With the decrease of Spanish interest in trade with England, English merchants were able to strengthen their position, but the strict enforcement of the Spanish navigation acts and the deterioration in relations between Henry VII and Ferdinand after the death of Isabella for the moment neutralised their advantage.

Some indication of this decline in Anglo-Spanish trade is given by the surviving particulars of customs of the main English ports. The last Bristol account of Henry VII's reign is for the year 1503-4.[2] This is before Isabella's death, and the situation was by no means as bad then as it grew later. Nevertheless, the decrease in the trade was very marked indeed, and although twenty-two ships brought Spanish commodities into the Gloucester port in this year, only nine took English exports to Spain. Most shipments from Bristol are entered as sailing for northern Spain, but nearly as many vessels returned from Andalusia as from the north coast ports. Henry VII's aggressive commercial policy is reflected in the fact that six of the outgoing ships and no less than eighteen of the incoming vessels were English. English merchants shipped 100 per cent of the cloths without grain exported to Spain, imported 95 per cent of the wine and shipped 94 per cent of all other commodities of the trade. An analysis of the figures, however, reveals the extent to which adverse factors in Henry VII's latter years had reduced

---

[1] *Vide* Finot, *Relations commerciales et maritimes entre la Flandre et l'Espagne au Moyen Age*, pp. 225 *seq.*
[2] P.R.O., K.R. Customs, 199/1.   *Vide infra*, Appendix A, p. 210.

the volume of the trade. The number of cloths without grain exported to Spain fell to less than half the figure for the first year of the reign. Only 975 (29 per cent of the total exported from the port) were shipped to Spain from Bristol in the year 1503–4, compared with 3,283 (58 per cent) during the year 1492–3. The importation of Spanish wines had fallen to 580 tuns from 746 in the same years. The value of commodities other than wine imported in the year 1503–4 was £1,148 15s. 2d., representing, with exports[1] valued at £235 3s. 4d., 13 per cent of the relevant total for the port. In the year 1492–3 it had been £6,495 11s. (54 per cent). It is probable that the following years showed a further decline in the Spanish trade of Bristol.

The decline of Southampton's direct trade with Spain at the end of Henry VII's reign may be seen from the local port books for the years 1502–3 and 1504–5.[2] In the earlier account the chief ship which almost certainly visited Andalusia was that of John Thomson, returning to the port on 14 March 1503 laden with oil, wine, soap and fruit for local merchants regularly trading to Spain and two freemen of London. The next voyage made by Thomson was to Bordeaux whence the regular Spanish traders shipped wine and woad. In the second account this preference for Bordeaux is much more marked, for the Spanish trade had further diminished. It is more difficult to assess the decline of the Spanish trade of the Devonshire ports from the particulars of customs. In the last full year of Henry VII's reign at least two Devon ships returned to Plymouth with goods from Andalusia,[3] and in the previous year at least four brought similar commodities into Exeter.[4] In both ports iron and iron goods were also imported in those years. But it is impossible to tell whether the southern Spanish goods were collected in an Andalusian port or came from Portugal.

London represents an even more difficult task, for surviving particulars of customs are of petty custom and wool exports only and thus the trade of Englishmen with Spain is not shown. Spanish merchants are seen importing large quantities of Toulouse woad, Alonso Compludo, Fernando de Aza, Martín Maluenda and Diego de Cadagua being prominent among them.

---

[1] Other than cloths without grain and tanned hides.
[2] Southampton Municipal MSS., Local Port Books, 1502–3, 1504–5.
[3] P.R.O., K.R. Customs, 115/12.
[4] ibid., 201/3.

The greater part of this woad was carried in English ships which now found that the operation of the Spanish navigation acts in the Andalusian ports rendered trade there too precarious. Undoubtedly their experience at Seville in the summer of 1505 deterred many English merchants from visiting that port for several years.[1] There had even been discrimination against Spanish ships carrying the goods of English merchants.[2]

At his death Henry VII left Anglo-Spanish relations and the trade between the two countries worse than he found them at his accession. Yet, during the first fifteen years of his reign both had been put on a firm footing. His commercial policy had undermined the dominant position of the Spaniards and encouraged English merchants and ships to take a greater part in the trade to Spain. His measures against the Spanish merchants must—for a time at least—have considerably increased his revenue from their trading activities and this was unquestionably his main consideration. The pre-occupation of the Spanish monarchs with the promotion of wool exports and their readiness to subordinate economic to political considerations helped at first to make Henry's policy extremely successful. The protection of native shipping, a prominent feature of Spanish policy, demanded retaliation against Henry's navigation acts, however, and when the *pragmática* of 1494 was enforced it struck a heavy blow against the increased amount of English shipping visiting Andalusia. Finally, the death of Isabella and anti-English feeling among powerful elements in Castile made the trade almost impossible. Only with the resumption of Anglo-Spanish friendship and strong government in Castile could the English merchants hope for a new period of prosperous trade with Spain.

[1] *Vide supra*, p. 51.   [2] *Vide supra*, p. 50.

CHAPTER III

THE YEARS OF PROSPERITY

THE death of Henry VII and the strengthening of Ferdinand's position in Castile seemed to promise a new period of prosperity to the English trade with Spain. The young king's intention to reverse the policy of his father's last years was clearly demonstrated by the prompt fulfilment of his marriage with Katherine and his readiness to support his father-in-law's continental schemes. Anglo-Spanish friendship in this period depended largely upon hostility to France and Henry VIII at this stage was bent on war against the traditional enemy. The treaty of April 1513 confirmed that the existing commercial agreements were still in force,[1] to the satisfaction of the English merchants. Their position in the trade had been secured by Henry VII's measures and with the resumption of amicable relations between England and Spain a flourishing commerce was again possible. Unfortunately, when this new treaty was solemnly agreed upon by the Spanish ambassador in London, Ferdinand had already secretly signed a truce with France. The outlook for the English merchants was not, after all, quite so promising.

A short while later a Spanish merchant, Domingo de Losa, suffered confiscation of his goods for selling a carrack to Henry VIII at a time when Spanish ships were co-operating with the English in the Channel. Apparently Henry had bought several vessels from Spaniards, although such sales were forbidden by Spanish law.[2] Ferdinand declared that on account of his friendship with Henry he would pardon De Losa on this occasion but instructed his ambassador to stress that his clemency would be criticised in Spain. It would be said that Ferdinand showed more favour to the English than Spaniards received in England. The Spanish king claimed that he observed English laws in his relations with English subjects and said he expected Henry to pay similar deference to the laws of Spain. At all events he could not allow Spanish ships to be sold abroad, and Henry was requested

---

[1] *Spanish Calendar, 1509–25*, no. 101.
[2] Larraz, *La Epoca del Mercantilismo en Castilla* p. 40.

neither to buy them nor allow his subjects to do so unless the seller could produce a royal licence in proof that he was permitted to sell.[1] Dissatisfaction with the status of the Spanish merchants in England and a hint of anti-English feeling in Castile may be discerned in this otherwise reasonable protest.

In the following year far more serious differences arose. Henry, stung by his father-in-law's duplicity, forestalled him in making peace with France and even toyed with the idea of reviving Henry VII's scheme of interfering in Castile, advancing a claim of his own through Katherine.[2] Now it was the turn of the English to make difficulties for the Spaniards. In December 1514 Luis Carroz, Ferdinand's ambassador, complained that Spanish captains were ill-treated in England and forbidden to lade cargoes for the Levant. The English claimed that there existed an old statute prohibiting all ships from taking part in this trade without special licence from the king. Members of the Privy Council assured Carroz that the enforcement of this statute was not directed against the Spaniards but had been effected for the protection of the king's interests. If the six ships sent by Henry VIII were unable to carry all the merchandise for the Levant the Spanish captains could lade it in their ships. The ambassador declared this was merely a pretext. He saw quite clearly that the resuscitation of the statute was a measure of retaliation against the enforcement of the Spanish navigation laws and an attempt to force the Spaniards to relax them. The Spanish captains complained bitterly of the heavy losses they sustained by being forced to sail from England with empty ships[3] and this prohibition was a severe blow to their growing interest in the carrying trade to the Levant. The incident recalls the occasion in 1505 when a large number of English merchants received similar treatment in Seville.[4]

The unnatural alliance between England and France did not long survive the death of Louis XII, however, and a new Anglo-Spanish treaty was concluded in 1515.[5] It contained three commercial clauses. Clause 2 re-affirmed the general agreement contained in the Treaty of Medina del Campo that the subjects of either of the kings had full liberty to travel without passport

---

[1] *Letters and Papers*, i(2). nos. 1866, 2131; *Spanish Calendar, 1509–25*, no. 122.
[2] *Spanish Calendar, 1509–25*, no. 192.
[3] ibid., no. 201.
[4] *Vide supra*, p. 51. [5] *Spanish Calendar, 1509–25*, no. 229.

and conduct commerce and other business in the dominions of the other, provided they respected the laws and privileges of the town or city in which they resided. Clause 5 stated that no letters of marque or reprisal were to be given by either of the contracting parties against subjects of the other. All vessels belonging to subjects of either monarch were to give security amounting to double the value of the vessel and its merchandise that they would keep the peace at sea with subjects of the other monarch. If any captain or crew of any vessel violated this clause the victims should be compensated from the security. In clause 9 it was declared that if a ship belonging to subjects of one party should be wrecked on the shores of any of the dominions of the other all possible assistance would be given in saving its cargo. The goods recovered were to be collected and restored to the owners, who should be bound to pay only a moderate sum, settled by four experts, as reward for the work of salvage. Shortly after this treaty was concluded Ferdinand died.

The accession of Charles and his subsequent election as the Emperor were of great importance in the development of Anglo-Spanish commerce in the early Tudor period. There had been for a number of years an increase in the proportion of trade between England and Spain by way of the Low Countries. The trend was for a triangular movement of trade between the three countries. Now that these two important markets for English cloth were under the same ruler, commercial relations between England and each of them could hardly be separated, although they were, in effect, upon a different basis. English trade with the Low Countries was older and better established than with Spain and the position of the English merchants there much stronger. Often commercial ties between the Low Countries and England had determined the foreign policies of both parties. The trade with Spain had no such influence except at this time as a part of England's general commercial interest which demanded friendship with the Emperor. Spanish economy was becoming increasingly concerned with the importation of precious metals from the New World and Anglo-Spanish trade consequently more important to the English merchants than to the Spaniards, although the Andalusian wine and oil trades depended a great deal upon their English customers[1] and Spanish shipping con-

[1] *Vide infra*, p. 185.

tinued to carry a large proportion of the trade. If relations between Henry VIII and Charles became hostile, Anglo-Spanish trade would be the chief sufferer.

The accession of Charles V promised certain advantages to the English merchants trading to Spain. As ruler of the Low Countries and later as Emperor, Charles did not pursue a national policy in the interests of Spain, whose economy was subordinated to his European schemes. The establishment of strong rule in Castile after the crushing defeat of the *Comuneros* and Charles' tolerance of foreign merchants increased the prosperity of the English in Spain, especially in Andalusia where native commercial enterprise had already suffered a severe blow by the expulsion of the Jews in the previous reign. Economic conditions on the whole favoured the English in Spain for the remainder of Henry VIII's reign. Their misfortunes arose mainly from political and religious causes. The Hapsburg-Valois struggle which dominated European politics during this period had a twofold effect upon Anglo-Spanish commercial relations. England's support was sought by the Emperor whenever he went to war with France. At such times the position of the English merchants trading to Spain was relatively secure; the early years of Charles V's reign were probably their most prosperous in this period. Eventually the Franco-Spanish wars were to prove a leading factor in the decline of the trade, however, for they never ended satisfactorily and always encouraged privateering and piracy.

The English merchants were anxious to have their privileges confirmed by the new king. In the Low Countries they demanded the confirmation of the treaty of 1506 which they alleged had not been observed by the Flemings.[1] But Charles was not willing to comply with their demand and the treaty of 1520 left the matter undecided.[2] He was equally anxious to avoid committing himself on the question of the privileges of the English in Spain until he had studied it more closely. The English merchants therefore petitioned Henry VIII to confirm that their position was secure. This the king did, issuing letters patent on 13 July 1519, setting out 'the articles touchinge the liberties graunted to the said marchantes there (i.e. Spain) by the king of Romaines

---

[1] *Letters and Papers*, ii(1), nos. 540, 723, 724, etc.
[2] ibid., iii (1), no. 739.

and Spayne in the last generalle league betweene the said kinges.'[1] The early 1520's were undoubtedly among the most prosperous years enjoyed by the English merchants trading to Spain in the Tudor period. Their privileges at San Lucar de Barrameda had been re-affirmed in a charter in 1517, and the notarial records of Seville show that their trade there and in other Andalusian ports was also flourishing. Further evidence of the prosperity of the trade is furnished by the ledger of Thomas Howell covering the years 1517–28[2] and the wills of Howell and Robert Thorne whose fortunes were largely built up in these years. Some of the most enterprising English merchants of the time were attracted to Andalusia, including the Thornes of Bristol, Roger Barlow and Thomas Howell. These and other Englishmen were also taking part in the trade to the New World in accordance with the treaties.[3]

Surviving particulars of customs of English ports concerned in the Anglo-Spanish trade convey only an impression of this prosperity. A detailed analysis of the particulars of customs of Bristol is possible only for two years during the whole of Henry VIII's reign—1512–13[4] and 1517–18[5]. The first of these years shows a marked increase in the volume of the Spanish trade of the port over the last available figures for Henry VII's reign.[6] The export of cloths without grain rose from 975 to 1,681, of tanned hides from 14½ dickers to 218; and the value of other merchandise exported to Spain was £346 18s. 1d.—higher than any previous year analysed. The amount of wine imported from Spain increased only slightly, from 580 to 593 tuns. The value of other imports more than doubled, however, for in this year it was £2,986 5s. 2d., compared with £1,148 15s. 2d. in the year 1503–4. Iron was by far the biggest of these imports with a customs valuation of £1,565 16s. 8d., followed by woad (£882 5s.) and oil (£157). These figures, though much smaller than those of the year 1492–93,[7] represent a greater proportion of the overseas trade of the port. Cloths without grain exported to Spain were 77 per cent of the total shipped from Bristol in the year

[1] B. M., Harleian MS. 36, f. 18.
[2] *Vide supra*, pp. 20 seq.
[3] *Vide infra*, pp. 71 seq.
[4] P.R.O., K.R. Customs, 21/1. *Vide infra* Appendix A., p. 211.
[5] ibid., 199/2. *Vide infra* Appendix A., p. 212.
[6] *Vide supra*, pp. 53–54.
[7] *Vide supra*, p. 41.

1512–13; the wine imported from Spain 77 per cent of the total and the value of all other commodities (except tanned hides) 37 per cent. This was a year of war against France which adversely affected the volume of trade but enhanced the comparative amount of Spanish wine imported into Bristol. In the second of these accounts exports to Spain (except tanned hides which dropped to 117 dickers) show a definite increase, cloths without grain numbering 1,988 and other merchandise valued at £528 19s. 7d. But there was a slight decrease in imports. Wine from Spain amounted to only 561 tuns and the value of other commodities £2,767 6s. 6d. Iron was again the biggest import (reflecting the more bellicose policy of Henry VIII) with a customs valuation of £1,821 11s. 11d. Oil (£454), woad (£110 6s. 3d.) and soap (£108 17s. 6d.) were the next most important commodities imported. In this year the number of cloths without grain shipped to Spain represents 70 per cent of the total exported from Bristol, but with the renewal of peace with France the amount of wine imported from Spain decreased to 34 per cent of the total. The value of all other merchandise of the trade (except tanned hides) fell to the same percentage of the corresponding total for the port.

As in the previous reign, local merchants dominated the Spanish trade of Bristol in these years. Among the most prominent were John and William Shipman, John Ware, John Drewes and Roger Dawes. Robert Thorne and Martin Pollard, an associate of Thorne in Seville, are shown trading to Spain, and in the second account Nicholas and John Thorne also made a number of shipments there. Thomas Batcock, now firmly established in Renteria, made one shipment of cloth to north Spain in the year 1517–18. Thomas Ashhurst and John Thomas, Bristol pioneers in voyages of discovery during Henry VII's reign,[1] continued to trade to Spain in these years. William Ostriche appears for the first time in the particulars of customs for the year 1517–18 and Roger Barlow made one shipment to Spain from Bristol during the same year. John Cappes and Richard Pryn, later important Spanish traders of the port, also appear in this account, but the Vaughan and Browne families made fewer shipments than in previous years. George Monox is not shown trading in these accounts, for he had long since migrated to London

[1] *Cal. Pat. Rolls, 1494–1509.* p. 224.

and become a freeman of the Drapers' Company of the capital.[1] A few London merchants also traded to Spain through Bristol in these years, notably Thomas Malliard.

Since detailed analysis of the particulars of customs of Bristol is not possible after the year 1517–18 no further figures for the Spanish trade can be estimated.[2] An impression from the accounts of the years 1522–23 and 1525–26,[3] however, indicates a definite increase in the volume of the trade over the earlier years of Henry VIII's reign. The same Bristol merchants dominated it as before. The name of Robert Thorne does not appear in these accounts, but although he was now in Seville he probably traded through Bristol in these years in co-operation with his brother Nicholas. He is shown trading through London at about this time.[4] Nicholas Thorne made many shipments to Spain in both years, and imported a consignment of oil and soap valued at £253 10s. in a Spanish ship in July 1526. It is of interest that one of their sisters, Katherine Woseley (wife, or perhaps by this time widow, of a Bristol merchant), also traded to Spain in that year. John Cappes and Richard Pryn shipped more goods to Spain in these years; so did William Ostriche. For the first time the name of John Sweeting appears in the Bristol customs accounts, though it is not known which of the brothers made the one shipment recorded. In December 1525 a ship of Exeter, the *Marie Spert*, Robert Spert master, put into Bristol with a Spanish cargo consisting of 112 tuns of wine and other merchandise valued at £186. Several of the merchants shipping these goods, including John Blackaller, Gilbert Kyrke and John Maynard, are shown from the Exeter customs accounts of the same period as regular Spanish traders from the Devon port. The Spanish trade of Exeter and Dartmouth and that of Plymouth and Fowey appear from the few surviving particulars of customs to have increased in the first fifteen years of Henry VIII's reign. Among the leading Plymouth merchants trading to Spain in these years were William Hawkins and other members of his family. William himself was master of the *Jesus* of Plymouth when she made a voyage to Andalusia towards the end of 1525. It could not have been his only visit to those parts. Nicholas

---

[1] *Vide supra*, p. 35.
[2] *Vide supra*, Introduction p. xviii.
[3] P.R.O., K.R. Customs, 21/4, 21/5.
[4] ibid., 81/8.

Horsewell, a member of another prominent Plymouth merchant family friendly to Hawkins, is also shown as a Spanish trader of the port; so is Peter Grisling, their bitter enemy in the 1530's.[1]

Particulars of customs of London for these years are even more unsatisfactory since, as in the latter years of Henry VII, almost all of those surviving are of wool exports or the petty custom only. Particulars of the collection of the subsidy of tunnage and poundage in the year 1519–20[2] alone give an indication of the Spanish trade. These show that Spanish shipping still carried a large proportion of Spanish goods into the capital, though mostly for English merchants. Most prominent of the Spanish merchants was Martín de Guinea, resident in London, who figures in a number of lawsuits in these years and occasionally acted as arbitrator between other merchants.[3] It is of interest that De Guinea acted as factor in London for a number of his fellow countrymen in Rouen. In 1525 Margaret of Savoy demanded restitution of a ship belonging to Alonso de Sevilla plundered near Lisbon by Englishmen, although Martín de Guinea, Alonso's factor, had obtained a safe conduct in England.[4] Other merchants on whose behalf De Guinea had sold wares in London sued him for breach of contract in 1527[5] and the decision went against Martín.[6] Other Spaniards prominent in the trade of this year were Alvaro de Castro, also trading through Bristol[7] and Southampton[8] at this time and Alvaro de Medina who later took out papers of denization.[9]

English merchants trading to Spain from London in the year 1519–20 included many of the leading citizens of the capital and prominent Spanish traders of the period. The drapers were well represented. William Roche, sometime lord mayor of London and one of its members of Parliament, to whom Thomas Howell was apprenticed, imported goods from north Spanish and Andalusian ports. Thomas Howell himself and Robert Lesse, another London draper acting as his agent in the capital, also traded to

[1] *Vide supra*, p. 10.
[2] P.R.O., K.R. Customs, 81/8.
[3] *Letters and Papers*, iv (2), nos. 3014, 3086, etc.
[4] ibid., iv (1), no. 1598.
[5] ibid., iv (2), no. 3240.
[6] ibid., iv (3), no. 5287.
[7] P.R.O., K.R. Customs, 21/5.
[8] Southampton Municipal MSS., Local Port Book, 1523–24.
[9] *Vide supra*, p. 17.

Spain during this year. So did Thomas Malliard and Francis Bawdwyn. The latter, a London draper who also enjoyed burgess rights in Southampton, acted for a time as Howell's factor in Spain.[1] After his death there was a dispute over his affairs between Richard Reynolds, mercer, also shown in this account trading to Spain, and Oliver Leder, fishmonger of London and husband of Bawdwyn's daughter Frances. In a lengthy suit before Thomas Cromwell, Paul Withypoll, William Roche and other arbitrators, a great deal of evidence of transactions in Spain was heard. Robert Palmer, Andrew Woodcock and Nicholas Lambert, Spanish traders appearing in this account, were also involved in the lawsuit.[2] There are a number of documents concerned with the settlement of Bawdwyn's affairs in the *Archivo de Protocolos de Sevilla*. On 29 December 1526, for example, Robert Thorne gave powers of attorney to Pedro Cavallero of San Lucar de Barrameda to act on behalf of Roger Barlow in a suit against Woodcock concerning transactions with Bawdwyn.[3] Woodcock, then in San Lucar, was representing Bawdwyn's heirs.[4]

Robert Thorne is shown in this London account trading to Spain and the prominent Merchant Adventurer to whom he had been apprenticed, Paul Withypoll, also made shipments from Spain this year. Other interesting figures in the Anglo-Spanish trade named in this account are Roger Basing, William Wilford, Thomas Traves and Henry Patmer. Basing, who also traded to Spain through Bristol,[5] later went to Andalusia on a special mission for the king.[6] He became imprisoned for debt during that visit but was subsequently released and served as a vice-admiral in the last French war of Henry VIII's reign.[7] William Wilford was a member of a prominent family of Spanish and Levant traders.[8] Traves was one of a number of wealthy London merchants residing in Bilbao at this time.[9] Patmer, a freeman of the London Drapers' Company[10] and trader to Spain through

[1] Ledger of Thomas Howell, f. 2v.
[2] *Letters and Papers*, iv, *passim*.
[3] Archivo de Protocolos de Sevilla, *Oficio* V, 1526, *Libro* IV, f. 345v.
[4] ibid., *Libro* I, f. 453.
[5] P.R.O., K.R. Customs, 21/7, 199/3 etc.
[6] *Vide infra*, p. 118
[7] *A.P.C.*, 1542–47, p. 60.
[8] Hakluyt, *The Principal Navigations*, v., p. 69.
[9] *Vide supra*, p. 8.
[10] *Roll of the Drapers' Company of London* (ed. P. Boyd), p. 140.

Bristol[1] and Southampton[2] as well as the capital, is by far the most interesting of these merchants. He was the English pilot accompanying Roger Barlow on Cabot's voyage to La Plata in 1526. Harrisse calls him Latimer, although his own transcriptions of the Spanish documents concerned with the voyage show him as 'Enrique Patimer',[3] and English historians have repeated this error.[4] Patmer is named by William Pepwell as pilot of one of the Emperor's ships in an expedition in search of new spiceries in 1534.[5]

Some indication of the Spanish trade of Southampton in the early years of Henry VIII's reign may be obtained from surviving local port books. Several ships brought in commodities from Andalusia for Southampton burgesses (including Francis Bawdwyn) in the year 1509–10 and others brought iron into the Hampshire port. It is recorded that a number of Spanish merchants exported wheat in this year, and Spanish shipping was prominent in the Levant trade of Southampton, very often carrying the goods of Italian merchants residing in London.[6] Three years later[7] there was a marked increase in the amount of Spanish goods imported into Southampton, especially iron. More ships also brought in wine, oil, soap and other commodities from southern Spain, sometimes collected on their way from the Levant. Several London merchants traded to Spain through Southampton in this year, including Thomas Malliard, John Maynard and Robert Elliott. Juan de Castro, Pedro de Miranda and Fernando de Aza, Spanish merchants residing in the capital, also made shipments. Prominent local merchants trading to Spain were Nicholas Cowart, John Perchard, Peter Stonard and Thomas Lyster. In November 1514 several ships returned from Andalusia with goods for Cowart, Francis Bawdwyn and other leading burgesses of Southampton and Thomas Malliard of London. A number of Spanish vessels bringing in iron during the year returned to their home ports laden with wheat.[8] A great

---

[1] P.R.O., K.R. Customs, 199/2.
[2] Southampton Municipal MSS., Local Port Book, 1520–21.
[3] H. Harrisse, *John and Sebastian Cabot*, pp. 415, 416, etc.
[4] e.g. E. G. R. Taylor, *Tudor Geography, 1485–1583*, p. 46; J. A. Williamson, *Hawkins of Plymouth*, p. 9.
[5] B.M., Cotton MS. Vespasian CVII, f. 62.
[6] Southampton Municipal MSS., Local Port Book, 1509–10.
[7] ibid., 1512–13.
[8] ibid., 1514–15.

deal of wheat was exported to Spain in these years, especially when Spanish troops in the north had to be provisioned. Among other prominent Spaniards Juan de Castro was granted a licence, to export 1,000 quarters in November 1516[1] and Juan de Soto, Queen Katherine's apothecary, received a similar licence in the following January.[2] In the same month Thomas Batcock obtained a licence to export 1,000 quarters of wheat and other foodstuffs.[3]

An incomplete Southampton port book for the year 1515–16[4] shows a further increase in the amount of trade to Andalusia, often by way of the Low Countries. Ships from the Levant brought in Spanish commodities for London merchants, including Italians, but the local burgesses usually traded direct with Spain. Nicholas Lambert and Robert Palmer, Spanish traders of London involved in the lawsuit following the death of Francis Bawdwyn, traded through Southampton in this year. So did Bawdwyn himself. The local port book for the year 1520–21[5] contains the names of a number of Spanish ships anchored off the port but gives no indication of any goods unloaded. This illustrates the function of Southampton as a rendezvous for Spanish vessels returning from the Low Countries. Henry Huttoft, one of the most prominent burgesses of the port in the early Tudor period, appears in this account with his brother Thomas importing wine, fruit, sugar and tunny fish. Antonio Guidotti, a Florentine who became a prosperous burgess of Southampton and was soon to marry into the Huttoft family,[6] also appears in this account importing Spanish goods.

Surviving particulars of customs of the English ports give an inadequate picture of this period of the Anglo-Spanish trade. Fortunately, sources elsewhere provide considerable evidence of the prosperity of the English merchants trading to Spain in the early years of Charles V's reign. The *Archivo de Protocolos de Sevilla* contains documents showing transactions of Englishmen in San Lucar de Barrameda, Cadiz and Jerez as well as Seville itself. The leading English merchant in Andalusia at this

---

[1] *Letters and Papers*, ii (1), no. 2588.
[2] ibid., ii (2), no. 2817.
[3] ibid., no. 2851.
[4] Southampton Municipal MSS., Local Port Book, 1515–16.
[5] ibid., 1520–21.
[6] Ruddock, *Italian Merchants and Shipping in Southampton, 1270–1600*, pp. 247–9, etc.

time was Robert Thorne of Bristol who, it appears like other prominent Spanish traders, had migrated to London as a young man and become apprenticed in one of the city companies. It is not known when he took up residence in Seville, but by the early 1520's he was very well established there. Lee, the English ambassador in Spain, spoke highly of Thorne, whom he described with Thomas Bridges as being of 'great credence' in those parts.[1] In partnership with Thomas Malliard, Leonardo Cattaneo, a Genoese, and Alonso de Melgar, a Seville banker, Thorne owned a soap manufacturing business supplying soap to Spanish customers and for export to England. Notarial documents show that at least two future governors of the Andalusia Company had dealings with the soap factory at this time.[2] Martin Pollard, too, acknowledged on 10 October 1523 that he owed a debt of 68,250 *maravedís* to Robert Thorne, Leonardo Cattaneo and Alonso de Melgar for 65 quintals of soap bought from them.[3] Other documents drawn up for Thorne and Cattaneo show the association of the Bristol man with the Genoese.[4] Robert Thorne is seen in these records trading on his own behalf, delegating powers to factors and attorneys to do business for him and handling the affairs of other English merchants. At one time he acted as attorney for his old master, Paul Withypoll, but in October 1524 transferred his power to Thomas Tison,[5] later to act as Thorne's factor in the West Indies. Among other merchants acting on Thorne's behalf was William Pepwell.[6]

Thomas Malliard, sometime factor of Thomas Howell and partner of Robert Thorne, was another of the most prosperous English merchants in Seville at this time. Malliard died in the early 1520's and his brother John, whom he had made his heir, went out to Seville to claim his inheritance, a fair-sized fortune accumulated in the Spanish trade. A number of documents drawn up by Francisco de Castellanos, public notary of the city, in the autumn of 1523 refer to business transactions concerned with the soap factory. John Malliard finally received the sum of 716,000 *maravedís* from his brother's partners on this account.

[1] B.M., Cotton MS. Vespasian C III, f. 237.
[2] William Ostriche and Richard Cooper. Archivo de Protocolos de Sevilla, *Oficio* V, 1523, *Libro* III, ff. 120v, 136v.
[3] ibid., f. 156 v.
[4] ibid., 1524, *Libro* II, f. 557; ibid., 1526, *Libro* IV, f. 266, etc.
[5] *Vide infra*, Appendix C, p. 229.
[6] Archivo de Protocolos de Sevilla, *Oficio* V, 1526, *Libro* IV, f. 409.

Payment was made partly in bills of exchange payable in England, issued to him by Robert Thorne and a balance of 39,500 *maravedís* in new gold ducats. The money was handed over to John Malliard when a document listing the assets and liabilities of his brother in the business was signed in the house of Thomas Bridges in Calle de Bayona in Seville. The notary tells us that since Malliard did not understand Castilian the document was read over to him in English by Bridges and Martin Pollard before he signed it.[1] Malliard subsequently gave Robert Thorne and Roger Barlow powers of attorney to settle his affairs and collect any debts still owing to his brother.[2] One of his debtors was William Ostriche. On 2 October 1523 Ostriche, describing himself as a citizen of Bristol living in San Lucar de Barrameda, acknowledged that he owed John Malliard as Thomas's heir the sum of 515 gold ducats for certain transactions made on his brother's behalf. This sum included payment for one hundred quintals of white soap and a number of silks sold by him. Ostriche had also received money totalling £25 in Bristol from John Thorne, John Cappes, Richard Pryn and John Udall and 60 ducats by exchange.[3] The following day Thorne and Barlow, acting on John Malliard's behalf, acknowledged before Francisco de Castellanos that Ostriche had settled this debt.[4] In another document John Malliard gave a 'quetans' to Thomas Bridges, Robert Thorne and Roger Barlow as executors of his brother's will.[5]

An interesting reference to John Malliard is contained in a letter from Sampson, Lee's predecessor as ambassador to Charles V, to Wolsey from Valladolid in November 1524. Sampson told the cardinal that he had been compelled to borrow 600 ducats by 'cambeo and recambeo'[6] from a certain Malliard, brother of a merchant who died in Seville three years earlier. The ambassador claimed that he had assisted John Malliard to recover 6,000 or 7,000 ducats by making representations to the Emperor. Sampson, who had no previous experience of taking up money by exchange, denounced it as cloaked usury and said usury was the chief

---

[1] Archivo de Protocolos de Sevilla, *Oficio* V, 1523, *Libro* III, f. 96.
[2] ibid., f. 98.
[3] ibid., f. 120v.
[4] ibid., f. 123.
[5] ibid., f. 100.
[6] i.e. by exchange.

merchandise in those parts. But he asked Wolsey to redeem the
bill he had issued as soon as possible. Sampson declared that his
efforts alone had enabled Malliard to recover his inheritance and
complained bitterly of his ingratitude. Malliard had not even
thanked him for his services yet told people he had given the
ambassador large gifts. This was not true.[1] Sampson's bitterness towards the merchants is in marked contrast with the cordial relations between Lee and the Englishmen trading to Spain.

The registers of the Seville notaries contain many references
to the business activities of Thomas Howell, whose ledger in the
Drapers' Hall gives an account of his affairs in these years.
Howell had become a freeman of the Drapers' Company in the
year 1506–7 through apprenticeship to William Roche, a prominent London merchant. It is possible, however, that he came
originally from Bristol for he traded a great deal through the
Gloucester port and left money in his will for charitable purposes there. Moreover, in his ledger he refers to Hugh Elliott of
Bristol as his former master.[2] Elliott traded to Spain during the
reigns of Henry VII and Henry VIII[3] and his name occurs from
time to time in Howell's accounts. He is perhaps better known
as one of the early pioneers of voyages of discovery whom Robert
Thorne mentioned as an associate of his father in his famous
letter to Dr. Lee in 1527.[4] In June 1538 Howell stated he had
been in Spain on and off for some twenty-six years.[5] The
reference to Hugh Elliott as his master when he first came
suggests he may have been employed in Spain as a factor when
he first went out there. At all events, by the time his ledger opens
Thomas Howell was firmly established in Seville on his own
account, which is clear from a list of outstanding debts owing
to him at the beginning of his book.

The notarial documents show Howell dealing most often in
oil, and numerous Spanish merchants acknowledged debts they
owed him for this commodity.[6] An entry in the ledger instructing Alonso de la Lonja, one of his factors, to invest more than
£1,000 in oil confirms the size of Howell's transactions in this

---

[1] P.R.O., State Papers, Henry VIII, vol. 32, f. 157.
[2] Ledger of Thomas Howell, f. 31v.
[3] P.R.O., K.R. Customs, 20/9, 199/1, 199/2, etc.
[4] Hakluyt, op. cit., ii, p. 178. *Vide supra*, p. 48.
[5] *Vide infra*, p. 70.
[6] *Vide infra*, Appendix C, p. 227.

important product of Andalusia.[1] Alonso de la Lonja is also shown in the notarial documents acting as Howell's agent.[2] No reference has been found to transactions between Howell and other leading Englishmen in Seville in these records, however, although we know from the ledger that several acted as his factor[3] and that he had dealings with many others. Mention is made of Robert and Nicholas Thorne in Howell's book and of Roger Barlow.[4] William Pepwell, the leading petitioner to Henry VIII for permission to form the Andalusia Company, dealt on occasion with the London draper.[5] So did William Ostriche, governor of the company in its darkest days when the Inquisition threatened the lives as well as the goods of many of its members.[6] There is also reference to Thomas Pery, whose own account of his ordeal at the hands of the inquisitors gives the most graphic details of an important phase in the history of Anglo-Spanish trade in the sixteenth century.[7] Andrew Woodcock and Richard Reynolds are among other well known London traders to Spain shown by the ledger as having dealings with Howell. The latter gave evidence in the *Reynolds v Leder* case concerning the will of Francis Bawdwyn. Howell's evidence of book-keeping by English merchants in Spain is of interest. He said on 10 June 1528:

that he hath beyn in the partyes of Spayne goyng and comyng by the space of xxvj yeres or theraboutes by all whiche tyme he hath vsyd marchaundyse and beyn allowed in cumpanye of marchauntes as well straungers of all nacions as Englysshe men and he never sawe any accompt gevyn by any marchaunt of what nacion soever he were of / but the playnnes therof myght be easelly perceyved by every man that hath any knowlege and not to be gevyn yn suche forme as noo man can vnderstonde yt but hym selfe orelles the marchauntes of Spayn wyll call hym noo playn marchaunt. [8]

Howell's ledger contains the only reference discovered in an English source to an English merchant despatching goods to

[1] *Vide supra*, p. 21.
[2] Archivo de Protocolos de Sevilla, *Oficio* V, 1525, *Libro* I, ff. 390, 607, etc.
[3] *Vide supra*, pp. 20 *seq.*
[4] Ledger of Thomas Howell, ff. 59v, 65v.
[5] ibid., ff. 13v, etc.
[6] *Vide infra*, pp. 119 *seq.*
[7] *Vide infra*, pp. 111 *seq.*
[8] P.R.O., State Papers, Henry VIII, vol. 48, f. 158.

the New World in this period,[1] but the notarial documents of
Seville contain ample evidence of this trade. One of the first
Englishmen to take part in the trade to the Indies was Thomas
Malliard. The register of Bernal González Vallecillo shows that
he supplied goods for transportation to San Domingo as early
as 1509.[2] Four years later a Spanish broker, acting on behalf of
Malliard, gave powers of attorney to two of his fellow countrymen in the Indies to recover money owing to the English merchant there.[3] The register of Juan de la Cuadra for the year 1516
contains a number of references to Thomas Malliard's affairs,
including an obligation of Sebastian Cabot, then in Seville as a
royal pilot,[4] to repay 55 ducats of gold which he had borrowed
from him.[5] John Malliard's power of attorney to Robert Thorne
and Roger Barlow to handle his interests specified gold and
other commodities due from the Indies.[6] On 30 September 1523
Roger Barlow gave the necessary power to John Malliard to
claim:

seys cientos e setenta e *qua*tro pesos de oro . . . rregistrados *de* las Yndias *del* mar oçeano en el rregistro del rrey . . . el qual d*i*cho oro con el
mas oro que la d*i*cha nao traya se rregistro ante los señores juez*e*s *de* la
Casa *de* la Contrataçion *de* las Yndias que rresiden en est*a* d*i*cha
çibdad.[7]

This gold had been brought back to Seville by the master of a
Spanish ship who had taken out wine for Barlow and sold it in
the Indies on his behalf. As the wine had been Thomas Malliard's,
however, Barlow was making over his claim to the gold to the
latter's heir.

Robert Thorne and Roger Barlow themselves took a prominent part in the trade to the New World. It is of great significance
that the Anglo-Spanish trade during the reigns of the first two
Tudors attracted such men and brought them into contact with

[1] *Vide supra*, p. 24.
[2] Archivo de Protocolos de Sevilla, *Oficio*, XV, 1509, *Libro* I, f. 724v.
[3] ibid., *Oficio* V, 1513, *Libro* II, f. 904.
[4] Cabot did not become Pilot Major until 1518.
[5] Archivo de Protocolos de Sevilla, *Oficio* I, 1516, *Libro* I, 9 *de Mayo*.
[6] ibid., *Oficio* V, 1523, *Libro* III, f. 98.
[7] '. . . six hundred and seventy four *pesos* of gold . . . registered from the
Indies of the Ocean Sea in the king's register. . . the which said gold with more
gold the said ship was carrying was declared before the officials of the House
of Trade of the Indies resident in this said city.' Archivo de Protocolos de
Sevilla, *Oficio* V, 1523, *Libro* III, f. 97v.

Spanish maritime power. The discovery of new trade routes and new sources of wealth for England was a matter of concern to these two patriotic merchants, but neither of them received the encouragement from Henry VIII that their enterprise deserved. The letters of Robert Thorne to the English king and Dr. Lee, his ambassador in Spain,[1] attempted, without success, to arouse interest in English projects of discovery. Roger Barlow's *Geographia* was no more successful.[2] Thorne had previously invested money in Cabot's voyage to La Plata especially to secure places on the expedition for Barlow and Henry Patmer. His object was to obtain information of a possible English route to the Spice Islands.[3] One of the first general agreements between Cabot, Thorne and other investors was drawn up by Francisco de Castellanos and signed on 2 December 1524.[4] It is recorded among the papers of the same notary that on 7 February 1526, prior to his departure on the voyage, Roger Barlow gave full powers of attorney to Robert Thorne to look after his business interests during his absence, including consignments from the Indies.[5] On the same day he had a will attested before Francisco de Castellanos in which he named Thorne as his heir and the latter and Martin Pollard executors.[6] Later in the same year there is evidence of Thorne's use of the powers granted him by Barlow in managing his affairs in San Domingo.[7]

There are numerous references in the *Archivo de Protocolos de Sevilla* to the trade of Barlow and Robert Thorne to the New World which throw interesting light upon their methods of conducting this commerce. The charter party drawn up on 18 July 1522 by Manuel Segura, public notary of the city, between Diego Rodríguez Pepino, master of the *San Antón*, and Roger Barlow and Luis Fernández of Seville may well be for the voyage referred to in the power given by Barlow to John Malliard in the following year.[8] Pepino agreed to lade in his ship,

[1] *Letters and Papers*, iv (2), no. 2814.
[2] Taylor, op. cit., p. 58.   [3] ibid., p. 46.
[4] Archivo de Protocolos de Sevilla, *Oficio* V, 1524, *Libro* II, f. 557.
[5] ibid., 1526, *Libro* I, f. 445v.
[6] ibid., f. 447. A transcription of this document appears as an appendix to my article, 'English Merchants trading to the New World in the early sixteenth century' in *Bulletin of the Institute of Historical Research*, vol. xxiii, no. 67 (May 1950), p. 66.
[7] Archivo de Protocolos de Sevilla, *Oficio* V, 1526, *Libro* IV, f. 234v.
[8] ibid., *Oficio* IV, 1522, *Libro* III, f. 393v.

then lying in the Guadalquivir by the city, 70–80 pipes of wine for Barlow and 25 tuns of wine and other merchandise for Fernández and to transport them to San Domingo. Freight charges were fixed at 2,400 *maravedís* per tun and in addition there would be the usual *averías*.[1] Pepino was to be paid the freight charges within thirty days of the ship's arrival at San Domingo, but the *averías* were to be paid before her departure from Seville. On this occasion no factor was to be sent with the goods and it is to be presumed that Barlow and the Spaniard had representatives in San Domingo to collect them and pay the master.

A more interesting charter party was made between Pedro de Agustín, owner and master of the *Santa Ana*, and Robert Thorne on 22 November 1525. The master agreed to transport 40 tons of merchandise for Thorne to the New World. The first ports of call were to be Puerto Rico and San Domingo, but if Agustín could not dispose of all the cargo there he was to proceed to Santiago in Cuba or to a port of New Spain. Freightage rates varied for the different ports. Agustín stated that:

devo av*er* de flete por cada tonelada de las sobre d*í*chas q*ue* en la d*í*cha mi nao cargada *es* de la qu*e* diere en Puerto Rico o Santo Dom*í*ngo a dos mill e qui*n*ient*o*s m*a*raved*í*s desta mon*e*da de Castilla e mas çient m*a*raved*í*s de av*e*rías e de la q*ue* diere en Cuba a tres mill e seteç*i*ent*o*s e çincuenta m*a*raved*í*s syn averias porq*ue* me han de ser pagad*a*s en esta d*í*cha çibdad a los d*í*chos çient m*a*raved*í*s por tonelada e de la q*ue* diere en la d*í*cha Nueva España a ocho mill m*a*raved*í*s p*or* tonelada e mas dosy*en*t*o*s m*a*raved*í*s de averías.[2]

The great difference between the freight charges to San Domingo and Puerto Rico and those to New Spain perhaps reflects the increased risks of attack by French corsairs around those coasts. The increase in distance certainly cannot account for it.

A form of *compañía*[3] between Robert Thorne and Juan de

---

[1] Averages.

[2] 'I am to have freightage for every ton of the aforesaid (merchandise) laden in my said ship that I deliver in Puerto Rico or San Domingo two thousand five hundred Castilian *maravedís* and an additional hundred *maravedís* for averages; and for (every ton) I deliver in Cuba three thousand seven hundred and fifty *maravedís* without averages, for (the latter) have to be paid me in this said city at the said one hundred *maravedís* per ton; and for what I deliver in the said New Spain at eight thousand *maravedís* per ton and in addition two hundred *maravedís* for averages.' Archivo de Protocolos de Sevilla, *Oficio* V, 1525, *Libro* IV, f. 244v.   [3] *Vide supra*, p. 23.

Murcia, a merchant of Cadiz, executed on 17 February 1525 provides an example of another type of business arrangement. The Spaniard agreed to travel with the goods of both partners to the Indies in a ship named the *San Juan*. Thorne's goods, valued at 455,000 *maravedís*, were laden at Seville and registered in the name of Juan de Murcia. They included flour and other foodstuffs, tallow candles, white soap, wrought tin, iron goods and esparto. De Murcia was to lade his own merchandise at San Lucar de Barrameda. Then:

con todas las quales dichas mercaderias me obligo de yr a las dichas Yndias e llevandome Dios en salvamento con ellas de las vender todas en los puertos de la ysla de Sant Juan o Santo Domingo o en otro qualquier puerto de las dichas Yndias que a mi me paresçiere e sea mas pro de las dichas mercaderias e por los mayores preçios que pudiere de contado no pudiendo fiar ni fie mas contra de hasta çient pesos de oro e sy mas fiare que esta a mi cargo e rriesgo.[1]

On his return to Seville Juan de Murcia promised to give Thorne a full and true account of his transactions and the profits were to be divided between them according to the value of the goods they had furnished. Thorne may have been dissatisfied with the Spaniard, however, for in the following year he gave powers of attorney to Thomas Tison and Francisco Núñez, then in San Domingo, to take over all his business interests from his former partner.[2] Two days later (14 November 1526) Thorne gave the two factors similar powers on behalf of Roger Barlow, whose interests in those parts had also been handled by Juan de Murcia.[3]

Robert Thorne also employed agents to purchase commodities on his behalf for transportation to the Indies. On 11 December 1525, for example, Bartolomé Sánchez was authorised not only to purchase 150 *fanegas* of wheat[4] but also:

[1] '. . . with all the which said merchandise I bind myself to go to the said Indies, and, God bearing me there in safety with them, to sell them all in the ports of the isle of San Juan or San Domingo or in any other port of the said Indies which shall seem to me most profitable and where I shall get the highest prices for the said merchandise in cash. I am not to give credit above one hundred *pesos* of gold and if I give more it is to be at my own charge and risk.' Archivo de Protocolos de Sevilla, *Oficio* V, 1525, *Libro* I, f. 315v.

[2] ibid., 1526, *Libro* IV, f. 218v.

[3] ibid., f. 234v.

[4] Equivalent to approximately 240 bushels.

las traer e trayga a los molinos de Marchenilla para alli las moler e faser harina e fecho harina . . . lo (sic) traer e trayga a la carreteria desta dicha çibdad o Triana para de alli lo cargar para las Yndias del mar oçeano.[1]

Nicholas Thorne, Robert's brother, also took part in the trade. A reference to him in the register of Francisco de Castellanos on 2 January 1527 furnishes an example of an English merchant sending a Spanish factor with his goods to the New World. Alonso de Torices acknowledged before the notary on that day that he had received certain goods from Nicholas Thorne which were already laden in the *Trinidad*, master Juan López, then lying in the river at Seville. These goods, consisting chiefly of English cloths and valued at 22,318 *maravedís*, were destined for the port of Cubagua in the island of Las Perlas. Alonso agreed to sell them for cash, which he would either send or bring back in person and render a full account to Thorne. As commission, the Spaniard said:

yo aya por mi trabajo e factoria la terçia parte de la ganançia que Dios nuestro Señor en ello diere quitas todas costas asy de seguro como de fletes e otras que fisyere e sacado el dicho vuestro prençipal.[2]

Thomas Bridges, the other executor of Thomas Malliard, is also known to have traded to the New World.[3] Besides Thomas Tison at least two other Englishmen, Nicholas Arnote[4] and John Martin,[5] are shown by these records to have resided in the Indies at this time.

Further evidence of the prosperous state of the Anglo-Spanish trade in these years is furnished by the wills of two of the leading English merchants taking part in it. The fortunes left by Robert Thorne and Thomas Howell must have both been accumulated largely in the early years of Charles V's reign. Thorne's will is of particular interest for its references to his associates in Bristol,

---

[1] '. . . to bring them to the mills of Marchenilla, there to be ground to flour and to bring the flour to the carters' of this said city or Triana and from there lade it for the Indies of the Ocean Sea.' Archivo de Protocolos de Sevilla, *Oficio* V, 1525, *Libro* IV, f. 482.

[2] 'I should have for my trouble and work as factor a third share of the profit our Lord God shall grant from it less all costs, including insurance, freight charges and any others there may be and excluding your said capital.' Archivo de Protocolos de Sevilla, *Oficio* V, 1527, *Libro* I, f. 3.

[3] ibid., *Oficio* I, 1513, *Libro* II, f. 823v.

[4] ibid., *Oficio* XV, 1516, *Libro* II, 28 *de Agosto*.

[5] ibid., *Oficio* I, 1525, *Libro* I, f. 924v.

London and Spain. Members of the Cattanei family with whom Thorne was in business partnership in Seville were given custody of his son Vincent whom he had left behind in Spain. Vincent was left £3,000 by his father while his mother, Anna Garcia, received £50 on condition that she renounced all pretence to his inheritance. This legacy to his former mistress was exactly half the sum left by the pious merchant to provide for the marriage portions of poor maidens in London and Bristol. Paul Withypoll, William Pepwell, Thomas Tison, John Shipman and Bennet Jay were among many Spanish traders who benefited under the will. Richard Reynolds, the London mercer, was one of the witnesses. Thorne's loyalty to both the city of his birth and that of his adoption is seen in the division of his charitable bequests between Bristol and London.[1] The same is true of Howell.[2] The draper left 1,000 ducats to the poor in each of these cities and an additional 1,000 ducats to supplement Robert Thorne's settlement to provide for young men of Bristol wishing to follow the cloth trade. Howell's executors in England were William Roche, his old master, and Robert Lesse, his agent, who also received bequests under the terms of his will. It is of interest that the draper's executors in Seville were Pedro and Antonio Espinosa, members of the prominent Spanish banking family. The latter was to take over the lease of Howell's house in Seville. Howell's largest legacy was 12,000 ducats to the Drapers' Company which occasioned a great deal of trouble to William Roche's son when he visited Seville to collect it after Howell's death.[3]

In May 1526 Charles V decided to conclude a fresh commercial treaty with Henry VIII. The new Imperial ambassador learned from his instructions that the Emperor would be sending him shortly a copy of the ancient treaties of commerce concluded by the Catholic Kings so that he could draw up a new agreement on similar lines. But Don Iñigo de Mendoza was cautioned to do nothing without consulting Charles and ascertaining his wishes on every point under discussion.[4] In the meantime war against France had not improved commercial relations between England and Spain. There had been depredations at sea and Dr. Lee, the English ambassador in Spain, wrote in March 1527

---

[1] Somerset House, P.C.C. Wills, 18 Thower.
[2] ibid., 24 Alen.
[3] *Vide infra*, p. 108.
[4] *Spanish Calendar*, *1525–26*, no. 410, p. 681.

of the rough handling of some English merchants detained by captains of Fuenterrabia while attempting to trade with France.[1] A few months later Thomas Traves of Bilbao complained to Lee that the English merchants in northern Spain had been greatly troubled by a commission sent to Biscay to enquire into their transactions over the previous twenty years. It was suspected they had been exporting gold.[2] An earlier letter from Lee to Wolsey hints at further difficulties of the English merchants in Spain. The ambassador had been told to make certain unspecified demands to the Emperor in connection with their privileges but said he had little hope of success. The merchants therefore had asked that Wolsey should have their demands granted as part of the new commercial treaty. Lee expressed his anxiety to help them, for, he declared, they were always ready to serve him and most loyal to the king.[3]

Lee also reported that English cloths were being more heavily taxed than had been agreed upon in the privileges granted by Ferdinand and Isabella. The ambassador said he had been asked by a representative of the merchants of Seville to request the Emperor that English cloths imported into Spain should be as free as the Spanish. Lee advised the Spaniard to present the merchants' petition to the president of Charles' council. It seems that this advice was not taken, however, and later the same merchant accompanied Lee to beg the Emperor that all laws passed against English cloths should be declared void. Lee reminded Charles that his own subjects had submitted the petition and the Emperor promised his council would consider it. One of his ministers admitted the justice of the English claim but affirmed that the Imperial ambassador in England had already a commission to deal with it.[4] In March 1527 English merchants had complained to Lee that the false making of cloths was doing them great harm.[5] This seems to imply dishonesty on the part of the home merchants sending out cloths to Spain, although it may refer to the Spanish regulations for cloth making.[6] In either event it was a serious matter, for in that

[1] *Letters and Papers*, iv(2), no. 2986.
[2] ibid., no 3152, p. 1437.
[3] P.R.O., State Papers, Henry VIII, vol. 38, f. 150.
[4] *Letters and Papers*, iv (2), no. 2987.
[5] ibid.
[6] *Vide supra*, p. 2.

same year it was reported that a number of towns in the Low Countries were refusing to accept English cloths, thus stimulating local manufacture to the detriment of English interests and increasing the demand for Spanish wool.[1] The Spaniards, too, had their grievances. In the previous May they were protesting that, in spite of the treaties, the English admiral had seized a Spanish wreck which was by no means derelict.[2] They also complained of injuries inflicted by the French upon Spanish shipping in English ports and waters which the English did little or nothing to prevent or punish.[3]

By the end of the year 1527 the political situation looked so grave that many of the English merchants in northern Spain were making preparations to despatch all their possessions to England. Nicholas Wilford, John Shaa, Thomas Traves and other Englishmen in Bilbao sought safe-conducts for a number of Biscayan sailors to assist them in this task as no English seamen were available.[4] Charles later alleged that Englishmen had been ordered not to take merchandise to his dominions because of the expected rupture.[5] War was eventually declared in January 1528 but it was short and there were no hostilities. English ships and goods in Andalusia which had been arrested were very soon released although Lee, who reported this, did not know if the English merchants in Biscay and Guipuscoa had fared so well.[6] There were a number of clashes at sea, particularly during the interval between the truce and the final peace. At Camber in December 1528 six Spanish ships became involved in a *mêlée* with French vessels. Two were sunk and the others subsequently arrested.[7] Juan de Acorda, a Spanish shipowner, declared that this violation of the truce had cost him 30,000 ducats,[8] and although it was agreed that restitution should be made, the Imperial ambassador feared a large part of De Acorda's goods had been hidden by the English.[9] Depredations at sea continued well into the next year.[10]

[1] *Letters and Papers*, iv (2), no. 3433.
[2] ibid., no. 3106.
[3] ibid., nos. 3782, etc.
[4] ibid., no. 3648.
[5] ibid., no. 3844, p. 1716.
[6] P.R.O., State Papers, Henry VIII, vol. 48, f. 213.
[7] *Letters and Papers*, iv (2), nos. 5000, 5017; ibid., iv (3), nos. 5137 etc.
[8] ibid., no. 5134.
[9] ibid., no. 5255.
[10] ibid., no. 5683.

During the difficult year of 1527 there occurred a significant event in the development of English interest in the New World. Henry VIII was more concerned with European schemes than oceanic enterprises, and while his relations with Charles V remained cordial he gave little encouragement to the bolder spirits among his subjects. His interest in exploration was at best spasmodic. But it is evident that when Anglo-Spanish relations became less friendly English interest in the newly-discovered lands became more active.[1] 1527 was such a year, when, after the defeat of Francis I at Pavia, Henry temporarily changed sides. In March 1527 a Spanish caravel met with an English ship off Puerto Rico. Reporting the encounter[2] the Spanish captain, Ginés Navarro, said he had at first thought it was a Spanish vessel and made to board it, but found himself confronted by a pinnace containing some twenty-five armed men and two guns. The men said they were English and had set sail with another ship from London to seek the land of the *Gran Can*, but a storm had separated them. When the Spaniard asked them what they were doing in those parts, they replied that they wished to trade and make a report to their king from whom they had written instructions which they offered to show Navarro. The latter, being unable to read Latin, had not examined them. The Englishmen left for San Domingo, where they were fired upon and did not land. Later they returned to Puerto Rico and traded with the inhabitants before finally disappearing.[3] Their brief appearance was a portent of things to come when friendly relations between England and Spain finally broke down.

The short period of war in 1528 shows clearly how vital the Emperor's friendship was to English commercial interests and emphasises the triangular flow of trade between England, the Low Countries and Spain. A truce was made first with the Low Countries as the most important English market. Henry then complained that Spaniards were enabled to visit Flanders although Englishmen could not go to Spain. Moreover the Regent was not bound to make restitution out of Spanish property in the Low Countries for injuries committed by Spaniards upon Englishmen. He was informed, however, that Eng-

---

[1] Other instances are the voyage of the *Barbara* and the Reneger Incident. *Vide infra*, Chap. vi.

[2] Archivo General de Indias, Patronato, *Legajo 265, Ramo 1*.

[3] J. A. Williamson, *Maritime Enterprise, 1485–1558*, p. 256.

land would benefit equally from being able to trade with Flanders. She could obtain oil and other Spanish merchandise there and sell cloths which otherwise would have been sent to Spain.[1] The question of obtaining oil was extremely important. Norfolk told Wolsey in May 1528 that the condition of the cloth industry in the Midlands was serious; it was said that unless some oil came from Spain many clothiers would be compelled to stop work.[2]

Events of the last years provided ample warning to the English merchants in Spain that new measures would have to be taken if their position was to be maintained. The precarious political situation and the recent discriminaton against English cloths in Spain were already undermining their prosperity when a new factor entered into Anglo-Spanish relations. Rumours of the English king's intention to separate from the Emperor's aunt were already abroad in Spain in the summer of 1527. Soon the significance of this news must have been the subject of anxious speculation among the English merchants in Andalusia. Doubtless it helped to convince them of the need for greater unity to meet their new difficulties and they petitioned Henry VIII to grant them a licence to form a stronger union. In September 1530 the Andalusia Company came into being.

[1] *Letters and Papers*, iv (2), no. 4404.
[2] ibid., no. 4239.

CHAPTER IV

THE ANDALUSIA COMPANY

THE charter granted by Henry VIII in September 1530 to the English merchants trading to Andalusia strengthened and extended an association which had been in existence for many years in the port of San Lucar de Barrameda. The latter, situated at the mouth of the Guadalquivir, was one of the most important Andalusian ports in the sixteenth century. From very early times San Lucar had been the centre of a flourishing wine industry and its favourable position had enhanced its importance after the discovery of the New World. Lordship of the town had been granted to Don Alonso Pérez de Guzmán, *El Bueno*, by the king of Castile in 1297 as a reward for his services in the wars against the Moors. The sixth member of the Guzmán family to be lord of San Lucar was created Duke of Medina Sidonia in 1446 after the confirmation by King John II of his possession of the port and successive dukes enjoyed the suzerainty of San Lucar until it was incorporated in the crown of Spain in 1645.[1] Its independence of royal authority was a great factor in the development of the town because of the encouragement given by the dukes to foreign merchants. The prosperity and growth of San Lucar de Barrameda owed much to the influx of *extranjeros*, particularly Bretons, Flemings and English, in the fifteenth and sixteenth centuries. Efforts were made to attract more. In the year 1499, for example, Don Juan de Guzmán wrote to the Doge of Venice requesting him to send the Flanders Galleys to San Lucar and promising good treatment to all Venetian subjects.[2] In 1517 his son expressed concern at the decrease of the former flourishing English trade of his town whereby in past years 'the said towne and the dwelleres thereof were inriched and brought to great estimac*i*on and my rentes encreased'[3] and issued a new charter of privileges to induce the English merchants to return to the port.

[1] P. Barbadillo Delgado, *Historia de la Ciudad de Sanlúcar de Barrameda*, pp. 24–35.
[2] *Calendar of State Papers, Venice, 1202–1509*, no. 801.
[3] B.M., Harleian MS. 36, f. 39v.

Englishmen had frequented San Lucar de Barrameda long before the beginning of the Tudor period. Indeed, according to the preamble to the charter of 1517, they had been granted privileges by Don Alonso *El Bueno* himself who had died more than two centuries before. At the accession of Henry VII they were thus already very well established there. An incident towards the end of Edward IV's reign indicates this and also shows the interest of the Dukes of Medina Sidonia in commercial enterprise. Hakluyt records that in 1481 the king of Portugal sent envoys to Edward IV to protest against the preparation of an expedition to Guinea by two English merchants, John Tintam and William Fabian, under the Duke's patronage. The Portuguese demanded the prohibition of the voyage as an infringement of their monopoly.[1] It is not known whether the project came to anything, but the incident is important for its bearing on the question of English interest in voyages of discovery in the earlier period.[2] Little is known of the activities of the English merchants in San Lucar in Henry VII's reign although the surviving particulars of customs of Bristol indicate that it was a favourite port of call for English ships visiting southern Spain. It must have become even more popular in Henry VII's last years when animosity between the English king and Ferdinand and the increased power of the hostile council of Castile caused great difficulties for the English merchants in Andalusia. Hostility to the English was felt even in the independent town of San Lucar, however, for early in Henry VIII's reign the merchants complained to the Duke that their privileges were not being observed and petitioned for their confirmation.

On 14 March 1517, in response to this petition, the privileges of the English merchants were set out in letters patent and publicly proclaimed.[3] The English trading to southern Spain, the document said, had for many years made San Lucar their

---

[1] *The Principal Navigations*, vi, p. 123; J. W. Blake, *Europeans in West Africa, 1450–1560*, vol. 2, pp. 295–297.

[2] cf. D. B. Quinn, 'Edward IV and Exploration' in *The Mariner's Mirror*, vol. xxi, no. 3 (July 1935), p. 275.

[3] There are several copies of all the documents concerned with the Andalusia Company mentioned in this chapter among the British Museum collections and in the Public Record Office. There is a copy of Henry VIII's grant in the Escurial Library. cf. Zarco Cuevas, *Catálogo de los Manuscritos Castellanos de la Real Biblioteca del Escorial*, II, p. 414. All quotations, unless otherwise stated, are from copies contained in P.R.O., State Papers, Miscellaneous, vol. 107, pp. 1–30.

staple and chief place of residence. They had received trading concessions from Don Alonso *El Bueno* and these had been renewed by successive lords right up to the time of the present Duke, Alonso Pérez de Guzmán. At the beginning of the latter's rule[1] the English merchants declared that they had become:

lesse favoured and their liberties not regarded nor kept, as they were wont to be for the customers and receauers of the towne made noe matter to take more custome and other duties then they were wonte and in truth ought to doe, and the justices making smale account how they wer vsed there either touching their parsons or otherwise shewed such fauour to the inhabitauntes as such of them as owe any money to Englishmen when the daies of payment com had no care nor regarded how long they draue them of by apeles and other delaies to their greate hindraunce and vexation and many tymes the debtes thereby quite lost.

Moreover, the English merchants affirmed, they were also maltreated by the customs officials and tax farmers of Cadiz, Seville, Jerez and other ports and towns of Andalusia who disliked their conducting most of their business in San Lucar because of the loss of revenue it caused them. The merchants complained that these officials had 'greately maligned them comensing suite against some, and threttening others to arrest theire parsons and goodes when they found them in their townes'.

The English had declared (according to the preamble to the letters patent) that unless they were given further safeguards they would be unable to continue trading in San Lucar. They had accordingly determined to bring their grievances to the Duke's notice. The latter, after consultation with his council, ordered the English merchants to draw up 'in certen articles' the injuries for which they sought redress and also 'such other matters as his fauor might stand them in steede to succour and aid them in for the better establishing of their trade in his said towne'. The English thereupon submitted a new list of complaints and requests to each of which the Duke added his answer, 'permitting and graunting them (in a manner or verie litle altered) in such forme as they praied to haue them'. Finally, they were issued as a body of privileges and openly proclaimed

[1] Don Alonso Pérez succeeded his stepbrother in 1513.

in the presence of a notary in the town. There were thirteen articles.

In the first of these the English merchants asked for a piece of land on which they could build a church of their own. They claimed that the Duke's father had promised them some ground by his own warehouse 'in *the* streete downe towardes the water-side'. The church would be built at their own expense and they would have to obtain permission from the ecclesiastical authorities. The Duke now granted them this land and ordered his officials to hand it over to them. The church was to be named in honour of the 'blessed martir St George', the patron saint of England, and there would be sufficient ground to provide a burial place for English merchants dying in San Lucar de Barrameda. The ostensible reason for desiring a church was 'to th' entent devine service might there be said and the name of Jhesus Christ called vpon', but it would be more than a place of worship. It would serve them as a place of assembly and for conducting business transactions. There is evidence of important meetings being held in the church of St. George, including the election of William Ostriche as governor in 1538.[1] Calle San Jorge[2] in San Lucar still bears the name it derives from the English church. There is to-day a church of St. George in the street, now derelict, the third built by the English merchants in San Lucar. In the early days of the Andalusia Company it was most advantageously placed near the river, but to-day it is several hundred yards from the shore just off the main street of the town.

Article 2 concerned the complaint against officials of other Andalusian towns frequented by the English merchants. The Duke:

having a privilege for his said towne for this, graunted to his progenitors tyme out of mynde from the kinges of Castill, sithence it was for the mayntenaunce of his privileges was content to take vpon him the defence of the nation in this behalf and to cause the sutes when any such were to be followed at his costes and charges, and by his appointment, and so every way to sett cleere, and saue them harmelesse for the same.

In the third article the English merchants complained of the Duke's own officials in San Lucar who, they declared, exacted

---

[1] *Vide infra*, p. 95.   [2] St. George Street.

The English Church at San Lucar de Barrameda

higher customs duties than they used to do, in violation of their ancient privileges. The Duke promised that a new table of rates should be drawn up so that the Englishmen could see what they had to pay and no more than these charges should be exacted from them.

The most serious protest of the Englishmen was against their inability to obtain justice in lawsuits against the townsmen, particularly in collecting payment of debts owing to them (article 4). In the course of trade they delivered merchandise to Spaniards in San Lucar by contracts and obligations to be paid at a date agreed between the parties. Knowing that the local justices would favour them against the English, however, the townsmen often failed to settle at the appointed date. Under their obligations the Spaniards' goods should have been distrained without appeal once judgement was given against them, but instead they were allowed to lodge interminable appeals. Often the English merchants, 'being not skilfull in suites, thought it as good to lesse the debt quite as to prosecute the recoverie thereof by the lawe'. The Duke commanded his justices and their officers to remedy this complaint and see that the English received prompt justice. He promised that settlement of their debts should follow immediately after judgement had been given in their favour and long appeals brought merely to cause delay of execution would not be permitted. Such a promise was easier made than fulfilled and delays in obtaining justice in foreign courts was a constant complaint of merchants in these times—certainly no less of the Spaniards in England than of the English in San Lucar.

The fifth article was also concerned with difficulties experienced by the English merchants in collecting payment for their merchandise. They said that when their goods were exchanged for wine and fruit to be delivered 'at their seasonable tymes' very often when payment was due the Duke's own receivers and rent-gatherers seized the whole yield for debts owing to him. The other creditors therefore had no hope of being paid. Moreover, the English merchants suffered further losses. Most of them acted as factors for other merchants in England to whom they had arranged to despatch the wine and fruit. When the Spaniards failed to deliver these goods the Englishmen had to pay dead freight and also lost their commission as factors. To remedy this the Duke proposed that English merchants giving credit to any Spaniard should obtain a certificate stating how much money he owed the Duke at the time the bargain was made. Then, when the day of payment arrived, they should produce the note and the Duke's receiver would take from the Spaniard only this amount before he settled with the Englishmen, even if the debt owing to the Duke had become much greater in the meantime. Moreover, if this bill from the receiver:

declared the partie that was then to be credited to owe the Duke nothing at that daie, then when the tyme of payement came he could not distraine in any of the goodes, at least wise as much as was owing for to the English man, thereby to debarr him of his debt, but the creditor, being of the English nation was to haue it.

The Duke's rent collectors had created a further difficulty for the English merchants (article 7). Some Englishmen, hosted with Spaniards in the town, were often absent on voyages to England or in other parts of Spain, and during their absence their hosts made purchases and sales on their behalf. Sometimes, too, newly-arrived Englishmen, inexperienced in Spanish business methods, might be helped by their hosts. The farmers of the 'brokerage rent' of the town alleged that these Spaniards were acting in the capacity of brokers for the English merchants and demanded payment of the tax levied on brokerage. The Englishmen denied the allegation. In reply, the Duke agreed to allow the hosts to continue to assist the merchants as before, but he decreed that, should it be proved they did in fact receive payment for brokerage, they would be fined a sum equal to five times the amount they had received.

The sixth article dealt with a custom among the 'barkemen'[1] of San Lucar which had caused a great deal of inconvenience to the English merchants using their lighters to take goods out to ships in the port. The town lighters came up to the wharf in strict order to load up, and until one was filled to capacity no other would take in merchandise. Thus, if an English merchant had only a small quantity of goods he would either have to pay the whole freight or the lighterman would not take it; nor 'might any other (nor yet would) by reason of the order amongst them take it in'. This complaint is difficult to understand since there seems to be no reason why the merchants could not have

[1] i.e. lightermen.

made arrangements among themselves to co-operate in providing full loads. But the Duke ordered that henceforth the
lighterman whose turn it was to load should either take whatever
goods the merchant offered or else the latter might freight any
other lighter he wished. If possible it was to be one belonging
to the town, but if none were available any other could be used.

Articles 12 and 13 were also concerned with lading merchandise. In the former the Duke granted the English merchants
permission to lade their goods at any part of the water-side
from the monastery of St. Dominic all along the town. Previously
they had been obliged to take all their goods to the customs
house at great trouble and expense. In his answer to the thir-
teenth article of the petition the Duke gave a ruling for the disposal of wines which had already been through the customs
house and taken out in the lighters but for which there was no
room on board ship. It was decreed that cheaper wines such as
'bastardes' and 'cuytes' might be landed and stored without any
reference to the port officials. In the case of other wines such
as sacks and romneys, however, the town and port authorities
had to be notified and only ten butts could be brought ashore
from any one ship. These must be stored in a house or cellar
having two locks. The key of one lock was to be kept in the
custody of a town official and the other should remain with the
merchant owning the wine so that the latter (in theory at least)
could not have access to the wine without the knowledge of the
official. Then, when the merchant had made arrangements to
ship it, he could do so without paying any further customs duties
upon it.

In the eighth article the Duke declared he took the English
merchants under his special protection:

and their goodes and marchaundize, that neither they shalbe killed
nor hurt nor ill intreated, neither their wares nor goodes deteyned
by restrayntes or arrestes, neither in warr nor peace, nor their shipps
nor wares in them, with their masters and marriners, which shalbe
either in the towne or porte and haven of the same.

The Duke commanded his council and justices to see that this
pledge was kept, and it was publicly proclaimed in the market
place and other streets of the town 'that noe man may pretend
ignoraunce that it was vnknowne vnto him'. Any townsman dis-

regarding its provisions would incur the full penalty the law 'doth appointe to be laied vpon such as be breakers of the assuraunce and defence giuen to any by their naturall lord, and in that case to haue the penalties executed vpon their parsons and good*es* wit*h*out respect of favour'. After this letter of protection had been publicly proclaimed the Duke ordered the notary present to hand it over to the English merchants 'that they might keepe it as a certificate by them, for the defence of their right'. Moreover, the Duke confirmed their ancient privilege permitting all members of the English nation in San Lucar, 'litle and greate', to carry for their protection both offensive and defensive weapons by day and night without interference from the town authorities. They might carry arms both within and without the town so long as they did not misuse them nor cause 'disquiet broyles and stirr' in the town. If they misbehaved themselves the local justices were to proceed against them in the law with the co-operation of the consul of the nation (article 9).

More about the governorship of the English nation in San Lucar in the early Tudor period before the formation of the Andalusia Company is given in articles 10 and 11 of the Duke's grant. The first of these was concerned with the lodging of the merchants. In order to give them more privacy and safer storage for their merchandise the Duke agreed that eight houses in the town should be made available to them in addition to the consul's own residence. No guests but their own should be billeted upon them. Article 11 gives a great deal of detail about the powers of the consul, which were greatly enhanced by its provisions. It stated that the English merchants had long been permitted to have a consul and governor as judge of their affairs, but:

being as he is lymitted, and his jurisdicion as it were restrayned to deale but in certen matters, and the justices of the towne in all the rest, by w*hich* the Englishmen receaue sundry iniuries, in that they cannot haue justice touching the recovering of their deb*tes*, as also in the ill intreating both in worde and deede of their parsons, for they being strangers, the justices rather favour th'inhabitaunt*es* being of their owne country, wheretby (as is said afore in the fowerth article) by long and many delaies, they driue of the English marchaunt*es* from speedie recovery in of the deb*tes* that are owing them by the townes men.

By article 11 of these privileges the consul was granted power to hear and determine:

all causes as well civill as crymynall, as of all striffes and controversies that should fall out as well in ordynary pleas as executyue, and in all such matters as by anie other ordynary course touched them, or any of them any way, and that he might commaund execucion to be had of obligacions and paymentes to be made of debtes whatsoever, were the suites and accions either depending betweene Englishman and Englishman, or betweene Spaniardes or anie other nation and Englishman./ And briefely in all matters of these two waies, which be both civill causes, wherein the nation some of them, or, anie one of them shall haue any dealing, and be therein either plainetiffe or defendant.

If, however, English merchants preferred to have their cases tried by the town justices this should be allowed them. Otherwise their own consul was to hear any civil case, and once it had been brought before him it should not be lawful for the justices of the town to interfere. In criminal cases affecting English merchants the latter were to act in co-operation with the consul, informing him of any arrest and the nature of the offence. Any infringement of this clause would incur a penalty of 50,000 *maravedís*, half to be paid to the Duke's treasury and half towards the cost of building the church of St. George. The consul was permitted to delegate his authority to a deputy when he was away from the town.

Having answered each of the thirteen articles contained in the English merchants' petition the Duke then confirmed them 'all ioyntly together' and issued them by letters patent as a body of privileges to them 'aswell to those *that* now are, as to those that shall come hereafter to trade and traffique in the said towne of St. Lucar'. He charged all the inhabitants of his town to see them observed and obeyed upon pain of a fine of 10,000 *maravedís* to his treasury, and his justices were to be fined the same amount if they failed to execute them. The justices were commanded to proclaim them in the market places and open streets and other 'vsuall places of the towne' and to give a testimony and certificate of their privileges to the English merchants:

which said letteres of privilege drawne out and written in parchement skyn firmed with his name, and sealed with the seale of his armes, and signed by his secretarie Hige Grace comaunded to be giuen to *the* said English marchaun*tes.*

The grant of these extensive privileges must soon have brought a considerable increase in the number of English merchants trading in San Lucar. The particulars of customs of Bristol for the year immediately following (Michaelmas 1517–Michaelmas 1518) show San Lucar as the provenance of all but one of the ships returning from Andalusia.[1] This is the last Bristol account in which these details are given. Unfortunately, too, the notarial records of San Lucar, which must have contained a wealth of information about the affairs of the English merchants there, have been destroyed.[2] The *Archivo de Protocolos de Sevilla* contains references to the port in the 1520's, however, including the names of several important English merchants residing there. William Ostriche was already established in San Lucar in 1523;[3] so, three years later, was Andrew Woodcock.[4] In 1523 Richard Cooper, consul of the English nation when the Andalusia Company was formed, is described as being in Cadiz in a power of attorney granted by Robert Thorne and his partners to a Spaniard to collect payment of a debt of 181,717 *maravedis* from him in October of that year.[5] Reference to English merchants in San Lucar is made in a letter from Margaret of Savoy to Henry VIII in August 1525 demanding restitution of a ship belonging to a certain Alonso de Sevilla, a Spaniard domiciled in Rouen, which had been plundered near Lisbon by Englishmen pretending to be Portuguese. These Englishmen, according to the Regent, had carried off the Spanish ship to San Lucar and disposed of her cargo there.[6] Richard Cooper declared subsequently that Alonso was, in fact, a Frenchman[7] and reported to Thomas Cromwell that judgement had been given in Spain that the ship and French goods in her should be retained as good prizes but the Spanish goods returned to their owners.[8]

---

[1] P.R.O., K.R. Customs, 199/2.
[2] *Vide supra*, Introduction, pp. xiv–xv.
[3] Archivo de Protocolos de Sevilla, *Oficio* V, 1523, *Libro* III, f. 122.
[4] ibid., 1526, *Libro* IV, f. 345v.
[5] ibid., 1523, *Libro* III, f. 136v.
[6] *Letters and Papers*, iv (1), no. 1598. *Vide supra*, p. 63.
[7] cf. The case of William Hawkins and Juan Quintanadueñas. *Vide infra*, p. 182.
[8] B.M., Cotton MS. Vespasian C IV, f. 332.

Meanwhile, the position of the English merchants in Spain had been growing more insecure. It is not known whether the Duke kept his promise not to arrest English ships and property in San Lucar during the short period of war between England and Spain in 1528, but by then the situation must already have greatly deteriorated since the prosperous days following the grant of 1517. In April 1529 Cooper, probably already consul of the English nation in the port, wrote to Cromwell from San Lucar to report the difficulties of the merchants there. Economic conditions were particularly hard in that year because of a bad harvest; lack of rain had caused an increase in the price of wheat to more than a ducat per *fanega*.[1] The English merchants were again finding themselves 'lesse favoured and their libe*r*ties not regarded nor kept'. Cooper complained that 'in all owr cawsses at the p*r*esynt whe be dysfavord in this cort'[2]. Since he was writing from San Lucar it was presumably the Duke's court to which he referred; at all events a year later he was to protest to the justices of the town against their failure to enforce the merchants' privileges. In England at about this time William Pepwell and others were petitioning Henry VIII to give his approval to new measures to meet their growing difficulties.

Henry VIII's grant of privileges to the English merchants in Andalusia clearly marks the end of a prosperous era. The English in Spain did not cling together instinctively. The greatest of the Anglo-Spanish traders like Robert Thorne and Roger Barlow had made their own way among the Spaniards and foreign merchants in Spain. Their names are not associated with the Company and Thorne and Barlow were back in England shortly after it was formed. Moreover the consuls complained time and again that in their adversity the English merchants were divided. Now a stronger association was imperative and Henry's grant was made to provide 'better help and gouernement in those part*es*, and for reformac*i*on and redresse to be had of certen wrong*es* and iniuries hetherto susteyned, and other *that* may hereafter be offired by sundry vexations ymposition*s* newe duties and customes.' It was also necessary to provide for the maintenance of the 'newly edified' chapel of St. George. This is the first intimation that the church had been built. The charter was

---

[1] Equivalent to approximately 1.60 bushels.
[2] B.M., Cotton MS. Vespasian C IV, f. 332.

to apply to all merchants of England, Wales and Ireland trading to Andalusia.

The merchants were permitted to assemble once a year, or more often if needefull, in 'a reasonable and competent number' in Seville, Cadiz, San Lucar de Barrameda or Port St. Mary for the purpose of electing a consul or consuls. This should be done with 'th' aduice and consent of *our* subiect*es* the marchaunt*es* of London', two merchants of Bristol and two of Southampton 'vsing the trade of marchandize in those part*es*'. The vague wording of this statement suggests that the London merchants had a preponderant voice in the election of the consul since no limit was placed upon the number who could take part. It is also of interest that Bristol and Southampton were placed on a parity, since all available evidence indicates that many more merchants of the Gloucester port took part in the trade than Southampton men.[1] The rewards of the office of consul were left to the discretion of the merchants themselves. Those holding it were to have 'for their travell*es* and paines in exercising the said function or office such benifitt*es* aucthoritie and prehemynence, as to you (i.e. the merchants) shall seeme reasonable meete and convenient'. Moreover, the merchants could remove the consul from office at any time they thought it necessary.

The consul (or consuls) and the company were also granted authority to choose from amongst themselves twelve 'auncient. and expert parsons' to be assistants to the consul, and when any of these died or gave up their trade in those parts they might choose others to replace them. The consul was given full power to levy upon all English merchants trading to Andalusia, their factors, agents and ships such imposts as he and the assistants considered necessary on both imports and exports. Should any merchant refuse to pay the imposition the consul could enforce payment 'by way of distresse penaltie or amercem*entes*' or by any other means which he and the assistants deemed expedient. The officers of the company had full power over all the English merchants in those parts and could make acts and ordinances 'for the generall comodety of them all', provided that the consul

---

[1] It is, of course, more difficult to identify the trade of Southampton to Spain (*vide supra*, Introduction, p. xviii) but among the Englishmen known to have resided in Spain in this period few can be identified as burgesses of the Hampshire port compared with the number of Bristol men.

himself and eight of the assistants were present when acts were
made. If these conditions were not fulfilled or the ordinances
were not for the common benefit of the merchants 'then in such
a case, they shalbe void and of no force nor value'. Finally, the
king declared:

we comaund all and everie one of *our* subiect*es* marchaunt*es* maisters
and mariners and others frequenting and vsing the trade of marchaundize and that from hensforth shall vse it in those part*es*, that
they shall allwaies assist with their aide counsell and advise, *the* said
consull or consulls their assistaunt*es* and successors, and this still
from tyme to tyme, as to them shall appertaine.

Henry VIII's grant was dated at Westminster, 1 September
1530.[1] On 15 October Richard Cooper, the governor of the
English nation, appeared before the ordinary judge and justice
of the town of San Lucar de Barrameda and presented the letters
patent granted thirteen years earlier by the Duke. He demanded, in the name of the English merchants, that these
privileges should be observed and publicly proclaimed in the
presence of a notary. Juan de Illescas, public notary of the town,
records that:

forw*ith* m*aster* judge said that w*ith* all due, and humble reverence he
did obey and obeyed the said privilege, and commaunded and doth
comaund *that* it be publiquelie proclaimed in the com*m*on meeting
places and open street*es* of the towne, as his grace had comaunded, and
forthwith in the open meeting place of the said towne before a multitude of people, then and there gathered together . . . the said
priviledge was openly word for word proclaymed.

Again, the following day in the town down by the river 'in a
greate and large streate of the same, being a publique *and* open
place' the privileges were again publicly rehearsed. The necess-
ity for this action of Cooper's is a further indication of the
growing difficulties of the English merchants in Spain.

The first available evidence of an assembly of the merchants
in accordance with Henry VIII's charter is an account of the
election of William Ostriche as the new governor in 1538. The
name of Ostriche's immediate predecessor is not known, nor

[1] There is a document in the Cotton MSS. (Vespasian C VII, f. 57v) purporting
to be a confirmation of Henry's grant by Charles V on 28 Sept. 1530 which
has been calendared in *Letters and Papers*, iv (3), no. 6640. It is clear from its
wording, however, that it is, in fact, a copy of the confirmation of 28 Sept. 1538.
Vide infra, p. 94.

do we know how often the consulship had changed hands since
1530. Richard Cooper seems to have returned to England some
time before August 1535 after a difficult career during which he
was for a long time in trouble with the Spanish authorities. In
March 1532 he complained that an unjust sentence had been
given against him by the Spaniards, who, he declared, gave it
out of a general grudge against the English nation in Spain.[1]
In November of the following year William Pepwell wrote from
San Lucar that two English merchants, Mathew Lambert and
Robert Dothyerne, previously imprisoned, had been set free
upon finding sureties, while Richard Cooper had received sentence as the most guilty of them all.[2] Again, the nature of his
offence is not mentioned. Finally, in August 1535 Thomas Batcock, forwarding some letters in Spanish to Cromwell, said
Richard Cooper would be able to translate one of them for him,
thus showing the latter was then in England.[3] Further information about the governorship is provided by evidence given in a
case before the High Court of Admiralty in the year 1537 between Richard Field (to whom Pery later wrote an account of
his sufferings at the hands of the Spanish Inquisition) and the
owners of the *Erasmus* of Erith. Thomas Pery stated that in
February 1537 he was in San Lucar when James Fitzjames
'Judge of the Englis nacyon' and Edward Lewis[4] his deputy
had heard evidence in the case.[5] Pery's statement not only
names the governor but shows the office was functioning at that
time although the state of the company was far from satisfactory.

In the following year the English ambassador requested the
Emperor to confirm the merchants' privileges. It is evident from
the wording of Charles' confirmation that Henry VIII's charter
was in danger of becoming a dead letter because many of the
merchants were refusing to pay the imposts levied by the consul
and his assistants. According to the ratification the English
merchants had petitioned:

that sithence the said *lette*res patent*es*, and the ordynaunces in them
contained, were to the com*m*on benifitt of the said English traders
into this our realmes, and *that* yet notwithstanding some of them

---

[1] *Letters and Papers*, v, no. 885.
[2] ibid, vi. no. 1430.
[3] ibid., ix, no. 33.
[4] Later to dispute the consulship with Hugh Tipton. *Vide infra*, p. 124.
[5] *Vide supra*, p. 14.

would not pay that w*hich* according to the purporte and meaning of them they were charged w*ith* by the said consulls. By reason whereof it falleth out that the *lette*res patent*es* are like to come to be of none effect, whereby they all shall receaue greate hindraunce, for the w*hich* cause (as is said) they besought that it would please vs to approue ratifie *and* confirme them, that they might take effect, and to giue them lycence and facultie to vse them, within these our realmes.

Charles granted this request and ordered his council to see that the privileges were observed. The next step was for the English merchants themselves to enforce the rules of the company.

A document drawn up by Pero Hernández, one of the public notaries of San Lucar, records that on 24 April 1539 an important meeting of the English merchants was held in the church of St. George. There were present John Sweeting, Richard Wigmore, William Southworth, Nicholas Lawford, Thomas Ridley, James Wake, and Blase Saunders, resident in Cadiz; Thomas Kingsman resident in Port St. Mary; and George Masters, John Norton, Edward Lewis, John Bedell, Richard Darrell, George Mason, Thomas Wall and George and Thomas Turnbull of San Lucar itself. It is unfortunate that these merchants are not designated by their towns of origin, for it is impossible to determine whether the representation of the three main English ports was in accordance with Henry's charter. It is of interest that no English merchants from Seville attended this meeting. The purpose of the occasion was to confirm decisions made at a previous assembly, doubtless because they had not been effective. On 6 December 1538, the merchants declared before the notary, they and 'diuers other marchaunt*es* of the said English nation' had elected as 'judge consull and gouerno*r*' William Ostriche resident in San Lucar. Ostriche, shown by documents in the *Archivo de Protocolos de Sevilla* to have traded in the town for at least some fifteen years,[1] was formerly a Bristol man. He traded a great deal to Spain through Bristol and is described by Hakluyt as a Levant trader.[2] The merchants also stated that on the previous occasion, in accordance with the privilege granted them by Henry VIII and confirmed by the Emperor, they had agreed upon certain impositions to be paid upon their imports

---

[1] *Vide supra*, p. 90.
[2] Op. cit., v, p. 69.

and exports by all English and Irish merchants trading in Andalusia. The 'average' had been fixed at 1 per cent since Henry's grant.

The assembly then proceeded to 'retorne anewe to the election choise and nomynation of the said William Ostrich' and bound themselves and all other English merchants in Andalusia to obey him and carry out all that he should order as their consul 'in such sort, and in like manner as they haue obeyed *the* ordinaunnces and actes of other governors which haue byn before him'. The powers now conferred upon Ostriche were very wide. The consul, or any person to whom he should delegate the necessary powers of attorney, was authorised to:

doe and passe all those thinges and matters to the said English nation and marchauntes and traffiquers of the same belonging or any wise apperteyning, and to their duties accions, doinges *and* affaires, and to anie one or either of them as well vniuersall and generall as speciall and particuler.

He was to demand and recover from all merchants the goods or money they paid for the average of 1 per cent and any other dues levied in accordance with the king's charter, and he or a deputy appointed by him was authorised to 'graunt their acquittaunces and discharges for, which shalbe as firme and in as good force strength and effect, as if *the* said marchauntes themselues, or any of them or all those of the said nation, ioinctly together had giuen and graunted them'.

Moreover, he was also given the power:

that as well in judgement as out of the same he might make all actes demaundes, requestes, protestations, take certificates take out and gett any manner of letteres, schedulls and prouisions that were requisite and cause them to be intymated *and* executed, *and* to demaund all in them conteyned, and that it should be kept and held for good, and *that* he might doe say reason treate of and procure all other thinges, *and* euerie one of them which apperteine to the said nation *and* marchauntes and traffiquers of the same / and which they themselues would doe, and might doe being present, yea although *the* matters be such as it were requisite for the same to haue their speciall lettere of atturney order and personall presence.

These powers were much wider than those conferred in the letters patent of Henry VIII and there is no mention of the assistants, only of deputies appointed by the governor himself and deriving their power from him. This is perhaps a measure of the more difficult times.

The English merchants ratified the powers William Ostriche had already conferred upon Thomas Harrison and John Field, residing in Seville, to collect the average—presumably from Englishmen trading in that city. Harrison and Field were leading figures in the Anglo-Spanish trade in the later years of Henry VIII's reign and both were mentioned by Thomas Pery as his benefactors during the time of his imprisonment. It is of interest that these two, like Sweeting, clearly well established among the Spaniards, were nevertheless also closely associated with the company of English merchants during the difficult period now beginning. Harrison is shown from documents in the *Archivo de Protocolos de Sevilla* as one of the few English merchants able to continue trading in the late 1530's[1] He is also shown as one of many English merchants trading to the Indies in the early Tudor period and was part owner of a vessel named the *Trinidad* which made voyages to the New World on his behalf. On 22 May 1542, for example, when the ship was lading her cargo at Seville for a voyage to the Indies, Harrison agreed before Alonso de Cazalla, public notary of the city, to the appointment of his partner as master:

puede ser e sea maestre de la dicha nao este dicho viaje que a la dicha Nueva España ha de haber e como tal maestre la rrija e govierne e a la compaña della e quite marineros e ponga marineros e faga todas las otras cosas e cada vna de las que buen maestre deve faser.[2]

When Robert Reneger of Southampton waylaid the *San Salvador* off Cape St. Vincent in March 1545, a consignment of gold belonging to Thomas Harrison formed part of the booty.[3]

John Field, the other collector of the average in Seville, figures in one of the most interesting of the earlier voyages recounted by Hakluyt—that of Robert Tomson into New Spain in 1555.[4] Hakluyt said that Field had then been in Seville 18

[1] *Oficio* XV, 1539–40, *passim.*
[2] 'He may and shall be master of the said ship the said voyage which is to be to the said New Spain and as such master shall rule and have charge of her and her company and discharge and take on mariners and do all the other things and each one of them which a good master should do.' Archivo de Protocolos de Sevilla, *Oficio* XV, 1542, *Libro* I, f. 956.
[3] *Vide infra*, Appendix D, p. 241.
[4] Op. cit., ix, pp. 338 *seq.*

or 20 years and had a wife and children there. Tomson stayed with Field for a year to learn Castilian and study the customs of the country, and when the latter subsequently decided to emigrate to the New World with his family Tomson accompanied them. John Field later fell sick and died in Mexico but Tomson survived many adventures to tell his story which had, for him, a happy and most profitable ending.

Ostriche had also conferred similar powers upon John Sweeting, Thomas Kingsman and Robert Spencer. John Sweeting performed the duties of deputy to Ostriche in Cadiz. Kingsman resided in Port St. Mary and presumably collected the average there. Reference was made to Thomas Kingsman in the case of *Austin v. Castelyn* in the High Court of Admiralty during the year.[1] He and a certain Thomas Wilson had been in charge of the repair of the *George* before she set sail for England.[2] He later demanded the observance of the Englishmen's privileges in Port St. Mary when a Spanish mat-maker was put over the merchants as consul.[3] It is not known where Robert Spencer collected the average. The powers granted to these three deputies were also confirmed and, finally, the assembly declared:

they graunted and doe graunte in such manner and sorte, as well they might doe both for themselues, and in the name of *the* rest of the said nation, w*ith* such full and ample faculty and power, as the lawes the termes and cercumstaunces to them apperteyning, and vse and custome doe in this case any way require, And for that so it should be held kept cumplid and had for firme, in forme afore expressed, they said they did bynde, and doe bynde their bodies and good*es* and the parsons and good*es* both ymmoueable and moueable had and to be had of the other marchaunt*es* traffique*rs* of *the* said nacion, in whose name they graunted the said power, as well as in their owne.

Armed with these wide powers William Ostriche became governor of the Andalusia Company at the most crucial moment of its existence and the most difficult the English merchants had so far experienced in Spain during the early Tudor period. When Henry VIII granted the company its charter he was already fully embarked upon a course of action destined eventually to lead to a break-down of Anglo-Spanish trade. Since

[1] *Vide supra*, p. 25.
[2] P.R.O., H.C.A. Examinations, 4, 31 August, 1539.
[3] *Vide infra*, p. 195.

then lack of co-operation among the merchants themselves had prejudiced the success of their new association. Now events beyond their control became the determining factor in the fortunes of the company The next recorded assembly of the English merchants in Andalusia was to rehearse the story of their sufferings at the hands of the Spanish Inquisition.

CHAPTER V

THE MERCHANTS AND THE INQUISITION

IT is not easy to assess with accuracy the extent of the persecution of English merchants by the Spanish Inquisition and its effect upon Anglo-Spanish trade in the first half of the sixteenth century. Statistical evidence of the volume of the trade is fragmentary;[1] nor can the number of victims be estimated from Spanish inquisitional records. Almost all the evidence of this important question is drawn from English sources which include several accounts of their sufferings by the victims and their associates. These convey an impression of widespread persecution met by forthright loyalty to the English king and the religious changes which occasioned their misfortunes. J. A. Williamson saw the English merchants upholding the royal supremacy in the face of great ill-treatment. 'It speaks much for the loyalty and patriotism of Englishmen', he says, 'that they held firm on what was to most of them a purely political quibble, even when the shores of England were far away, and the dungeons of the Holy Office gaped close at hand'.[2] J. B. Williamson declared that this persecution was, in effect, a manifestation of Spanish hatred of the English and that 'in the tortures of the Inquisition the national antipathy found a pitiless expression'.[3]

Closer examination of the question shows that both these opinions must be modified. There is evidence that the persecution was spasmodic and not so widespread as the complaints of the English merchants would suggest. Moreover, many Englishmen residing in Spain for trading purposes conformed outwardly at least to the Catholic religion and few placed their lives or prosperous businesses in jeopardy for the sake of a 'political quibble'. Hakluyt wrote in the later period of his contemporaries that:

[1] *Vide supra*, Introduction, p. xvii.
[2] *Maritime Enterprise, 1485-1558*, p. 221.
[3] *The Foreign Commerce of England under the Tudors*, p. 24.

the covetous merchant wilfully sendeth headlong to hell from day to day the poor subjects of this realm. The merchant in England cometh here devoutly to the communion, and sendeth his son into Spain to hear Mass. These things are kept secret by the merchants; and such as depend upon the trade of merchandise are loth to utter the same.[1]

How much more easily could an earlier generation of merchants stifle its conscience when there had been few doctrinal changes. The story of Thomas Pery[2] can hardly be considered typical. Had it been so, no Englishman could have remained in Spain during the difficult periods, whereas there is ample evidence that some did, and continued to prosper.

It appears, however, that a certain number of English merchants did leave Spain as a result of the activities of the Inquisition and as the English became more Protestant it must have been increasingly distasteful to them to conform to the old religion. Probably, too, as J. A. Williamson suggests, Protestantism was to find some of its staunchest adherents among Englishmen receiving injury at the hands of the Papists.[3] It is evident that even if the complaints of the English merchants were exaggerated they contained a large element of truth. Moreover, they were believed by their fellow countrymen, and this impression, far more than actual numbers of victims, was to be important in Anglo-Spanish relations and undoubtedly most adversely affected the trade.

One aspect of the question is quite clear. As the warmth of the friendship between Henry VIII and Charles V depended largely upon the rivalry between the Emperor and Francis, the treatment of the English merchants in Spain was always best when the Emperor needed England's support against France. It is certain, too, that although Charles said on one occasion that the Holy Office was concerned solely with matters of faith and he could not interfere with it,[4] persecution of the merchants was most severe when political relations between the allies were most strained. These periods were from the Truce of Nice until the new alliance against France—when there occurred the worst persecution the English merchants endured before Elizabeth's

---

[1] *The Principal Navigations*, xii, pp. 33–34.
[2] *Vide infra*, pp. 111 *seq.*
[3] *Maritime Enterprise, 1485–1558*, p. 223.
[4] *Letters and Papers*, xv, no. 38.

reign—and again after the Peace of Crépy. It was then that the most serious English complaints were made.

Henry's intention to divorce the Emperor's aunt was known to Charles at least as early as the summer of 1527; he may even first have learned of it through the English merchants.[1] Lee, the English ambassador in Spain, later reported news of the divorce obtained by a fellow countryman at the fair of Medina del Campo.[2] Henry's break from Rome did not become definite before 1533, however, and until then there is little evidence of Imperial plans against him. Chapuys, Charles' ambassador in England, believed then that if an ecclesiastical interdict forbade trade between England and the Emperor's dominions there would be a rift between Henry and his council,[3] and the people would rise against the promoters of the new marriage.[4] At the same time Chapuys advised his master not to allow the English merchants residing in Spain and Flanders to be ill-treated, for they would be instrumental in fostering the goodwill and affection of the English people towards the Emperor.[5]

Meanwhile the Spanish merchants in England, more conscious of the precariousness of the situation, were trying as far as possible to withdraw their merchandise from the country. Even Chapuys' creditors, fearing he might have to leave in a hurry, were after him for settlement.[6] These precautions were unnecessary, however, for neither Henry nor Charles was anxious for a breach just then. Thus, when the citizens of London tried to force all foreigners to contribute towards the coronation expenses of Ann Boleyn, Spaniards were apparently exempted.[7] Cromwell promised Chapuys, too, that Spaniards residing in London should be exempted from swearing obedience to the new statute confirming the recent changes.[8] According to the author of the *Spanish Chronicle* this concession was made only to Spaniards, all other foreigners in the city being summoned by the commissioners to take some form of oath.[9] This anxiety

---

[1] *Letters and Papers*, iv (2), no. 3400.
[2] ibid., iv (3), no. 5856.
[3] *Spanish Calendar, 1531–33*, no. 1047, p. 598.
[4] ibid., no. 1058, p. 631. This was a favourite theory of Chapuys which he was still advocating when Henry VIII died. *Vide* ibid., *1545–46*, no. 386, p. 557.
[5] ibid., *1531–33*, no. 1058, p. 632.
[6] ibid.
[7] ibid., no. 1073, p. 682.
[8] ibid., *1534–35*, no. 58, p. 164.
[9] *Chronicle of King Henry VIII. of England*, ed. M. A. S. Hume, p. 38.

for conciliation was evidently reciprocal, for there is no evidence
that the Inquisition persecuted English merchants in Spain
during the year immediately following Henry's new marriage.
When, in the spring of 1534, two Englishmen were imprisoned
for having heretical books in their possession, they were released by Charles' orders.[1] This doubtless was a reflection of the
Emperor's unwillingness to take strong action against Henry
for fear of driving him into an alliance with Francis. In England
the church had undergone little doctrinal change and the new
religious arrangements would hardly have been felt by the
great majority of English merchants and probably not at all
by those resident in Spain.

In the summer of 1534, however, John Mason,[2] writing from
Valladolid to his friend Thomas Starkey in Padua, mentioned
that two English merchants had brought a book written against
the Pope into Spain and were likely to be burned for doing so.[3]
By the following October Cromwell's general praise of the
good treatment of the merchants in Spain was qualified by a
reference to the Inquisition.[4] Early in the next year he protested
against the severity of the inquisitors in dealing with some
English merchants. Cromwell asserted that if they had been
convicted of real heresy, the king and his council would have
been glad they had been burned,[5] but he hoped it would be
realised that those taken at Seville were merchants' factors and
that the goods confiscated belonged to others.[6] In March 1535,
however, Chapuys again reported that Cromwell had praised the
Emperor for showing great clemency in ordering the release of
some Englishmen imprisoned by the Inquisition, the restora-
tion of their property and the release of their ships arrested for
the use of the Imperial fleet. Such acts on Charles' part, Cromwell said, would greatly strengthen the friendship between the
two countries.[7] The Emperor was anxious at this time to find

[1] *Spanish Calendar, 1534–35*, no. 58, p. 164.
[2] Mason was later ordered by Henry VIII to investigate the complaints of
the English merchants in Spain but was recalled when Wyatt was brought to
trial. *Vide infra*, p. 126.
[3] *Letters and Papers*, vii, no. 945.
[4] ibid., no. 1297, p. 496.
[5] Later, the English ambassador emphasized to the Emperor that since
Henry VIII also punished heresy the status of the Pope was the only point
of difference between the two rulers. *Vide infra*, p. 110.
[6] ibid., viii, no. 189, p. 67.
[7] ibid., no. 327.

some means of reaching an understanding with Henry and had instructed Chapuys to sound English opinion on certain proposals. These stipulated good treatment for Katherine and Princess Mary and the end of Henry's intrigues with Denmark and the Germans in return for the suspension of the Papal sentence against the English king.[1] Thus the Emperor came to intercede with the Spanish Inquisition on behalf of Henry's subjects. Such intercession was not often to be repeated, however, and time was to show that the inquisitors would be allowed a free hand when there was no particular reason for conciliating the English.

At this time there was good reason for so doing, however, for a fresh war between Charles and Francis had become inevitable. A rapprochement between the old allies was made easier by the death of Katherine in January 1536, and the subsequent execution of Ann Boleyn removed another obstacle to a closer friendship. When he heard of Ann's impending fate, Charles wrote to Chapuys of possible marriages for both Henry and Princess Mary.[2] Henry's position was thus considerably strengthened and he stood very much on his dignity when, in the following July, he protested strongly against the imprisonment of one of his subjects in Seville for exhibiting before a Spanish court a power of attorney in which the king was styled sovereign head under God of the English church. Henry declared he could conceive no greater insult nor injury than an attempt to deprive him of that title and prerogative which God and human reason had conferred upon him. Chapuys, anxious not to dispute the matter with the king, assured him he knew nothing of it, but if he were given details he would write immediately to Spain. The ambassador received no further information, but heard subsequently that the Englishman was released eight days after his incarceration.[3]

Despite Charles' efforts to secure his assistance, Henry remained neutral during this phase of the Hapsburg-Valois struggle, and relations between England and Spain gradually worsened, aggravated by the depredations at sea inseparable from these wars. When, as the year 1537 drew to a close, Charles

---

[1] *Letters and Papers*, viii, nos. 272, 433.
[2] ibid., x, no. 888.
[3] ibid., xi, no. 40.

and Francis sought a truce and Henry began making overtures
to Protestant Europe, the position of the English merchants in
Spain became more difficult than ever before during this period.
Already in August of that year William Spratt, a leading Bristol
merchant engaged in the Spanish trade,[1] had received disturb-
ing news from Hugh Tipton, his factor in northern Spain.[2] Tipton
wrote that in the previous July he and Thomas Shipman,
another Bristol merchant, had been sentenced by the inquisitors
not only to:

go to the churche in the saide towne of Sainte Sabastianes accom-
paned *with* the best of the same and duringe the tyme of the masse and
sermon stonde at the highe altar *with* tapers in their hand*es* *with*owte
cappes capes girdles and shoes.

but also to pay between them a fine of 600 ducats and 120
ducats costs. Moreover, they were forbidden to leave the city
of San Sebastian within the following two years upon pain of a
fine of 10,000 ducats, for which they had given sureties. Their
offence, according to Tipton, had been to declare, six years
previously, that they did not believe in the authority of the Pope
nor in prayers to the saints and to assert that King Henry's
laws were in accordance with God's laws. Nor were Tipton and
Shipman the only victims. A boy from Bridgewater was fined
20 ducats for words spoken in England 'or ell*es* to have had an
hundreth sott*es* and . . . but a very boye'; more serious still, a
Londoner had been burned. '. . . let all those that come owte of
England beware what they speake before Spannyerd*es* ffor if
they come hither they shalbe punyshed for that they speake
there.'

On 4 August Tipton wrote another letter to his master, this
time from Renteria.[3] This reveals that very soon after receiving
sentence from the Inquisition he was going about Spratt's
business as before. It is a typical factor's letter, informing his
master of goods despatched to England. Within four days of
writing this second letter, Tipton said, he intended to go to
Bilbao to sell cloth for Spratt and other merchants. Clearly,
the order forbidding him to leave San Sebastian was not strictly
enforced. He declared he had to sell the cloths to pay his debts

[1] P.R.O., K.R. Customs, 21/5, 21/7, etc.
[2] P.R.O., State Papers, Henry VIII, vol. 124, f. 252.
[3] ibid., vol. 123, f. 218.

for he was penniless, probably the result of paying the fine. Tipton told Spratt that more goods were despatched to him with the second letter in a Spanish ship, the *Saviour* of Renteria, whose master was Domingo de Zubieta. Tipton said there was another Spanish ship sailing with her and warned Spratt against meddling with any of the Spaniards but Domingo and his brother, for they were not to be trusted. It is of interest that the latter, apparently good friends of the Bristol merchants, were accused of piracy shortly after their arrival in England—by men of Southampton.[1]

Domingo arrived in Bristol on 23 August[2] and doubtless was questioned by Spratt about the contents of the letters. Subsequent events reveal the English merchant's agitation. On 18 September, after a month's procrastination, he showed Tipton's letters to the mayor of Bristol and other merchants of the city, amongst whom they undoubtedly caused great consternation since so many of them had staked their fortunes in the trade to Spain. The mayor, Richard Abingdon, immediately informed Cromwell of the contents of the letters, requesting him 'to be goode lord in that trade of the said Willyam and other *marchauntes* of the same towne is in the said *parties* in Spayne', but above all to be discreet in dealing with the matter as otherwise it would be disastrous for the Bristol merchants.[3] So distraught was Spratt that he could not let the matter rest there, but himself wrote to Cromwell enclosing a copy of his factor's second letter. He stressed that he would be in very great danger of losing his goods and Tipton his life if the Spaniards knew he had made this accusation against them.[4] Whatever action Cromwell took, however, Spratt certainly continued trading to Spain for some years[5] and Tipton resided there for a part of Elizabeth's reign.[6]

After the Truce of Nice in June 1538 feeling against the English in Spain became more pronounced and by the autumn the fortunes of the merchants were at low ebb. At a moment when they should have united in the face of danger many failed

---

[1] *Letters and Papers*, xii (2), nos. 596, 606, etc.
[2] P.R.O., K.R. Customs, 199/3.
[3] P.R.O., State Papers, Henry VIII, vol. 124, f. 251.
[4] ibid., vol. 123, f. 220.
[5] P.R.O., K.R. Customs, 21/10, 199/4, 21/12.
[6] *Vide infra*, p. 124.

to fulfil their obligations under the charter—to the detriment of them all.[1] It is evident that the religious changes in England were received with mixed feelings among the English in Spain. Some were not prepared to prejudice their interests there by condoning publicly what were considered in Spain their king's heresies; others were more loyal.[2] There was much bitterness between them, which is reflected in the letters of Richard Abbis, a London merchant,[3] to Cromwell, written during a voyage to the Mediterranean. Abbis arrived at Cadiz on 5 September 1538 after visiting Corunna on his way. In both places he learned that his fellow countrymen had been unpopular in Spain ever since the peace. He alleged they were hated as heretics and Lutherans and reported that the Spaniards said they hoped soon to make war against England on the Pope's behalf. Englishmen therefore had to be very careful in both actions and words for fear of the Inquisition, except those of the 'popyshe lawe', both English and Irishmen, 'that dothe dayly invent slander to the reme of Ynglonde'.[4] There were many such Irishmen and Abbis mentioned one English merchant by name whom he accused of dying in Spain a traitor to the king—Thomas Howell.[5] Abbis does not state the nature of Howell's treachery and it can only be surmised that his accusation arose from the draper's prosperity and the friendly terms upon which he remained with the Spaniards until his death. Whatever Howell's attitude towards Henry's Supremacy—which we do not know—he cannot be accused of forgetting the country of his birth, for he left the bulk of his money to good purposes in England. He doubtless committed an offence by dying in Spain, for in doing so he could hardly have died otherwise than as a good Catholic.

The religious question during this earlier period was clearly not yet one of doctrine. Most English merchants were probably good Catholics and attended Roman services in Spain without demur. Their difficulty arose from Henry's Supremacy and their loyalty to him. As doctrinal questions did not arise at first it

---

[1] *Vide supra*, p. 94.

[2] Even their loyalty was not disinterested because the merchants had interests in England where they would wish to be considered loyal subjects of the king.

[3] Abbis or Abbs, figures in a number of Admiralty cases in this period. *Vide supra*, p. 12.

[4] B.M., Cotton MS. Vespasian C VII, f. 87.

[5] *Letters and Papers*, xiii (2), no. 660.

was possible when the Inquisition was more tolerant for a tactful merchant to go about his business without interference.

The official policy of the Spanish Inquisition towards the English merchants at this time is revealed by correspondence in the records of the *Inquisición de Aragón*. Among letters written to the Prior of San Sebastian in June 1539 concerning some Englishmen (including boys) accused of heresy is a statement which was apparently to be given in answer to the English ambassador. This says, first of all, that the inquisitors should proceed according to the law against any Englishmen having in their possession books by Luther or his followers, or books containing errors or heresies contrary to the Catholic Faith or due obedience to the Holy See. They should deal likewise with Englishmen reported for speaking or writing anything against the doctrine of the Catholic Church or the Papacy. If, on the other hand, Englishmen were provoked into defending Henry VIII's measures, but did not voice any erroneous opinions of their own, they and those who had provoked them were to be reported to the Council. Meanwhile, such Englishmen should not be arrested unless it was suspected they would absent themselves and if they did not give sureties that they would not do so without permission.[1] Moreover, when Charles was anxious to conciliate Henry, he gave orders that the English in Spain were not to be molested unless they spoke words defamatory of the Pope.[2]

During times when the Inquisition was most aggressive and relations between the two countries were strained, however, English merchants were often forced to give their opinion of Henry's religious changes. One aspect of the religious problem was to be a constant source of difficulty to the merchants—the refusal of the Spaniards to admit in their law courts legal documents in which the king was described as Supreme Head of the English church. Henry himself had complained of this in 1536[3] and Richard Abbis reported in October 1538 that when Mr. Roche's[4] son came from London to Seville to recover the

[1] Archivo Histórico Nacional, Madrid, Inquisición de Aragón, Cartas, 322, ff. 240v–242.
[2] *Vide infra*, p. 187.
[3] *Vide supra*, p. 104.
[4] William Roche, Thomas Howell's former master.

12,000 ducats left by Thomas Howell to the Drapers' Hall, the Spaniards would not recognise the validity of his papers for that reason.[1]

In December 1538 the English merchants, assembled in the church at San Lucar, elected William Ostriche as their governor with wide powers to meet the more difficult situation. In the following April they met again to confirm before a public notary the decrees of the previous meeting.[2] Among other witnesses of this declaration was Francisco Hermoso, a Spanish priest. His presence in the English church on this occasion is of special significance, for it shows that the merchants as a whole could not have been regarded as heretics at that time, otherwise no Spanish priest would have dared to take part in such an assembly. This document also confirms that the church of St. George was still being used—further proof that the majority of the English merchants were conforming to the old religion.

This was the period of Henry VIII's flirtation with the German Protestants, and news of such incidents as the desecration of the tomb of St. Thomas served to stir up Spanish feeling against the English. William Ostriche told Abbis in January 1539 he had heard from Seville that the Emperor had been urged by the Pope to wage war against Henry in alliance with the kings of France and Scotland and to proclaim the English king and his subjects schismatics and heretics, to be treated as Jews and infidels wherever seized. Spanish friends of the English merchants had warned them to look to their goods as war was imminent.[3] In the following March it was believed in London that the Pope had procured the burning of three English merchants in Spain and had granted remission of sins to anyone killing an English heretic.[4] To this period in all probability belongs an undated letter written by a certain Nicholas Danyell from his prison in San Sebastian. Thomas Batcock forwarded this letter to Cromwell and asked that the Emperor should be requested to command '*the* corigedor *that* ffrome hence fforth he inbrace none off *our* nacion *that* wee bee off Lutere is sect or erytick*es*'. Batcock declared the English had never been so badly treated in Spain as they were now and named a fellow

---

[1] *Letters and Papers*, xiii_(2), no. 660.
[2] *Vide supra*, p. 95.
[3] *Letters and Papers*, xiv (1), no. 158.
[4] ibid., no. 466.

countryman, John Young, as inciting the Spanish authorities against his compatriots.[1]

At the beginning of the following year Wyatt, the English ambassador, in attendance upon Charles in Paris, protested against the ill-usage of the English merchants in Spain at the hands of the Inquisition. The Emperor replied that the Holy Office had been established for good reasons which he was not prepared to contest, and that Englishmen residing in his dominions would have to obey his laws. Wyatt reminded Charles that he had agreed earlier to a relaxation of the rigour of the Inquisition for the sake of the commerce with England. He pointed out that Henry VIII also punished heresy and the only point of difference between them was the status of the Bishop of Rome. Charles insisted the matter concerned the Faith and said he would communicate with Henry about it. He did promise, however, to write to the Cardinal of Toledo, the chief inquisitor, after he had examined a statement of the merchants' grievances. Wyatt also complained of the activities of Robert Brancetour, whom he accused of inciting Englishmen in Spain to disloyalty, and of English preachers defaming their king and country and stirring up the Emperor's subjects against their fellow countrymen. Charles' reply was unsatisfactory and the ambassador afterwards declared he had never seen him so vehement and imperious as on this occasion, especially when he spoke of the Inquisition. Wyatt believed Charles would do nothing to protect the English merchants, for he had said he would rather they did not come to his dominions than they should sow heresies there. The English merchants, wrote Wyatt, should be warned that henceforth they would trade to Spain at their own risk. The ambassador himself, however, was not convinced that Charles' attitude was governed solely by considerations of religion. He believed the Emperor wished to keep Henry neutral until he went into Germany, showing the English king by ill-treating his subjects that he could repay the injury Henry did him by his friendship with the German Protestants. At the same time this ostentatious unfriendliness towards the English would encourage Francis to keep negotiating for Milan.[2]

During this particularly bad period in Anglo-Spanish rela-

---

[1] P.R.O., State Papers, Henry VIII, vol. 92, f. 204v.
[2] *Letters and Papers*, xv, no. 38.

tions there occurred the persecution of Thomas Pery, a wealthy London merchant residing in Ayamonte, whose own account of his ordeal throws a great deal of light upon the methods of the inquisitors and the difficulties of a loyal Englishman in the face of them. Moreover, it reveals something of the earlier attitude of such men towards the religious changes in England and helps to explain why they were later to be among the most zealous adherents of the new faith. Although the majority of English merchants must have kept their opinions to themselves in the company of Spaniards, there can be little doubt that as time went on an increasing number of Englishmen came to share Pery's sentiments. The latter's experience, re-told among his fellow countrymen both at home and in Spain, must have helped to stir up patriotic feeling against the Spaniards.

Thomas Pery, citizen and clothworker of London, where he lived in Fenchurch Street in the parish of St. Denis,[1] had been trading to Spain since his mid-twenties,[2] making Ayamonte his headquarters during his visits there. He was assisted in his business by his wife, Alice, who appears to have managed his affairs at home during his absences in Spain,[3] while his servant Francis Bolde looked after his interests in Ayamonte when he was in England. Pery must have travelled backwards and forwards quite frequently, for he is known to have been in England during the years 1537 and 1539 when he gave evidence in cases before the High Court of Admiralty.[4] From these it appears that he was born in either 1499 or 1500.[5] On 27 June 1539 Pery was examined before the court in the case of *Austin v. Castelyn*[6] and shortly afterwards he returned to Spain in the company of one Thomas Edwards. Pery's story is contained in two letters written by him from his Spanish prison, one to a fellow merchant, Richard Field,[7] the other to Mr. Ralph Vane 'belonginge

---

[1] P.R.O., H.C.A., Examinations, 2, 3 July 1537.

[2] He was approximately 39 years old at the time of his persecution when he declared he had been trading to Spain at least 14 years. *Vide infra*, p. 115.

[3] In a case before the Admiralty Court Pery declared his wife sold tunny fish on his behalf. *Vide supra*, p. 29.

[4] P.R.O., H.C.A., Examinations, 2, 92 *passim*. *Vide supra*, pp. 13, 26.

[5] ibid., 2, 3 July 1537, when he is described as 37 years of age, and ibid., 92, 28 May 1543 (actual date 1544) when he is 44. These details in Admiralty cases are not always accurate but this consistency suggests their reliability in Pery's case.

[6] ibid., 92, 27 June 1539.

[7] B.M., Cotton MS. Vespasian C VII, ff. 91v *seq*.

to my lorde prewe seyll'.[1] As Pery's account, which is the same in both letters, is the most detailed document bearing upon the question of the persecution of the English merchants by the Spanish Inquisition in the early Tudor period it is worthy of close examination.[2]

On 9 October 1539, according to Pery, he was in his warehouse at Ayamonte in the dwelling of his host, Gômez Malmazeda,[3] brushing some cloths. The previous evening he had given seven pieces of 'northern dozens' to his host in part payment for the board of his servant Francis Bolde for the two years just ended.[4] While he was thus engaged a local priest and several other Spaniards entered the warehouse. The priest drew Pery's attention to a 'brassyne' bell of about two quintals weight brought by Thomas Edwards on their last voyage together from England and which up to that moment Pery did not realise was in his warehouse. 'What a goode crysten is yowre kinge of Ynglande to pwte downe the monesterys / and to take awaye the belles?' asked the priest.[5] After challenging the Spaniard to go to England and put the matter to Henry himself, Pery declared he did consider the king a good Christian and he was certainly regarded as such in his own realm. The priest said Henry was a heretic who had suppressed the monasteries, sold their bells and 'ys pope with in hym selfe in his reyme'. He asked Pery if he approved this. The merchant pointed out, naturally, that he had nothing to do with such matters 'for hys gracce and hys consell knowythe what they hawe to do in his reyme', but vehemently denied that the king was a heretic. He went further. He declared himself ready to affirm his opinion before a public notary—a rash act if conditions were as the merchants later described them. The priest called upon his companions to bear witness to the Englishman's words and Pery repeated them before they departed.

The English merchant left Ayamonte the following day to go

---

[1] B.M., Cotton MS. Vespasian CVII, ff. 102 seq.

[2] A copy of the letter to Vane was transcribed by Sir Henry Ellis in *Original Letters illustrative of English History*, Second Series, vol. ii, pp. 139–156. Ellis made only one short comment on the contents and apparently included the document to show the opinion of Henry VIII's conduct held in the Catholic countries of Europe.

[3] Malvaseda?

[4] This suggests that Pery had spent the previous two years in England.

[5] This and all subsequent quotations from Pery's account of his persecution, are taken from his letter to Richard Field.

to Lepe, about four leagues away, to arrange the lading of a ship he had chartered, thinking he would hear no more of the matter. Perhaps other merchants of his acquaintance had been questioned in the same way and heard no more of it. In pursuance of his business Pery bought a hundred pipes of bastard wine from the Duke of Bejar which was subsequently laden on the ship by two London merchants, Thomas Edwards and William East.[1] On 11 October he was arrested in Lepe by order of the vicar of the town and sent to prison. There he remained for eleven days chained by his left leg. On 21 October he was examined by the *alguazil mayor*[2] of the Seville Inquisition in the presence of a public notary, who recorded Pery's answers to the questions put to him by the inquisitor. The *alguazil's* questions were all concerned with Pery's valuables—what money and jewels he owned; what money was owed him in Spain and what goods of his own and other merchants he had in his possession. When Pery told him the extent of his property the official confiscated goods belonging to William Wood and Richard Field, and money, a gold ring and goods belonging to Pery himself. Then he removed the merchant from the prison and would have taken him in chains to Seville 'as thowgh I hade byne the strongest theyffe in the worlde' but for the intervention of the Duke of Bejar who entered sureties for two thousand ducats that Pery would present himself at the castle of Triana.[3] On 27 October the Englishman honoured the Duke's pledge and from then until 8 February 1540 he remained a prisoner in the castle. During all that time no one was permitted to speak with him except the Spanish officials.

On 2 November, at his own request, Pery was granted an interview with a *licenciado*[4] named Corro. The latter asked him if he knew why he had been imprisoned and the Englishman answered that he did, repeating the words he had spoken in the warehouse and protesting that if he had said anything wrong it was because he had been provoked to anger by the priest. The *licenciado*, referring to a process against Pery sent him by the vicar of Lepe, asked the merchant if he knew any of his accusers

---

[1] These merchants were present when Pery was arrested. *Vide infra*, p. 119.

[2] The senior *alguazil*. The *alguazil* was a minor functionary of the tribunal whose chief job was the arrest of prisoners and seizure of their goods.

[3] This great fortress on the outskirts of Seville became the headquarters of the Inquisition shortly after its inception under Ferdinand and Isabella.

[4] A lawyer.

and told him their charge was more serious than he alleged. Pery answered that he knew none of them and his words had been those which he had confessed to the inquisitor. Two days later Corro sent for Pery again and questioned him about King Henry's orthodoxy, and his own. He asked him how he could prove Henry was a good Christian when the English king was known to be a heretic. Pery said the king was a good and faithful Christian, for he had commanded that all his subjects should observe the sacraments and all holy services be celebrated in every parish church throughout his realm to God's glory and honour. Moreover, Henry himself set them a good example by his own religious observances, hearing Mass daily in his own chapel and performing all duties 'acording to the lawdebwll vsse and costom of owr holly mother chwrche and so commandyth all hys swbgett*es* to do the same apone payne of deythe / and also to keype the yemberinge fastys and all other fasting dayes acordinge to the olde ansyent costome'.

On 15 November Pery appeared before Corro once more and was told to nominate any witnesses he would like examined on his behalf. Pery named forty persons, both Englishmen and foreigners, living in Seville, San Lucar, Cadiz, Ayamonte and Lepe. Sending for all these people cost him much money, but he did not know what transpired. On 24 November the *licenciado* again asked the English merchant if he believed Henry VIII was a good Christian and did well to suppress the monasteries. Pery re-affirmed his belief in the king's orthodoxy and concerning the other matter, said it must have been justified because Henry had not done it:

a pone hys owne heyde but be the consell of all hys nobyll*es* of hys reyme spyrytwall and te*m*porall and more that the arsbysshop*es* and bysshopys dowyth opynly preyche hit in the pwlpyt*es* throwthe owit the reyme and many wother docters whiche be takin for gret lernyde men and theye do declare that all that hys grace hathe downe he maye do hit be the atoryte of holly scryptwre / the whiche cawsythe me to gewye credanes vnto hit I beinge onlernyde.

Pery said that if the *licenciado* was able to show him that the king was not justified by authority of the scriptures he would submit and ask for mercy. The Spaniard did not reply, but dismissed the merchant with a warning that he would hear more of it later.

On 10 December Pery was called before Corro to hear the accusation presented against him. Henry VIII was declared a heretic and Pery one also for believing him to be a good Christian and approving his measures against the Roman Catholic Church. Corro would demand that the Englishman be punished in person and lose all his goods, half of which would be confiscated to the Emperor's use and the other half to the Holy Office. On being called upon to make answer Pery declared he knew Henry VIII was no heretic, but a faithful Christian; as for himself, he had traded to Spain for at least fourteen years and no man could say he was not a good Christian and of good Christian family.[1] Three days later he was ordered to declare before a public notary the extent of his own goods, those of other men in his possession and all debts owing to him. On 23 December the *licenciado* visited Pery in prison and asked him how he was and whether he lacked anything. He also warned him that a colleague, Doctor Pero Diez, would be coming shortly to discuss Pery's ultimate fate. The Englishman begged to be given justice and not left in a prison so full of vermin that he had 'no lyste of meytte nor dryncke' and with no proper bed to lie on.

On 20 January 1540 Pery appeared before Doctor Pero Diez who asked him three questions. Did he really believe in his heart that King Henry VIII was a good Christian? Pery answered that he did think so. Secondly, he was asked whether he had said at Ayamonte in Gómez Malmazeda's house that the king did well in suppressing the monasteries and confiscating their bells. This Pery denied. Lastly, whether he had said the English king was Pope in England, to which Pery replied he had not mentioned the Pope's name. When, in the following week, the merchant was again called upon to confess the truth of what the witnesses had alleged against him, he refused to do so and was sentenced to undergo torture. 'Than', in Pery's own words:

he commayndyd the alcaylde to hawe me in to the / prysson of tormento wher al thinges was preparyde for me and strypyde me fowrthe of my clowthis as nakyde as ever I was bowrne and then

---

[1] A Thomas Pere, citizen and fishmonger of London, died in Cadiz in 1532. *Vide* Somerset House, P.C.C. Wills, 15 Thower. It is possible he was the father of this Pery which would strengthen the latter's assertion that it was known in Spain that he came from a good Christian family.

the porter browghte me a payer of lynnen breches and then cam in the jwge and hys scrywano / and he sette hym downe in a chayer with in the prysson haweinge a kwsshin of tapstery worke vnder hys feytte and then / I knelyde downe apone my knewyes holdinge vp my handes to hym deysyring hym to be goode vnto me and to do me jwstys he sayeinge vnto me Confes yowe the trwthe and we axke no more. I answeryd and sayde I hawe confes the trwthe and ye wyll not be lewe me./ ther a pone the porter and a nother tooke me be the armes and cawsyde me for to set downe a pone the sayde of the bwrryco and browght the wone of my armes over the other and caste a rope v tymis a bowtte them bothe and so drewe the sayde rope with all ther myghte.

I thynking they wolde a plockyde the fleshe from the bownys and cryde a pone the sayde jwge to showe me mercy sayeing to hym yowe saye thys is a howsse of mercy but hit is more lycke a howsse of morder then of mercy wher a pone he commandyd me to be layde a pone the bwrryco and at the yende therof / ther was a nerthen panne which myghte holde iij or iiij gallones of watter / and in hit a tocke of fyne cotten contayenyng iij yardes longe or more. which I showlde a recewyde in to my boddy by dropys of watter in at my mowthe whiche is a greweus payne and to be bownde with ropys to the sayde bwrryco / and when I sawe so lyttyll mercy in hym I axkyde hym what he wolde that I showlde do he sayeinge I wolde ye showlde tell the trwthe I hawe sayde the trwthe and ye wyll not be lewe me. I mwste saye as yow saye or elles ye are dysposyde for to morther me he sayeing no morther but jwstys and so I confeste that I sayde hit and thowght hit and so he cawssyde hit to be wrytten and so went hys waye and I was onelowesyde a gayne.

Two days later Pery appeared again before Diez. A public notary read over to him what he had confessed in the torture chamber and the judge demanded that Pery should declare whether it was a true statement or not. When the Englishman tried to avoid a direct answer by saying that God knew all truth, he was warned that if he did not agree he would be sent back to the torture chamber. Whereupon he acquiesced and asked for counsel in saving his soul. Diez told him that ten or twelve years earlier Henry VIII had written more in condemnation of Luther, that great heretic, than any other Christian king. But now he was himself the biggest heretic in the world and 'a wery tyrante and a man qwyller' who 'kepythe no jwstys but doythe all thinges of hys owne ryall power'. Diez went on to accuse Henry of spending his time in all vicious pastimes; of cut-ting himself off from the Mother Church and from the Pope's authority because of the sentence given in favour of Queen Katherine; and of living with another woman and then beheading her. To all of this Pery replied that he knew the king was a good Christian, and whatever he did was with the advice of his council. When Ann was beheaded Pery was not in England —at least he had nothing to do with that.

On 8 February Pery was summoned from prison by the *alcaide*,[1] who had his irons removed and brought him before the court of the castle. There he knelt before some priests in the company of certain other English merchants, John Robins, Harry Holland, Robert Morgan and William Alcot, while they had the 'sawme of messerery' said over them. The Spaniards 'dysplyde' them with 'a fagget stycke' and ordered them to stand in a row beside the wall bareheaded in their 'cott*es*'. The porter[2] of the castle brought each of them a 'nabet of sent benett*es*'[3] of yellow canvas with two red crosses, which he put over their heads upon their backs, and each was given a wax candle to hold. So they went out of the castle into the street. Here some three or four thousand people were waiting, warned the previous day of what was to take place. Behind a cross and flanked on either side by guards the Englishmen proceeded to the parish church of St. Anne in Triana. Within the church a scaffold had been erected upon which the victims were set and remained during the hearing of High Mass. A sermon was preached by an Austin friar, one of the fathers of the Inquisition. He said the errors of the Englishmen had been innocent because they were ignorant of the scriptures. Then a public notary went into the pulpit and read out each man's sentence. Pery's offence was that he had declared the English king a good Christian when he was, in fact, a heretic; he had approved the suppression of the monasteries in England; and had said Henry VIII was Pope in England. All of which was heresy. As punishment Pery was sentenced to six months' imprisonment in the prison of 'perpetwe' being allowed out only each Sunday clad in his habit of penance to hear High Mass at San Salvador's. He was also to lose his goods.

[1] The jailer.
[2] The *portero* was a minor functionary of the Inquisition.
[3] i.e. the *sanbenito*, worn by penitents after sentence by the Inquisition.

'Then he was taken back in procession to the castle of Triana where he remained until three o'clock on Shrove Sunday afternoon. The English merchants were then summoned to hear a final admonition from Doctor Pero Diez. The doctor told them that their punishment had been that of a loving mother to her child, 'for yf she lowe hym she wyll chastyne hym and so hathe owr holly mother chyrche vssyde yowe'; but if they offended again, however slight the offence, they would surely be burned. From thence he commanded them to be taken to the prison of 'perpetwe'. There Thomas Pery was when he wrote, abiding, he said, the mercy of the Lord. He might have died, had it not been for the goodness of Mr. Harrison and John Field[1] who with many other English merchants had helped him 'of cheryte', for the Spaniards had not left him a single blanket or garment to his back, 'Gode a mende them'.

Pery's vivid and detailed account of his persecution at the hands of the Inquisition reveals quite clearly the nature of the religious problem confronting the English merchants in Spain following Henry's Reformation. A comparison between Pery's experience and the account of Robert Tomson's adventures some years later[2] throws considerable light upon the development of anti-Roman, anti-Spanish nationalism among English sea-going men and provides a remarkable commentary on certain aspects of the religious changes in Tudor England.

While Pery was languishing in prison Roger Basing was sent on a mission to Spain which included an investigation of the reports of ill-treatment of the English merchants.[3] In June 1540 Basing was in Bilbao whence he reported to Cromwell that it was indeed true that certain ill-disposed persons, mostly priests, spoke opprobriously of the English king and his council. If they could get an Englishman apart from his fellows they would question him about the Pope's authority and take advantage of his answer to report him to the inquisitors. They said the Pope and the cardinals constituted the *Ecclesia Catholica* and whoever denied it should be burned. On this account alone a Flemish mariner married in England had been burned recently in Bilbao. All the Englishmen who had been in trouble with the Inquisition

---

[1] Leading English merchants in Seville. *Vide supra*, p. 97.
[2] *Vide supra*, pp. 97–98.
[3] He was also to purchase horses for the King. *Vide supra*, p. 6.

had left for England except one, who was winding up his business and had arranged to leave within the next three weeks.[1] It is of interest that in this very month the Emperor's chief minister in Spain, Francisco de los Cobos, declared that the Inquisition was encroaching daily upon the civil power in cases involving capital punishment and told Charles that when he returned to Spain measures must be taken to curtail its authority.[2]

On 8 July a gathering of English merchants in San Lucar under their governor, William Ostriche, put their difficulties to Basing. According to a document sent home by the envoy[3] these were 'the mostt pryncypall*es* and honest of the nacio*n* resydent in these p*a*rties of Andolozea' whom the king had wished to be asked whether the complaints which had reached his ears of their ill-treatment in Spain were true. Basing produced 'one boke of complaynt*es*' of Thomas Pery, probably compiled from his letter to Vane, for the London merchant was still in prison,[4] and asked the assembled Englishmen whether they believed its contents were true. In reply, they declared that concerning Pery's account of the circumstances leading up to his arrest 'emonge the hole nacyon, it is publyke voyce and fame theffecte of the same as it is alledged by the same Thomas Pery, to be trew'.[5] Most of those signing the document had received their information from men like Philip Kydwar, William East, Thomas Edwards and Edward Deakyn who were present when Pery was sent to prison and witnessed everything that happened on that occasion. The English merchants were unable to give testimony to events in the castle of Triana where only the officials of the Inquisition and their servants were present. They were convinced that Pery spoke the truth, however, because all over Spain the Emperor's subjects vehemently denounced King Henry as a heretic and a Lutheran. Indeed, if any Englishmen trading in Spain said or wrote that their king was a good Christian they were 'with moche creweltye put in pryson and their goodis lost forever and theyr lyfe in gret daunger'.[6]

---

[1] *Letters and Papers*, xv, no. 787.
[2] *Spanish Calendar, 1538–42*, no. 110.
[3] P.R.O., State Papers, Henry VIII, vol. 161, ff. 76–78.
[4] Pery was released on 9 August. *Vide infra*, p. 125. J. A. Williamson is mistaken in thinking Pery was present at this meeting and related his sufferings there. *Maritime Enterprise, 1485–1558*, p. 222.
[5] P.R.O., State Papers, Henry VIII, vol. 161, f. 76.
[6] ibid., f. 76v.

Concerning Pery's allegation that he was compelled by torture to make a statement as the judge ordered, they said that
several English merchants who were prisoners with him had told
them that they were present when he was tortured. For the rest,
the merchants said Thomas Pery was such an honest, discreet
man that they did not believe he would speak anything but the
truth in this matter. Moreover, they knew he had long demanded a copy of the whole process against him which he intended to present to the king and council (if he could obtain it)
in order to prove his 'boke of complaynte' to be true. That concluded the answer of the English merchants to Pery's book.
They then proceeded to give an account of their own difficulties.

For a long time past, they said, all Englishmen trading in
Andalusia had been living in extreme fear of the Inquisition. The
latter and its deputies were active wherever the Englishmen
traded and, moreover, the ordinary Spanish people were hostile
to the English king, his council and his subjects. Every day
their sole topic of conversation with the English merchants was
whether Henry VIII had returned to the Holy Church or had
continued a heretic and a Lutheran. The Spaniards spoke so
slanderously of the king they dared not repeat their words. If
any Englishman said Henry VIII was a good Christian or spoke
any word in his favour he was reported to the inquisitors, who
treated him cruelly and confiscated his goods and all those of
other men in his possession to the use of the Emperor and the
Holy Office. This had happened to many Englishmen. Four or
five of them were still in prison, their goods lost, their persons
put to the greatest shame and dishonour that the Spaniards
could devise and all the goods of other men in their possession
in great danger of confiscation.

The assembled merchants further affirmed that the officers
of the Inquisition had been in Seville, Jerez, San Lucar and other
places enquiring about a great number of English merchants
and searching for their goods. Some of these merchants were
still in Spain but most had returned to England, not daring to
trade nor visit Spain for fear of the Inquisition. Such men had
been completely ruined by the stoppage of their trade. The
English merchants remaining in Spain went in daily dread of
the inquisitors and of the Spanish people generally, since they
might at any moment be taken for speaking some word to the

king's honour. So they did not dare to mix freely with the Spaniards as they used to do and thus lost a great deal of trade. All the merchants journeying backwards and forwards to Spain were likewise in great fear and danger:

that as men amased and vnquyet in theyr sprytes goo from place to place inquyryng of theyr frendys if they doo heare that any of theym be accused and inquyred for, and to dispache and delyuer theyr parsons out of that gret feare and daunger do not lett dailly to sell all their goodis and merchandes to theyr gret losse and hynderance / and some for feare to be accused and knowe not how to lyve but by their trade and occupieng into this cuntreth to dyspose theym self of all theyr goodis, and other mennys in theyr power and put it in the powers of othre of the nacion whome they take to haue mor fauor freendship and to be moste clerest owt of suspect of soche daunger.[1]

The majority of Spaniards were so evilly disposed towards the English that it was almost impossible to answer their malicious demands without incurring risk of arrest.

Englishmen arrested by the Inquisition were not only solemnly sworn to declare what they themselves had said and done, but by the same oath to accuse any of their fellow country-men whom they had ever heard say anything 'contrary to theyr pleasure and ordenances'.[2] In this way:

many of our nacion be secretly accused and know not therof so that all the hole company daylly dotth lyve in gret feare and daunger / and when in their demandes the prysoners make soche aunswers that they cannot take soche advantage of theyr wordys as they desyre, then they doo swere theym to declare what they doo thynke in theyr conscience and hartes. yf they thynke the kinge be a good Christen man / yf they thynke the kynge doo well to pulle downe abbays and monasteryes and to put the relligious men to deth / yf they thynke he can be, or be a good Chrysten man not beynge obedyent to the holly ffathers of Rome, and many othre demandes that were to long to wryte.

and finally, the merchants declared:

this is the trewth whervnto we haue fyrmed our names the day and yere beforesaid. //

God save the kynge.[3]

---

[1] P.R.O., State Papers, Henry VIII, vol. 161, f. 77.
[2] ibid., f. 77v.
[3] ibid.

The statement was signed by William Ostriche, the governor, Thomas Harrison, John Sweeting, William Folwode, John Field, John Bedell, George Masters, Edward Lewis, William Wilford, Thomas Kingsman, Thomas Wilson, Robert Hunt, Thomas Ridley, John Lonnor, Walter Frauncis, Nicholas Rochell, John Augustyn, Nicholas Saterley, Blase Saunders, William Redstone, Richard Hore, Nicholas Skyres, William Merycke, Nicholas Lawford and Christopher Sowthwerke.

This account of their treatment at the hands of the Inquisition by the leading English merchants in Spain describes a situation which, had it persisted, must within a short space of time have rendered English trade with Spain impossible. The question at once arises, how far it was exaggerated—and this is not easily answered. It is quite certain, however, that the intensity of the persecution must soon have abated, because the trade did not cease and English merchants continued to trade and reside in Spain. Apart from their loyalty to the king, which brought trouble upon their heads if they voiced it in public, the religious problem of the English merchants in Spain became more acute as the English church diverged further from the church of Rome. It became increasingly difficult not to take sides in the great religious struggle of the period. The merchants, having business interests in both England and Spain, would wish to be considered loyal subjects of Henry VIII in the one country and orthodox Christians in the other. Clearly it was thus in their interests to exaggerate their difficulties and emphasize their loyalty in the face of them. In fairness to the merchants, there is little doubt their inclinations were towards loyalty to their king and acquiescence on the whole in his religious changes. It must also be noted that there is very little evidence of the Spaniards denying the truth of their complaints. Nor is there any reason why they should have done so, for toleration of dissenting religious beliefs was not regarded as a virtue and Spain had no monopoly in the matter of persecution. The years 1539 and 1540, in which their most serious allegations against the Inquisition were made, were the worst the English merchants in Spain had to endure since the Reformation. Soon an anti-Protestant reaction in England and renewed Franco-Spanish hostility were to bring them another more secure period.

There is evidence that several of the merchants signing the

document lived in Spain for many more years. John Sweeting
is shown as a very important trader in Cadiz in the reigns of
Edward VI and Mary in the notarial records of the city.[1]
According to Hakluyt's account of Robert Tomson's adventures
Sweeting was living with his wife in Cadiz and sending a ship of
his own to the Indies in 1555.[2] Evidence of Sweeting's trade to
the New World in the last years of Henry VIII's reign is contained in the notarial records of Seville.[3] John Field is described
in Tomson's story[4] as residing with his family in Seville in 1553.
Harrison and Kingsman are also known to have been in Andalusia towards the end of Henry VIII's reign.[5] Edward Lewis
was later an unsuccessful candidate for the consulship.[6] Even
Thomas Pery, after a visit to England, was back in Ayamonte
in 1542.[7]

William Ostriche, as governor during this difficult period,
must have thought it politic to be on friendly terms with the
Spanish authorities. It is not known when his governorship
ended, but doubtless he was glad to relinquish the office. In
January 1540 he wrote to the Bishop of Chichester that he only
carried on in obedience to the king, for his affairs in England
were in need of his attention and the position of the English
merchants in Spain extremely difficult.[8] In 1545 Ostriche gave
powers of attorney to John Kidderminster, whom he mentioned
in his letter to the bishop, to attend to his affairs at home.[9] A
letter from Bonner, then English ambassador in Spain, to Henry
VIII in March 1543 makes a grave charge against Ostriche. In
it the ambassador warned the king 'how that the same William,
havyng suspecte acquayntaunce with dyverse naughtie freers in
Seville, intendeth shortly to presente Your Majestie with dyverse costelye boxes of marmelado, given to ·him by the saide
freers, and suspected to have within theim thinges of daunger
and great perill'.[10] No more has been found about this matter,
unless a letter written to Ostriche by the council on behalf of
Mr. Starkey on 12 July of that year had any bearing upon it.[11]

[1] Archivo de Protocolos de Cádiz, *Oficio* XIX, 1547 *seq, passim.*
[2] Op. cit., ix, p. 341.
[3] Archivo de Protocolos de Sevilla, *Oficio* XV, 1545, *Libro* II, f. 68v.
[4] *Vide supra*, p. 97.   [5] *Vide supra*, pp, 97, 98.   [6] *Vide infra*, p. 124.
[7] P.R.O., H.C.A., Examinations, 92, 28 May 1543.
[8] *Letters and Papers*, xv, 45.
[9] Archivo de Protocolos de Sevilla, *Oficio* XV, 1545, *Libro* II, f. 58v.
[10] *State Papers, Henry VIII*, ix, p. 330.   [11] *A.P.C., 1542–47*, p. 153.

It is significant that Bonner refers to Ostriche merely as an English merchant residing in San Lucar and not as governor. The notarial records of Cadiz show that William Ostriche, described as residing in the port, was still in Andalusia at the beginning of Mary's reign.[1]

Thus, in spite of the Inquisition, Englishmen were able to reside and conduct their business in Spain right through to Mary's reign when the situation improved considerably. Philip Kever, almost certainly the Philip 'Kydwar' in the document Basing sent home,[2] was able to die in Spain both loyal and a Catholic after three reigns of varying religion at home.[3] The most remarkable case, however, is that of Hugh Tipton whose career as an English merchant trading in Spain extends over four reigns. Tipton, who was persecuted in San Sebastian in 1537 when he was factor of William Spratt of Bristol,[4] returned to England in 1570 after being consul of the English nation in Spain for a great number of those years.[5] He is mentioned frequently in the diplomatic correspondence from Spain from 1561 until his return to England, for his good offices were constantly required on behalf of some of his compatriots in trouble with the Spaniards. It was Tipton who befriended Hawkins' men in 1570,[6] and whose letter to Challoner J. A. Williamson quotes in support of the theory that Hawkins himself visited Spain in 1563.[7] It is of interest that the Emperor had approved Tipton's appointment as governor instead of Edward Lewis.[8] Tipton attempted again and again to have the company's privileges confirmed and its regulations enforced, but complained that the merchants were disunited and quarrelling among themselves.[9] Conditions were reminiscent of the late 1530's.[10]

Basing sent home a copy of the merchants' statement in August 1540 and promised to despatch the original when he received the answer of the Emperor's council. He had not been to the Spanish court about the matter because shortly after

---

[1] Archivo de Protocolos de Cádiz, *Oficio* XIX, 1553, ff. 743v, 753v.
[2] *Vide supra*, p. 119.
[3] Somerset House, P.C.C. Wills, 31 More.
[4] *Vide supra*, p. 105.
[5] *State Papers, Foreign Series, Elizabeth, 1569–71*, no. 736.
[6] ibid., no. 711.
[7] *Sir John Hawkins*, pp. 90–91.
[8] B.M., Harleian MS. 36, f. 26v. The document is undated.
[9] *State Papers, Foreign Series, Elizabeth, 1561–62*, nos. 199, etc.
[10] *Vide supra*, p. 94.

buying horses for the king he had been arrested at the instigation of a Frenchman from Bordeaux who had alleged Basing was a Lutheran. Pery and his fellow prisoners had been released on 9 August after doing open penance and forfeiting all their goods.[1] They had served the full term of imprisonment to which they had been sentenced in the previous February. Pery must have returned to England shortly after his release, for it is recorded among the business of the Privy Council that he appeared before it on 21 November 1540. He declared the wrongful imprisonment and ill-treatment he had suffered in Seville merely for defending the king's measures against the Bishop of Rome. He was ordered to put his complaint into Spanish or French and attend upon the Duke of Norfolk who was appointed to take it up with the Imperial ambassador.[2]

Further reference to Pery is made in a despatch of Marillac, the French ambassador in London. Marillac reported on 4 December that the Imperial ambassador had been called before the council about the ill-treatment of English subjects in Spain on account of their religion. Amongst others, said Marillac, one rich English merchant had been sentenced to a long term of imprisonment and had lost all his goods because he had said his sovereign was right in severing the English church from Rome and suppressing the abbeys. This is obviously Pery. The Imperial ambassador was required to inform the Emperor that if he did not order that Englishmen in Spain should be better treated the trade between the two countries would be prohibited. Marillac declared that Chapuys was much put out over this, especially as he was already out of favour, and the French ambassador more graciously treated than usual.[3] The Imperial ambassador's version of the interview is very different. According to Chapuys, Henry's councillors prayed him as affectionately as possible to beg and entreat Charles that the king's subjects should be treated with a little more favour and kindness than they had been lately by the officers of the Inquisition and others.[4]

[1] *Letters and Papers*, xv, no. 977. The original has not been found. It is doubtful whether Basing received an answer from the Emperor's council.
[2] *Proceedings and Ordinances of the Privy Council*, vol. vii, p.86.
[3] *Letters and Papers*, xvi, no. 312.
[4] *Spanish Calendar, 1538–42*, no. 143. *Vide* J. A. Froude, *English Seamen in the Sixteenth Century*, p. 18. Froude believed that 'Henry spoke up stoutly to Charles V., and the Holy Office had been made to hold its hand'.

Meanwhile arrangements were made to send another envoy, John Mason, into Spain to clear up Basing's affairs and investigate the complaints of the English merchants.[1] Mason was also given secret instructions to find out certain information about the state of Spain in the Emperor's absence [2] He was recalled, however, when he became involved in Wyatt's trial[3] and no further missions were arranged. There is no record of Pery receiving satisfaction, but according to Chapuys, Gardiner, the new ambassador, had received assurances from the Emperor which rendered a further mission about the English merchants unnecessary [4]

The nature of these assurances is not revealed, but it is significant that little evidence has been found of further complaints of religious persecution from the English in Spain for several years. The next reference to the religious problem is the arrest of two Spaniards in England for speaking against Henry's Supremacy.[5] Political events were again moving in the English king's favour. As the last French war of Henry's reign became inevitable the Emperor was again eager for his friendship, while the execution of Cromwell and the Catholic reaction in England had already paved the way for a new alliance. The new war made it essential, and the English merchants in Spain enjoyed once more a period of relative freedom from religious persecution

---

[1] *Letters and Papers*, xvi, no. 354. Basing had been imprisoned for debt and his creditor also accused him of being a Lutheran. *Vida supra*.

[2] ibid.

[3] *Spanish Calendar, 1538–42*, no. 150.

[4] ibid.

[5] *Letters and Papers*, xvi, no. 1032.

CHAPTER VI

THE 'RENEGER INCIDENT'

ALTHOUGH the renewal of Franco-Spanish hostility made Henry's position more secure, strained commercial relations continued between England and the Emperor. In February 1539, a month before he arrested Flemish and Spanish shipping in England in view of the political situation and the activities of the Spanish Inquisition against the English merchants,[1] Henry VIII had made a concession to stimulate trade. It had been proclaimed that foreign merchants trading to England should pay only the same duties as English subjects on all goods except wool.[2] Now the crisis had passed and one sign of Henry's renewed confidence was his navigation act of 1540,[3] greatly diminishing the privileges granted to foreigners the previous year. By this new act aliens were to pay the same customs duties as English subjects only if they shipped their goods in English vessels. If they exported them in foreign ships they must pay at alien rates, unless there were no English ships available at the port of lading. As Chapuys observed, Henry had made the concession when he feared war and stoppage of trade, but now the danger had passed he wished to benefit his own shipping. It is of great interest that the Imperial ambassador declared that the new act would affect the Flemings most,[4] showing that Spain was much less concerned by English navigation acts than she had been in the earlier period. Disputes of this kind were to occur much more often with the Low Countries than with Spain during the remaining years of Henry's reign, but commercial relations between England and Flanders in this period cannot be separated from the Anglo-Spanish trade.

When Chapuys complained of the new navigation act, Henry's council told him it need not injure the Emperor, who could publish a similar order in his own dominions. The ambassador advised Charles to do so and said he believed there was already

[1] *Letters and Papers*, xiv (1), no. 487.
[2] ibid., no. 373.
[3] Stat. 32 Hen. VIII, c. 14.
[4] *Letters and Papers*, xvi, no. 13.

an edict in Spain forbidding foreign vessels to lade merchandise while Spanish ships were in port.[1] This was the *pragmática* enforced by the council of Castile against the English merchants at the end of Henry VII's reign, after Ferdinand and Isabella had granted them exemption in view of the betrothal of Prince Henry and Katherine.[2] Conditions were more favourable to the English now, however, because less Spanish shipping was available to carry the trade to England. The *pragmática* was more often enforced on other routes. Some years previously, for example, a certain Denis Harris, a Levant trader, had complained that he was detained at Cadiz while a Biscayan ship, also bound for Messina, took his lading by virtue of the 'prematicha':

and apon this, there was a crye made for this gere generall by the justice, that vpon payne of a thowsande ducatt*es*, that I nor no strange shipp shulde lade nothing, this youe may see howe we be intreated in this parties.[3]

Chapuys also wrote about the Spanish *pragmática* to Mary of Hungary, who had already retaliated against Henry's navigation act by measures against the English merchants in the Low Countries. He also advised the enforcement of the Spanish edicts against the importation of 'false cloths' by the English,[4] which, he declared, would greatly assist the Flemish cloth merchants.[5] In the following month (March 1541) Charles wrote to Spain about Chapuys' suggestion.[6] There had been a number of other incidents marring Anglo-Spanish commercial relations in the last few months. In September 1540 the Emperor was informed by his council in Spain that a caravel of Seville, laden with more than 5,000 ducats' worth of gold, amber and other merchandise, had been taken some eighty leagues off Cadiz on its way home from the Barbary Coast by an English ship and a sloop.[7] The English ship was the *Barbara* of London which then proceeded on its piratical course to the Canaries, Brazil and the West Indies.[8] In reporting their losses the Spaniards asserted that the Englishmen had declared that they were at war with the

---

[1] *Letters and Papers*, xvi, no. 214.
[2] *Vide supra*, pp. 51 seq.
[3] B.M., Cotton MS. Vespasian C VII, f. 45.
[4] *Vide supra*, p. 2.
[5] *Letters and Papers*, xvi, no. 524.
[6] ibid., no. 664.
[7] ibid., no. 73; *Spanish Calendar, 1538–42*, no. 128.
[8] R. G. Marsden, 'Voyage of the Barbara to Brazil, Anno 1540,' *The Naval Miscellany* (Navy Records Society) vol. ii, pp. 3–66.

Pope, the Emperor and France, and with the latter because the French king was giving Charles thirty thousand men for use against the English. They had even told the Spaniards of their future plans.[1] In January 1541 a number of Exeter merchants complained that they had been imprisoned and their goods seized in Biscay on a charge of exporting money and other contraband goods. They had been released and after a suit lasting some three years recovered their goods, but as no damages nor expenses were allowed them they had sustained the loss of £607 10s.[2] In the same year the English merchants in Spain complained bitterly of the intolerable delays and injustices they experienced in the Spanish courts. In particular, the case of a certain John Birmingham was specified which was still not settled when the Diet of Bourbourg met in 1545.[3]

There were more fundamental differences concerning the trade with the Low Countries. The Flemings had never been satisfied with the treaty of 1506, which Charles had refused to confirm in 1520.[4] Now they demanded a new treaty, asserting that the existing one had been concluded by Philip of Castile under compulsion when he was driven by a tempest to land in England.[5] Henry expressed surprise at this demand and affirmed his own wish to stand by the existing terms.[6] An agreement was reached in June 1542 by which the latest edicts in Flanders against English shipping were revoked and the Flemings and Spaniards exempted from Henry's navigation act. This agreement spoke of a treaty of closer amity between Charles and Henry,[7] now essential to the Emperor in view of his impending war with Francis. Even so commercial difficulties continued. Later in the year the Regent refused to confirm the 1520 treaty until certain duties had been revised in the Flemings' favour.[8] In February 1543 she imposed a 1 per cent *ad valorem* duty on all goods and merchandise exported from the Low Countries. She said this was an emergency measure to meet the expenses of the war with France; it was to last a year only and should

[1] Archivo General de Indias, Patronato, *Legajo 265, Ramo 2.*
[2] *Letters and Papers*, xvi, no. 486.
[3] ibid., *Add.* i (2), no. 1510, fn.
[4] *Vide supra*, p. 59.
[5] *Letters and Papers*, xvi, no. 1095.
[6] ibid., no. 1110.
[7] ibid., xvii, no. 440.
[8] *Spanish Calendar, 1542–43*, no. 72, p. 155.

not be considered a breach of existing treaties.[1] The English refused to accept the Regent's explanation of the need for making the new impost, in spite of Chapuys' efforts to justify it. The ambassador pointed out that the war was England's as much as the Emperor's and was especially the concern of the English merchants, many of whom had no other markets for their goods but the Low Countries and Spain. He also reminded the English deputies that they had been relieved by the Emperor of the duty of 2 per cent imposed on English goods at Cadiz.[2]

This last point affords a further illustration of the link between Anglo-Spanish commercial relations and those between England and the Low Countries. Some time earlier, when Chapuys informed the Queen of Hungary that he believed the English Parliament was going to pass measures injurious to the Low Countries, the Regent had declared that if this happened the Emperor would doubtless retaliate against the English in Spain.[3] This shows how England was in a stronger position in relation to the Low Countries and weaker in Spain, for Anglo-Spanish trade had become increasingly an English concern in this period. Chapuys stated in 1540 that there were only six of the Emperor's subjects residing as merchants in London, and although that was during a precarious period there is no doubt the number of Spanish merchants in England was very much less than that of the English merchants in Spain. The ambassador had reminded Charles how much greater damage he could do by confiscating the property of Englishmen in his dominions than Henry VIII could do by similar action against the Emperor's subjects in England.[4]

In February 1543 a new treaty was concluded between Charles and Henry, including an agreement that no letters of reprisal, marque or counter-marque should be issued by either against the subjects of the other.[5] Events at sea were soon to demonstrate how necessary was the reiteration of such a clause. Wars undertaken by England and Spain in alliance against France had always ended unsatisfactorily, while the attempt of either to remain neutral during these conflicts had occasioned par-

---

[1] *Spanish Calendar, 1542–43*, no. 106, p. 254.
[2] ibid., nos. 114, 147.
[3] ibid., Appendix, 273.
[4] ibid., *1538–42*, no. 144, p. 301.
[5] *Letters and Papers*, xviii (1), no. 144.

ticular difficulties on the high seas. Again and again the cry was raised that the enemy's goods were being 'coloured'[1] and that the neutral's ships were being despoiled on the pretext that they contained goods belonging to the enemy or destined for his ports. The treaties between England and Spain proclaimed that, in the event of their clauses being violated, letters of marque should not be issued until the government of the offending party had been petitioned to make restitution. Prompt justice was promised in such cases, but both parties alleged that this was not in practice carried out. On the English side the merchants, ever since the Reformation, had been loud in their complaints that they could not get a fair hearing in the Spanish courts, from which they were often excluded as heretics.[2] The Spaniards, for their part, complained bitterly of the long delays of the Admiralty Court.[3] Maritime relations between the two allies on the eve of this last French war were far from propitious in spite of the political alliance. The trade to Spain had suffered in recent years from the effects of the Inquisition,[4] and a number of English merchants and mariners who had received injuries at the hands of the Spanish inquisitors were only too ready to seize an opportunity to square their personal accounts with the Spaniards.

It was not long before the Imperial ambassador was complaining to the Privy Council of depredations at sea upon his master's subjects. In March 1543 a certain John Bowle was ordered to compensate within twenty days a Spaniard whose pinnace he had despoiled in the port of Lulworth.[5] Private merchants were not the only offenders. In the following month the Privy Council wrote to Richard Broke, captain of the king's fleet in the Narrow Seas, reprimanding him for not discriminating sufficiently between friends and foes.[6] In the same month the customers of Southampton were ordered to give an explanation for their arrest of a Spanish ship.[7] In May the Privy Council was enquiring into the embezzlement of gold from a Spanish vessel which had been taken by Frenchmen and driven by bad weather into Milford Haven.[8] Already Henry VIII was letting

---

[1] i.e. they were registered in the name of a friendly merchant.
[2] *Vide supra*, pp. 104, 108.   [3] *Vide infra*, p. 180.
[4] *Vide supra*, chap. v, *passim*.
[5] *A.P.C.*, *1542–47*, pp. 99–100.   [6] ibid., p. 123.   [7] ibid., p. 118.
[8] ibid., pp. 125, 128, etc.

loose his 'swarm of wasps'[1] against his enemies in the Channel by issuing letters of marque to certain captains with ships and arms at their disposal who had received real or imaginary injuries at the hands of the French. These men were given licence to capture as many French ships as they could, but had to undertake to attempt nothing against the Emperor's subjects.[2] It was inevitable, however, that some of them should find an excuse for attacking neutral ships, and one of the first to do so was Robert Borough, a Devonshire captain. Borough set out in May 1543 with two ships of Rye, the *Kate* and the *Nicholas*, both armed to make war on French shipping.

He and his company met with a hoy of Flushing laden with canvas coming out of St. Malo and commanded its crew in King Henry's name to strike sails and declare whether or not there were any French goods on board. This they refused to do, and Borough and his company:

in tyme of good peace betwene the kyng*es* highnes and themperors maiestie veryly supposyng the sayd hoy to be Frenche men*es* good*es* enymeys bothe to themperors subiect*es* and allso to this realme of Englond shott dyve*rs* pec*es* of ordin*n*anc*es* to the sayd hoye and so by force and stronge hand*es* toke the same as enymeys good*es*.[3]

Then, according to Borough, he took the hoy into Southampton, and, finding the master had neither safe-conduct nor any 'credable testimonye' to prove her lading belonged to subjects of the Emperor, detained her there while the Privy Council was informed. In the meantime he began to dispose of some of her cargo. The matter was referred by the council to the Admiralty Court and Borough was ordered to make restitution.[4]

The English authorities were not always so prompt to curb the activities of the seamen, however, and early in the year 1544 the Regent of the Low Countries complained that they were not honouring safe-conducts granted by the Emperor and herself.[5] An outstanding instance of this was the retention of a large cargo of herrings on its way from France to the Low Countries, taken at sea and brought into an English port. Members of the

---

[1] J. A. Williamson, *Sir John Hawkins*, p. 26.
[2] *Letters and Papers*, xviii (1), nos. 346, 474, etc.
[3] P.R.O., H.C.A., Examinations, 92, 18 July 1543.
[4] ibid.
[5] *Letters and Papers*, xix (1), no. 70.

Privy Council told the Imperial ambassador that, since their merchants had been unable to visit Iceland the previous year, they had been literally obliged to keep the herrings, but that the Emperor's safe-conducts would be respected in future.[1] The Flemish merchants protested, however, that they had been offered much less than the value of the herrings by way of compensation,[2] and the troubles at sea persisted, causing increasing friction between the English and the Emperor's subjects.

The Peace of Crépy in September 1544, which seemed to the English to be an act of desertion by their ally, was the signal for the virtual abandonment of such discrimination as they had hitherto exercised between friend and foe on the high seas. The Spaniards were particularly vulnerable in the Channel and their efforts to resume peaceful commerce with France met with increasing interference from their former allies. In the December following the peace Henry VIII issued a proclamation authorizing all his subjects to equip vessels to put to sea against the Scots and French. All officers of port towns were ordered to assist in making the proclamation effective and were forbidden to take mariners, munitions or tackle from ships equipped for this task.[3] Henry's action, although justified by the precarious situation caused by the Emperor's defection, further encouraged depredations at sea and aggravated relations between England and the Emperor's dominions. Complaints by the Spaniards and Flemings increased in the New Year and they protested bitterly that it would be better to have open war with England than to be treated worse than enemies under the colour of friendship.[4] Finally, on 5 January 1545, the Emperor was forced in retaliation to arrest the persons, property and ships of English subjects in the Low Countries.[5] The English replied by seizing more ships, but claimed that the goods they confiscated belonged to Frenchmen and were consequently good captures by law. As for the Imperial embargo, they contended that it constituted a breach of the treaties which provided that, in the case of a capture being made by one party, the other should not adopt reprisals but submit the dispute to arbitration.[6]

[1] *Spanish Calendar, 1544*, no. 27.   [2] ibid., no. 48.
[3] *Letters and Papers*, xix (2), no. 766.   [4] ibid., xx (1), no. 8.
[5] *Spanish Calendar, 1545–46*, no. 4.
[6] ibid., no. 21, p. 48.

The Peace of Crépy, besides increasing English animosity towards the Emperor's subjects, gave the English privateers a further excuse for molesting Spanish and Flemish shipping. Since the Spaniards and Flemings were now neutrals in the war between England and France, they began to carry more French goods in their ships. The English seamen considered this gave them much greater licence to interfere with shipping in the Channel and they seized ships carrying the smallest quantity of enemy property. It was inevitable that Spaniards and Flemings would 'colour' French merchandise and that Englishmen would seize everything of value on the pretext that it belonged to the French. Very soon the less scrupulous English privateers even disposed of their prizes in remote havens before inquiries could be instituted.

An interesting example of both the attitude and the methods of these privateers is seen in one of the exploits of a West Country syndicate in which Thomas Wyndham and the Lord Privy Seal were the chief figures. The interest of Russell also illustrates the practice of high ranking officials having shares in the privateering enterprises of the more daring sea-captains. Wyndham, a well known Tudor seaman, combined a naval career with legitimate trading, piracy and, later, exploration. He served against the Scots in 1544 and the French in 1545–46. In the autumn of 1547 he was given the office of 'Master of the Ordnance in the King's Ships' and was appointed vice-admiral of a fleet sent by Somerset to the east coast of Scotland to enforce his Scottish policy.[1] The character of the man is well shown by a letter he wrote in December 1547 in which he said he would leave 'nether towne nor vylage nor fyser bott vn bornyd frome Fyfenase to Comysynch' and trusted 'er ytt be longe to supprese a abby or to'.[2] After the peace of 1550 Wyndham turned to trade and exploration and was a leading spirit of the Barbary trade. It was, in fact, while expanding his range to Guinea and Benin that he eventually met his death in 1553.[3]

At the beginning of the year 1545 Wyndham was captain of the *Mawdelyn Russell*, a ship owned by the Lord Privy Seal, equipped as a privateer. In consort with him was 'another lytell

---

[1] *Dictionary of National Biography*, vol. xxi, pp. 1164–5.
[2] P.R.O., State Papers, Scotland, Edward VI, vol. 2, f. 143.
[3] J. A. Williamson, *Sir John Hawkins*, pp. 36–38, 40–42; Blake, *Europeans in West Africa, 1450–1560*, vol 2, pp. 314 *seq.*

barke of Plymmouth namyd the Mary Figge'.[1] The master of the *Mary Figge* was a certain John Landy who is another interesting figure. Landy had been master of the *Paul* of Plymouth, William Hawkins' ship, on a voyage to Brazil in 1540. J. A. Williamson suspected that he was a Frenchman brought in for that occasion and was fairly certain that he was not a Plymouth captain because he had found no references to Landy commanding Plymouth ships on other occasions.[2] J. W. Blake quotes a reference to Landy as captain of the *Mary Winter*, Thomas Winter's ship, in 1549. He is described as a mariner of Plymouth.[3] The probability is that he was a renegade Frenchman who had settled in the Devonshire port.

When Wyndham and Landy returned from their expedition they brought back with them a ship of San Sebastian, the *Santa María de Guadalupe*, laden with Gascon wine and Toulouse woad. They must already have decided upon a cunning plan to justify their capture, because before coming to land they sent word to Thomas Clowter, the mayor of Plymouth, who was obviously not a disinterested party, requesting him to examine the master and other members of her crew. It is recorded in a deposition of the mayor made on 2 March 1545, and later produced as evidence in the High Court of Admiralty, that he and a number of fellow officials went to the Guildhall to hear 'their examynacion and their confessions'.[4] According to the mayor's statement, Juan de Ramizo, the master of the Spanish ship, Domingo de la Chiço, the pilot, and Juan de Larrea, the boatswain, were 'examyned asondre one from a nother'. They all said that the goods in the *Santa María* belonged to a certain Bernardo de la Furtada, a citizen of Bordeaux, who had himself been present when the wine and woad were brought on board at the French port. They had seen him enter the goods in the customs house at Bordeaux in his own name and pay all the necessary charges. Then there came on board one Martín de Miranda, a Spaniard of San Sebastian, in the capacity of factor and attorney of Bernardo 'and not otherwise to their knowlege but a factor', who sailed with the ship. When Miranda was examined by the mayor and his brethren he declared that the goods were his own and that Furtada merely brought them on

---

[1] P.R.O., H.C.A., Libels etc., 14, no. 34.
[2] *Sir John Hawkins*, p. 15.
[3] Op. cit., vol. 2, p. 301.
[4] P.R.O., H.C.A., Libels etc., 14, no. 34.

board. His claims were rejected, however, and the Spanish master and crew departed with their ship after the freight charges had been paid them. That was the mayor of Plymouth's story. A very different version of the incident was to be told a little later.[1]

At about the same time one of the ships of William Hawkins, who had been granted letters of marque against the French in the previous September,[2] seized a ship belonging to Juan Quintanadueñas, a wealthy Spaniard domiciled at Rouen. According to J. A. Williamson, Wyndham was his associate in this capture,[3] but the appearance of the two captains before the Imperial ambassador at the same time[4] seems, however, to be the only link between them, unless Hawkins was at this time part owner of the *Mary Figge* as he apparently was at a later date.[5] Hardly had the Spaniards time to register protests against these depredations of Wyndham and Hawkins when the news reached England of an exploit which dwarfed them both with its boldness and its far reaching consequences for Anglo-Spanish relations—the capture of Spanish treasure on its way from the Indies by Robert Reneger of Southampton.

The career of Robert Reneger furnishes a striking illustration of the transition from the prosperous trading between the two allies in the earlier period to the widespread English attacks on Spanish shipping during Henry VIII's last French war. As a rising young merchant and burgess of Southampton Reneger's chief trading interest was the commerce with Spain, for which country he once declared he felt 'particular affection'. This is evident from the particulars of customs and the local port books of the Hampshire port. A more detailed picture of his trading activities is afforded by the excellent series of Southampton Brokage Books available for this period. These show him to have been one of the biggest distributors of merchandise from the town. Wine and woad form the bulk of the loads which he sent out of Southampton, while iron, oil, soap, raisins and figs appear in smaller quantities. Most of his goods went to Newbury, Winchester and Basingstoke, and he brought into the town mostly cloth and leather, and occasionally grain.[6]

---

[1] *Vide infra*, p. 181.   [2] *Letters and Papers*, xix (2), no. 340.
[3] *Sir John Hawkins*, p. 28.   [4] *Vide infra*, p. 182.
[5] *A.P.C.*, *1542-47*, p. 544.
[6] Southampton Municipal MSS., Brokage Books, 1537–43.

Corn was often in great demand in Spain during this period, and Reneger shipped it there on occasion. He probably used the licence he was granted in April 1543 for that purpose.[1] Apparently, also, he exported wheat to Spain without licence at a time when it was forbidden to do so, if there was substance in a charge brought against him in the Star Chamber.[2] The licence granted to Reneger permitted him to export 100 quarters of wheat and 100 quarters of barley. According to his accuser, he exported 150 quarters of wheat from Chichester, 150 quarters from Arundel and 700 quarters from Southampton in three vessels of his own and one other, without paying customs duties or being in possession of the requisite licence. All this wheat went to San Sebastian. It is not surprising to learn that a pinnace presumably at some time connected with Reneger was named the *Trego-Ronnyger*![3]

According to Hakluyt,[4] Reneger and another prominent Southampton merchant, Thomas Borey, carried on a regular trade to Brazil round about the year 1540. It is unfortunate that the records of Southampton are incomplete, and no other evidence of Reneger's participation in the Brazil voyages has been found to corroborate Hakluyt's statement. The information given to the latter by Anthony Garrard some sixty years after the event may well have no surer foundation than the likelihood that a captain of Reneger's reputation had taken part in all the most ambitious voyages of the earlier period. He was already a prosperous merchant who had probably acquired ships of his own by then, but it is unlikely that the speculative Brazil voyages would have appealed to a man like Reneger. If he did participate in them, he was soon to forsake them for enterprises promising quicker returns.

By the time Reneger had become well established in Southampton the trade to Spain, in which he was particularly interested, was no longer as profitable as it had been in the earlier period. The commerce which had yielded large fortunes to men like the Thornes of Bristol and Thomas Howell, the London draper, was now fraught with grave difficulties. Merchants such as these had

---

[1] *Letters and Papers*, xviii (1), no. 476.
[2] P.R.O., Star Chamber Proceedings, Hen. VIII., Bundle xxvii, no. 118.
[3] Sir Julian Corbett, *Drake and the Tudor Navy*, vol. 1, p. 35, n. 1, mentions a pinnace 'with the curious name, "Trego-Ronnyger", apparently Spanish'. If his surmise is correct the pinnace's name in English is *Reneger Wheat*!
[4] *The Principal Navigations*, xi, p. 25.

lived on the friendliest terms with the Spaniards, employing factors in all parts of the Spanish dominions and conducting business in close co-operation with Spanish subjects. The Reformation and the political situation it helped to aggravate were swiftly altering this satisfactory state of affairs and bringing about a deterioration of Anglo-Spanish relations from which they never fully recovered. The religious aspect of the quarrel with Spain, which was one of its great determining forces in Elizabeth's reign, was already affecting the fortunes of Englishmen trading to Spain.

Had he been born a generation earlier Robert Reneger might have made his fortune in the Anglo-Spanish trade, sending his younger brother out to Seville as his factor or even residing there himself and taking part in the legitimate trade to the New World. By the time he had established himself and was rich enough to buy ships, however, the situation in Spain had become precarious for prosperous trading; and hardly had it begun to improve when it was dealt another severe blow. The last French war of Henry VIII's reign encouraged another form of maritime enterprise at once more lucrative to its successful exponent and more productive of daring seamanship than the peaceful commerce which it crippled. The prosperous merchant under such conditions became the 'notorious pirate' with his daring capture of the Spanish treasure.

Robert Reneger was among the first English captains to be granted letters of marque against the French early in the year 1543, some time before the formal declaration of war between England and France.[1] These letters of marque enabled Reneger to continue, under more favourable conditions, a bitter quarrel which he had been waging against the French for a number of years. On several occasions Reneger's goods had been seized between England and Spain by Frenchmen, apparently in retaliation for acts committed against them by Reneger and other Southampton merchants. Two petitions among the records of the High Court of Admiralty throw interesting light on this quarrel. One of these was submitted by Reneger alone and the other in association with Henry Huttoft, one of the most important burgesses of Southampton.[2] The petitions are undated,

---

[1] *Letters and Papers*, xviii (1), no. 346; *A.P.C., 1542–47*, p. 109.
[2] *Vide supra*, p. 66.

but as they are addressed to Sir William Fitzwilliam, Earl of Southampton, they must have been submitted between the years 1536 and 1540 when he held the office of Lord High Admiral.[1]

Reneger's individual complaint was of the loss of cloth worth £135[2] taken out of the *Trinity* of Poole. According to his petition:

the seid shipe *with* goodes and marchaundise in here beinge laden repairinge toward*es* Byscae / mette *with* here aboutes viij leages frome Alleredo ij shippes of Frenchemen supposinge the oon of them to be of Depe and the other of Fecum and bourded the seid shipe of Poole demaundinge the sight of all the bylles of ladinge of the goodes *within* the seid shippe among*es* the whiche they *per*ceyvinge the billes of the seid ij pakkes beinge the goodes of yo*r* seid poore orato*r* ymedyately therevppon tooke the same yo*r* orato*rs* goodes oute of the same shipe / spoyllinge or hurtinge the resydue litle or nothinge sayinge that yf they knew the seid shipe or any of the other goodes therein to belonge to any of the towne of Southampton as they *per*ceyvid it the contrary they wolde have handelid them right crually so that yo*r* seid pore orato*r* there lost his goodes because he was of Southampton.[3]

The second petition submitted jointly with Henry Huttoft is even more interesting. Huttoft and Reneger declared that:

Where as a shippe of the same towne called the Fraunces belonginge to yo*r* seid orato*r* Henry Huttofte made a voyage into the *par*ties of Spayne and there was laden for the howne*r* and yo*r* seid orato*r* Robert Renneger by their facto*rs* Richard Pocoke and William Edge *with* se*c*kes bastardes oylles sope kewte almondes and fruytt*es* / In their weye homewarde was mett by a Frencheman of warre and a carvell of Portingale late before that by the seid Frenchem*en* taken / of whome they were most crually and extremely handelyd and dealyd *with* / beinge putt in moste grete feare of their lyves spoyllinge and robbinge them of all thing*es* that they myght cary *with* theym . . . And so crually they intreated the facto*rs* and s*er*vauntt*es* of yo*r* seid orato*rs* that after they hade to*r*mentyd them *with* pyncheinge their fleshe and drawinge them by the legg*es* aboute the shipe in threatninge theym to be caste over the bourde and provinge the seid shipe oone nyght saylinge in wille to haue caried here *with* theym

[1] R. G. Marsden, *Select Pleas in the Court of Admiralty*, vol. 1, Introduction, p. lix.
[2] The amount is given as £125 in the petition but as £135 in a statement apparently submitted with the two petitions.
[3] P.R.O., H.C.A., Oyer and Terminer, Examinations, 33.

yf they hade lyked here in suche wise that they lefte here neither victualle*s* except oon*e* bagge of almonde*s* nor other cordage to rule the seid shippe w*ith* all then oon olde jonnke all worne / spekeinge moost dispytefull word*es* of wrong*es* that the kinge*s* highenes his shippes hade don vnto them by takeinge a shippe at the landes ende of Englande / and of an other taken in Hampton Water / sayinge that they wolde not cease to make that to be repentyd lyke most errony-ouse lutheryans as yo*r* seid orator*s* *and* contrey men be / w*ith* other most detestable word*es* *and* demeanor*s* towarde*s* yo*r* seid orator*s* in somuche that they tooke the flagg*es* oute of yo*r* orator*s* shipe and in moste grettist dispyte did tere them vnder their fete. . . . And the seid Frenchemen seid by yo*r* seid orator* Huttofte / that yfe they coulde know the ship his as she was namyd uppon yo*r* orator* Robert Renneger they wolde have brent here.[1]

Nothing is heard of Reneger's fortunes as a privateer for nearly two years. Then on 1 March 1545 the ambitious Southampton merchant suddenly became a figure of national importance as the first Englishman to despoil a Spanish treasure ship coming from the Indies. The *San Salvador*, Francisco Gallego *El Mozo*[2] master, was on her way to Spain from San Domingo in Hispaniola. Like most of the ships from the Indies, she carried a number of passengers, official documents and a cargo consisting chiefly of gold, silver and pearls with some sugar and hides. The *San Salvador* was making the journey alone and there may have been some particular reason why she was not travel-ling in convoy, although nothing about her voyage was sub-sequently proved to have been irregular. Most of her cargo was consigned to merchants of Seville, amongst whom it is of great interest to find Thomas Harrison an Englishman resident in that city.[3] According to a statement prepared by the Spanish authori-ties,[4] Harrison's contribution to Reneger's plunder was 38 *pesos* of gold. Gallego himself had some sugar and hides on board[5] and perhaps a little gold which had not been entered on the ship's register.[6]

---

[1] P.R.O., H.C.A., Oyer and Terminer, Examinations, 33.
[2] i.e. the Younger.   [3] *Vide supra*, p. 97.
[4] Archivo General de Indias, Patronato, *Legajo* 265, *Ramo* 3.
[5] ibid., Contratación, *Legajo* 2439, *Ramo* 6, *no.* 2. Gallego's father was later compensated for his son's loss. Archivo de Protocolos de Sevilla, *Oficio* XV, 1551, *Libro* I, f. 279v.
[6] There was a suspicion of an agreement between Reneger and Gallego concerning some gold but it was not proved that the *San Salvador* was carrying much that had not been registered. *Vide infra*, p. 145.

The official Spanish version of the incident[1] stated that the *San Salvador* was attacked off Cape St. Vincent by four English ships and a pinnace, all armed and under the command of 'Roberto Reneguel' and his brother John. The Englishmen robbed the Spanish vessel of all the gold, silver and pearls she was carrying as well as 124 chests of sugar and 140 hides. The total value of the goods seized was 7,243,075 *maravedis*.[2] Before committing this outrage the Renegers had been at Cadiz and from there sailed to San Lucar de Barrameda where they seized a French ship and made off with it. In a report made by officials of the *Casa de la Contratación* it was stated that Gallego, his crew and the passengers had all declared that the robbery took place ten leagues from Cape St. Vincent and that three ships had taken part in it. Two of the ships were English and the third was a French prize taken by the Englishmen.[3] There is no other evidence of the number of ships Reneger had with him.

When Reneger returned to England he reported the incident to the Privy Council in person.[4] It was important for him to state his case as soon as possible since, apart from anything else, he had broken the conditions of his recognisance as a privateer.[5] In his statement to the council Reneger said that he had taken a French ship off the coast of Spain and, looking through its papers, found that some of the goods in it belonged to Spaniards. Partly owing to fear of the King's displeasure if he retained them and partly 'for the particular affection himselff hadde vnto the nation where he hath long vsed to trade' he lay off a Spanish port and sent word that he would meet the claims of those Spaniards whose goods might be in his possession. In response to this offer many came and he satisfied all their claims, until one, coming as Reneger affirmed, without 'all right or coullor of right' alleged that he was the owner of certain feathers which the Englishman declared were quite clearly French property. When Reneger refused to hand over the feathers the Spaniard used his influence to cause another of the Englishman's ships, which was lading nearby, to be arrested and

---

[1] P.R.O., State Papers, Henry VIII, vol. 199, ff. 146 *seq.*

[2] In a contemporary English translation of the Spanish document, ibid., ff 151 *seq.*, this sum is given as 29,315 ducats. As a *maravedⁱ* was worth 1/375 of a ducat, however, the sum involved was almost exactly 19,315 ducats.

[3] Archivo General de Indias, Contratación, *Legajo* 2439, *Ramo* 6, *no.* 2.

[4] P.R.O., State Papers, Henry VIII, vol. 200, ff. 95–96.

[5] *Vide supra*, p. 138.

Robert himself was ordered to go ashore. The latter said that he was afraid to comply with this order because he had heard of the general arrest of the English merchants in the Low Countries[1] and feared that a similar arrest was imminent in Spain. So he left his other ship and sailed away.

A short while afterwards he met with a Spanish ship and boarded her. He asked the master and crew what they were carrying and they answered upon oath that their cargo consisted of sugar and similar merchandise. On searching the ship, however, Reneger discovered a quantity of gold, silver and pearls. Thereupon he told the Spaniards of the unjust arrest of his ship in Spain and declared that for his own indemnity and until he should obtain restitution he would have to retain from their ship an amount equivalent to his losses. In the meantime he would give them a receipt for what he took, for it was his intention to return their property when he recovered his own. When he began to make an inventory of the gold, however, the Spaniards begged him 'in the reverence of Godde' not to mention it, for if he did so he would ruin them all, since it had not been declared to the Emperor's officers. And so he sailed away.

Reneger's version of what had taken place receives confirmation from the Spanish side on one important point—his statement that he promised his victims eventual restitution of their property. It is recorded that on 26 March 1545 Luis Fernández and twenty-six other merchants of Seville gave powers of attorney to Fernando de la Fuente and Juan Núñez to recover the gold and other goods taken out of the *San Salvador*. These powers stated that the English captain had agreed to restore what he had taken and had written for legal representatives to be sent to England to require it by law.[2] The willingness, even anxiety, to make the matter the subject of a lawsuit which Reneger displayed throughout the negotiations must not, however, be taken as the expression of a genuine desire for a just settlement. The Southampton captain had other reasons for constantly appealing to the law.

Reneger's story is altogether too plausible, with its air of injured innocence and scrupulous respect for the law. His capture of a French prize 'off the coast of Spain' undoubtedly in-

[1] *Vide supra*, p. 133.
[2] P.R.O., State Papers, Henry VIII, vol. 199, f. 147v.

volved the violation of one of the Emperor's harbours. It is ironical that this port was San Lucar de Barrameda, where his fellow countrymen had long been particularly favoured. In another English account of the incident it was alleged that Reneger took the French vessel coming from the Levant and repaired to the nearest Spanish port to restore the goods of Spaniards which he found in her.[1] This would probably be either Cadiz or San Lucar. The Spanish account stated that he had been to both. Reneger's presence in those waters with a number of armed ships is itself significant. His must have been a considerably more expensive expedition to fit out than he would have required for enterprises like those in the Channel, and he was hunting bigger game than ships on their way from France or Spain to the Low Countries. Perhaps Reneger was lying in wait for Frenchmen coming out of the Mediterranean. Cadiz was the chief port of call in Andalusia for the Levant traders of all nationalities and apparently he paid it a visit and found nothing worth taking there. Proceeding to San Lucar he found a French ship and seized her. Reneger subsequently claimed that he lost this French prize, but this seems unlikely because there is evidence that he had it with him at the time of the spoliation of the *San Salvador*.[2] Moreover a French prize, probably taken by Reneger, was serving with the King's fleet shortly after his return to England.[3]

It appears that Reneger did lose a ship during the episode in San Lucar or soon afterwards, because the Spaniards admitted that they arrested one of his vessels.[4] He may, of course, have taken more than one French ship. It is improbable that he put into a northern Spanish port and lost his prize there because although he may have been forced to put into port it is doubtful whether news of his exploit at San Lucar would have preceded him there.[5] It is much more likely that the whole incident took place in the Andalusian port. Perhaps Reneger sought to mitigate his offence in seizing a neutral in a friendly harbour by offering to give up Spanish goods in her, or even attempted to

---

[1] *Letters and Papers*, xx (1), no. 1086, p. 534.   [2] *Vide supra*, p. 141.
[3] *Vide infra*, p. 151. The possibility must not be overlooked that the *Marlyne* may have been one of the earlier fruits of Reneger's privateering activities, but the fact that she does not appear in any of the lists of serving ships prior to his return home is significant.
[4] *Letters and Papers*, xx (1), no. 1132, p. 558.
[5] M. A. S. Hume, *Españoles é Ingleses en el Siglo XVI*, p 99.

bribe the local officials. In either case the latter refused to entertain his proposals, arrested one of his ships and ordered him to come ashore and answer for his action. Reneger may even have lost his ship quite simply in a *mêlée* in the harbour. It cannot be believed that he went to another Spanish port and made the generous offer as he alleged.

There is always the possibility, by no means a remote one, that Reneger intended from the start to plunder a Spanish treasure ship. The fact that he possessed the necessary daring to rob one under any circumstances, and other evidence we have of the boldness of his character, support such a possibility. It may even be that he deliberately became involved in trouble with the Spanish authorities in order to have an excuse for making such a reprisal. That would be typical of Reneger. Perhaps he anticipated war between England and Spain, as he subsequently told the Imperial ambassador,[1] and was determined to strike an early blow. At all events, despite the fact that he had undertaken not to molest the Emperor's subjects, Reneger lay in wait for a Spanish treasure ship off Cape St. Vincent, a favourite haunt of French corsairs with the same object in view. There can be no doubt of the premeditation of his action.

The most important point in Reneger's statement, however, is his allegation that the Spaniards on board the *San Salvador* had begged him not to mention the gold in his inventory because it had not been declared to the Emperor's officers. Other references to this point in the diplomatic correspondence suggest that there was truth in the English captain's allegation. Martin Hume, the editor of this correspondence, believed that the gold taken by Reneger had been laden secretly in San Domingo and was unregistered, and for that reason the Imperial ambassador claimed it on behalf of the Emperor.[2] There is ample evidence in the Spanish archives, however, to prove this was not the case. The register of its cargo, which every ship proceeding to and from the Indies was required to carry, arrived safely with the *San Salvador* at Seville and is now in the *Archivo General de Indias*.[3] This contains the amount of gold actually registered

---

[1] *Spanish Calendar, 1545–46*, no. 62, p. 118.
[2] *Españoles é Ingleses en el Siglo XVI*, pp. 99–100.
[3] Contratación, *Legajo 2439, Ramo 6, no. 2.*

at San Domingo prior to sailing and comparison with the amount subsequently claimed by the merchants from Reneger[1] shows them to be almost identical. If some of the gold taken by Reneger was unregistered, as he alleged, he must have taken more than the amount claimed by the Spaniards; in fact he insisted that he took much less. The only possible conclusion in either case is that Reneger was lying.[2]

Although there is no proof that the merchants of the *San Salvador* had acted in any way contrary to the regulations of the *Casa de la Contratación*, the Emperor was determined to keep the gold for himself if he could lay his hands upon it. He informed his minister, Francisco de los Cobos, that he had instructed his ambassador in England that should restitution be made of the ship and its contents he was to confiscate them as Imperial property. In the meantime Cobos was to inform the Council of the Indies, order an inquiry and, if necessary, proceed against the culprits.[3] An inspection of the ship had already taken place some months before Charles gave these orders to his minister, however, and the fact that the Emperor thought the ship itself was in Reneger's hands illustrates his ignorance of the details of the case. There is no record of any of the parties concerned being punished and Francisco Gallego continued to sail with the *San Salvador* to the Indies.[4] The merchants eventually received some compensation, which, although only a part of what they had lost, probably represented the total amount handed back by Reneger.[5]

It is very likely Gallego did warn Reneger that the gold was Imperial property to deter him from taking it, but beyond that the Englishman's story cannot be believed. Yet Charles told Cobos that it was in view of Reneger's statement that he had instructed Van der Delft[6] to take possession of the goods as Imperial property if he could obtain restitution of them.[7] The

---

[1] Archivo General de Indias, Patronato, *Legajo* 265, *Ramo* 3.

[2] It is possible that there was a quantity of unregistered gold on the *San Salvador* taken by Reneger and that his booty was more than the amount claimed by the merchants. It was never proved, however, and if it was so it makes the Englishman a bigger rogue than ever, for he claimed at the same time that the amount he had taken was less than what we know was duly registered.

[3] *Spanish Calendar, 1545–46*, no. 111.

[4] Archivo General de Indias, Contratación, *Legajo* 1079, *no. 7, Ramo* 1. This is the register of the *San Salvador* for her next voyage to San Domingo.

[5] *Vide infra*, p. 194.   [6] Charles' ambassador in England.

[7] *Spanish Calendar, 1545–46*, no. 111.

mismanagement of the whole affair by the Spanish authorities is plain throughout the negotiations and this contributed greatly to Reneger's success. The question of the legal ownership of the treasure seriously weakened the Spanish case and it can hardly be doubted that Reneger deliberately fostered suspicion of Gallego and the merchants in the minds of the Imperialists. At a later date John Hawkins saw the value of sowing discord between the Spaniards and their masters.[1] He was not the first to do so.

When Reneger made his report to the Privy Council he was immediately ordered to return without delay to the place where he had left the treasure 'and so to assemble the peces as no iote thereof mynght be fownde to be missed to thintent that iustice might take place as vpon proofe sholde afterwarde appere'. A minute corrected by Paget dated 28 April stated that Reneger had departed from the council 'for thexecution of that His Graces plesure', which suggests Henry knew all about it. Despatched to Wotton and Carne in the Low Countries to acquaint them with all these details, it closed with the hope that similar promptness would be shown on the Spanish side in the matter of restoring Reneger's ship.[2]

We do not know where Reneger stored the bullion or even in what English port he unloaded it, but its ultimate destination was the Tower. Thirty-five years later, when Francis Drake's arrival in England with his treasure caused a similar problem for English and Spaniards alike, the precedent created by Robert Reneger was not forgotten by either party, and the Spanish ambassador of the later period reminded Philip II, who was himself, of course, a prominent figure in the Reneger episode, of the earlier incident. Referring to Drake's exploit, he said the English council had ordered a letter to be written that all the money was to be registered and handed over to the Queen's possession in the Tower of London '*en la forma que se hauia hecho quando Renegat pirata ingles robo vna nao en la carrera de las Indias en tiempo del Emperador*'.[3] Warrants issued by the Privy Council in December 1547 to the Master of the Mint and

---

[1] J. A. Williamson, *Sir John Hawkins*, pp. 175, etc.
[2] P.R.O., State Papers, Henry VIII, vol. 200, ff. 96–96v.
[3] B.M. Add. MS. 28,420, f. 30. i.e. 'just as was done when Reneger, the English pirate, robbed a ship on its way from the Indies in the time of the Emperor.'

the Clerk of the Wardrobe, whose departments were housed in the Tower, to hand over to Reneger the ingots of gold and silver and the pearls which he had delivered to them 'to the Kinges Majestes use',[1] substantiate the assertion made by the Spanish ambassador thirty-five years after the incident.

The presence of interested parties in high places in Reneger's exploit may be inferred, for the Southampton man swaggered about the Court and, according to the Imperial ambassador, was treated like a hero there,[2] whereas William Hawkins received a term of imprisonment when he seized other Spanish goods at about the same time.[3] It is unfortunate that more is not known of the circumstances under which Reneger set out on his greatest privateering expedition. It is possible that he was assisted in fitting out his ships by these same interested parties and that they accepted part of the Spanish treasure as their share of the profit. If so it must have far exceeded their hopes and they would have had good reason for protecting Reneger's interests.

Nevertheless, there must undoubtedly have been great consternation among some members of the Privy Council when Reneger arrived home with gold pillaged from a Spanish treasure ship. There must have been even more among the officials of the *Casa de la Contratación* at Seville when Gallego told his sorry tale. French corsairs had long been active against the ships from the Indies[4] but the French, after all, had always been the Emperor's enemies. On the other hand, in spite of the depredations in the Channel and the bitter recriminations which followed them, England was still Spain's old ally. Even the clerk who completed the *San Salvador's* register started to record that it was the French who had committed the outrage before he realised his mistake.[5] The fact that the treasure ships were no longer safe from English free-booters was far more important than the value of the gold itself. It is not surprising that the incident was the subject of so much diplomatic correspondence and had such important consequences for Anglo-Spanish relations.

The merchants despoiled by Reneger lost no time in submit-

[1] *A.P.C., 1547–50*, p. 155.
[2] *Spanish Calendar, 1545–46*, no. 77.
[3] *Vide infra*, pp. 182–183.
[4] Haring, *Trade and Navigation between Spain and the Indies*, pp. 68, *seq.*
[5] Archivo General de Indias, Contratación, *Legajo* 2439, *Ramo* 6, *no.* 2.

ting a petition to the officials of the *Casa de la Contratación*, demanding the immediate sequestration of the goods of Englishmen in the surrounding ports. They urged that there should be no delay for further inquiries as the facts were known to everyone and any procrastination would enable the English to carry away their goods. They reminded the officials of the many outrages perpetrated lately by Englishmen and asked for prompt justice on this occasion. The date of their petition[1] is not known, but it must have been earlier than 27 March because on that date the officials of the *Casa* issued an order for the embargo.[2]

At this time Charles V was in the Low Countries preparing the way for his onslaught on Germany, and Prince Philip was Regent of Spain in his absence. This fact is of importance, both because of the action taken by the Regent on learning of Reneger's exploit and for the association of the Southampton man with Drake in the minds of Philip and his ministers when the Spaniards suffered worse outrages in Elizabeth's reign. This division of royal authority also had the effect of weakening the Spanish handling of their case, and the Emperor was never properly informed of the true facts of the matter.[3]

Philip's reaction to the news from Seville was prompt. He issued a royal *cédula* from Valladolid on 20 March, instructing the Marqués de Cortés, and leading officials of the *Casa de la Contratación*, to hold an immediate inquiry into the incident. The Marqués was to ascertain not only the value of what Reneger had taken from the *San Salvador*, but also what the French prize and its contents were worth. Then he should proceed without delay to confiscate all manner of goods and ships belonging to Englishmen to be found in Seville, Cadiz, San Lucar, Port St. Mary and other ports of that coast to the value of both of Reneger's depredations and a further third of this amount to cover the expenses of the embargo and costs of indemnification.[4] A week later an order was issued from the *Casa de la Contratación* to the *alcaldes* and senior officials of the Andalusian ports, instructing them to sequestrate immediately the property of Englishmen in the districts under their juris-

---

[1] Archivo General de Indias, Patronato, *Legajo* 265, *Ramo* 59. *Vide infra* Appendix D, p. 239.
[2] P.R.O., State Papers, Henry VIII, vol. 199, f. 147.
[3] *Vide infra*, p. 187.
[4] P.R.O., State Papers, Henry VIII, vol. 199, f. 146.

diction. This order, it was stated, was made upon receipt of information contained in the royal *cédula* that a Spanish treasure ship had been robbed by Robert Reneger and his brother John. The value of this robbery had been assessed from the ship's register at 7,243,075 *maravedís*. The goods of Englishmen so confiscated were to be put in the hands of substantial persons for safe keeping in the presence of a public notary. Failure to

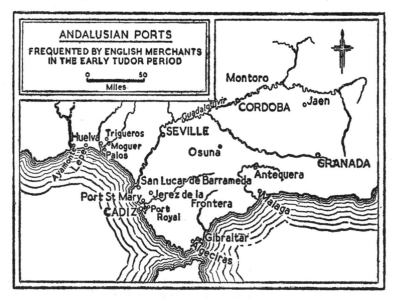

carry out these instructions on the part of the local officials would render them liable to contribute towards the compensation of the merchants themselves and to pay a fine of 50,000 *maravedís*.[1]

On the following day (28 March 1545) two officials of the *Casa*[2]

---

[1] P.R.O., State Papers, Henry VIII, vol. 199, f. 147.

[2] It is of great interest that one of them was Pedro Mexía, described in their report as *theniente de contador* (deputy treasurer). *Vide* Archivo General de Indias, Contratación, *Legajo* 2439, *Ramo* 6, *no.* 2 *et infra*, Appendix D, p. 235. In his introductory biography to Mexía's *Historia del Emperador Carlos V* (pp. xxiii, *seq.*) the well known editor of fifteenth- and sixteenth-century Spanish chronicles, Prof. Juan de Mata Carriazo, on the basis of documents in the Archivo General de Indias brought to his notice by Señr. Don José de la Peña y de la Cámara, challenges the traditional belief that Pedro Mexía was at some time *contador* at the House of Trade in Seville. Instead, from these documents, he says it appears that he was cosmographer. This report of the inspection of the *San Salvador*, however, proves that the famous Spanish humanist did at least on occasion act in the capacity of *contador* of the *Casa*.

boarded the *San Salvador*, which was lying at anchor in the river at Seville, and made an inspection of the ship and its papers. Francisco Gallego, his crew and the passengers were questioned and swore that, except for one or two small items which they named, nothing had been brought in the ship except the goods listed in the register. It was recorded by the inspectors that the ship had been thoroughly searched in accordance with the regulations of the *Casa* and that nothing more had been discovered. The register had been examined and found to be in order. It can safely be taken that, in spite of the later doubts of the Imperial ambassador and Charles V, this inspection cleared Gallego and the merchants of any possible charge of defrauding the authorities. It is stated in the report that on the same day Gallego handed over to the officials a number of despatches which he had received from the governor of San Domingo. The fact that Gallego carried these papers explodes the theory advanced by Martin Hume that the voyage was an illegal one.[1] Incidentally, it was stated in the report that one of these documents had been broken open by the Englishmen.

It is difficult to imagine what action Philip could have taken other than arresting the English ships and goods in Andalusia. Spanish ships had been subjected to almost indiscriminate plundering in the Channel from the early days of the last French war and redress had seldom been forthcoming. Reneger's action was little better than sheer piracy in spite of his brazen talk about law and justice. Apart from the particular merits of the case, however, on a matter of principle the Spaniards put themselves undoubtedly in the wrong by arresting English property in Spain as a reprisal for Reneger's act. The Treaty of Medina del Campo, which was still the basis of commercial relations between the two countries, stated quite clearly that reprisals were not to be made until redress had been demanded by the sovereign of the injured party.[2] A treaty concluded between Charles and Henry in February 1543 had re-iterated this point in view of possible depredations at sea.[3] Yet the commission for the arrest of English property issued by Philip definitely stated that it was given as a result of Reneger's act.[4] The English naturally were to make much of this point.

[1] *Vide supra*, p. 144.   [2] *Vide supra*, p. 38.   [3] *Vide supra*, p. 130.
[4] P.R.O., State Papers, Henry VIII, vol. 199, f. 146v.

The plunder brought back by Reneger from his privateering expedition may have been viewed with mixed feelings by Henry's councillors, but the arrival of the daring captain and his armed ships must have been very welcome at this crucial stage of the war. In the first phase of hostilities Henry had been able to take the offensive against Francis on the continent while his armed merchant ships wrought havoc among French commerce in the Channel. After the Peace of Crépy, however, the French king was able to concentrate on assembling a navy for a counter-offensive, and England, deserted by her ally, found herself on the defensive. As Francis gathered together his fleet in his northern ports Henry called in his merchantmen to take part in the defence of their country.

There can be little doubt that after Reneger had handed over the treasure—or some part of it—to the officials of the Tower, he made speedy preparations for joining the king's fleet then assembled off Southampton and Portsmouth. A list of these ships dated 19 April 1545[1] reveals that the *Trenyte Renygare*, the *Jamys Runygare* and the *Gallyone Runygare* were already in service by that date. Among ships in the same list named as prizes taken in the Narrow Seas is the *Marlyne* of 70 tons and a complement of 60 men. It is possible, however, that this was the French prize which Reneger seized in the harbour of San Lucar de Barrameda. The conviction that she was a prize of his is strengthened by the fact that he himself captained her later in this war.[2]

While Reneger was with the Fleet awaiting the French on-slaught the news of his daring exploit and the nature of his booty must have been the subject of discussion not only among members of the King's council in the council chamber, but among merchants and mariners throughout the ports and creeks of southern England. Its repercussions on the enterprises of English seamen were clearly demonstrated in the months immediately following Reneger's return.

---

[1] P.R.O., State Papers, Henry VIII, vol. 200, ff. 25v–28.
[2] Salisbury MS. 137, f. 79.

CHAPTER VII

'WORSE THAN OPEN WAR'

ROBERT RENEGER's feat had immediate and far-reaching effects upon the activities of the English seamen, causing a marked increase in both the number and the boldness of their attacks upon Spanish shipping. The arrest of English property in Andalusia as a reprisal for the seizure of the treasure was a blow not at the privateers and pirates, for whom it provided an excuse for more outrageous enterprises, but at the more honest merchants who had been struggling to continue to trade with Spain in the face of ever-increasing difficulties. These men were now given a further incentive to forsake the less profitable legitimate trading for the quicker returns of privateering and piracy, and eventually even merchants like William Aphowell and John Cappes of Bristol, who had plied the Spanish trade for thirty to forty years,[1] began to take part in these enterprises.[2] There were other reasons why the men of the West Country were prominent among the English adventurers on the high seas, but one undoubtedly arose from the deterioration of their long-established trade to Spain.

At first the merchants hoped that the arrest in Spain would be ended by negotiation, as the similar embargo in the Low Countries had terminated early in April 1545.[3] It was, in fact, promised at the same time, and, when their hopes were disappointed, they demanded the arrest of Spanish ships in England. Such action did not suit the policy of Henry and his council, however, for they were playing a more subtle game. Keeping strictly to the treaties, which they claimed the Spaniards alone had broken, they gave no official encouragement to the merchants.[4] It became increasingly clear to the latter that the remedy must lie in their own hands and the bolder spirits needed no further hint from the government.

[1] P.R.O., K.R. Customs, 199/1 *seq.*
[2] *A.P.C., 1542–47*, pp. 540, 558.
[3] *Letters and Papers*, xx (1), no. 494.
[4] *Vide infra*, chap. viii, *passim.*

Reneger's success itself gave encouragement to the English seamen, for as the months went by it became evident that the king, far from punishing his temerity, was making a justification of the Southampton captain an essential feature of his policy towards Spain. Reneger's triumph provided the clearest proof of the inability of the Spaniards to defend their ships against the English attacks, or to take effective counter-action against the adventurers. Charles' letters to Philip at this time show that he was fully conscious of the position. He told the Regent he was doing all that was possible short of declaring war on England. It was not a great deal. The Emperor deemed it inadvisable to authorise further reprisals or issue letters of marque since both the English and French had strong forces at sea and such action might give them a reason for settling their differences. Moreover, it would take a long time to assemble an adequate sea-force in Spain and then it would be too late to do anything effective.[1]

The Spaniards had, therefore, to be content with diplomatic representations. Their success in this field was very limited and matters did not improve when Charles' reluctance to resort to more forceful arguments became increasingly evident. The Emperor was told that Henry had commanded his captains to treat the Spaniards lovingly, but he must surely realise that men of war were apt to transgress their orders. The English seemed to remember that in the last French war, when they were neutral, the Spaniards had dealt them great injuries, quite against the wishes of the Emperor. The English ambassador stressed the strict legality of his country's actions in marked contrast with those of Spain. A whole multitude of English merchants, he said, was clamouring for the king to arrest the Emperor's subjects in England, but Henry would not break the treaties for the sake of private matters. Those sea-captains who had disobeyed the king's orders should be punished; more than that could not reasonably be asked.[2]

Van der Delft, the Imperial ambassador, protested that it seemed that the Spanish ships seized by English privateers were being held as security for the release of the property in Spain. He asked if this was so or whether they were held as French

---

[1] *Spanish Calendar, 1545–46*, nos. 112, 301.
[2] *Letters and Papers*, xx (1), no. 1132.

prizes. The councillors told him truculently that he could take it which way he pleased. He knew King Henry's mind. Let him have the arrests in Spain released, and Spanish ships and property in England would be restored, although, they said, they were able to prove some of the property was French.[1] Such an attitude, even though they were still ordered not to molest the Emperor's subjects, was bound to encourage the English sea-captains, especially when the most notorious of them was known to be in favour at the king's court.[2]

It is therefore not surprising to find that from this time onwards the enterprises of the English seamen became more numerous and considerably bolder. More and more English ships left the Channel to cruise off the coasts of Spain and Portugal looking for likely prizes. Juan Martínez de Recalde, the famous Biscayan sea-captain, who was later one of the principal commanders of the Spanish Armada, told Prince Philip in the summer of 1545 that the English plundered every ship they encountered on the Spanish and Portuguese coasts as well as in the Channel. He said, moreover, that he had heard they were much worse than the French.[3] Even Lord Russell, President of the Council in the West, himself involved in depredations upon the Spaniards,[4] wrote to the Privy Council expressing his pity for the Spanish mariners stranded in West Country ports, their ships despoiled, without wares or victuals to sustain them.[5] At the beginning of the following year the Spaniards declared that the English armed ships were doing as much damage as lay in their power, which was considerable.[6] Lord Lisle, the Admiral, admitted a little later that every Spaniard, Portuguese or Fleming coming from the south was robbed by English adventurers, some pretending to be Scotsmen and some wearing vizors.[7] The diplomatic correspondence is full of evidence of their activities and of the efforts of the Spaniards to obtain redress.

The records of the business of the Privy Council during this period also bear testimony to the frequent representations of the

---

[1] *Spanish Calendar, 1545–46*, no. 83, p. 156.
[2] *Vide supra*, p. 147.
[3] *Spanish Calendar, 1545–46*, no. 60 and fn.
[4] *Vide supra*, pp. 134 *seq.*
[5] *Letters and Papers*, xx (1), no. 1307.
[6] *Spanish Calendar, 1545–46*, no. 205.
[7] *Letters and Papers*, xxi (1), no. 563.

Imperial ambassador on behalf of Spaniards despoiled by English privateers. The ambassador constantly protested that these complaints were referred to the Admiralty Court, as indeed they were, but it is evident that a great deal of the council's time was also spent on them. An increasing number of letters was written to the mayors and other officials of coastal towns ordering inquiries into these complaints. References to suits in the Admiralty Court become more frequent. More safe-conducts were issued to Spanish captains and merchants and letters of recommendation sent to port officials on their behalf. Repeated instructions for the enforcement of the decisions of the Admiralty Court and threats of punishment for failure to carry them out tell of a boldness which was going further than official policy would approve. It is evident that the men of the West Country were well to the fore in attacking the Spaniards. The mayors of Dartmouth, Plymouth and other Devon and Cornish ports were the most frequent recipients of orders and admonitions from the council.[1]

Typical of these were letters issued to Antonio de Mazuelos, Antonio Guarras and other Spaniards who claimed they had been robbed of a quantity of cloth by English adventurers on the seas. On 11 September 1545 they received letters addressed to all the king's officers upon the coast ordering search to be made in the surrounding towns and villages for bales of cloth bearing the marks of the Spanish merchants.[2] Three days later Juan Bautista San Vitores, factor of Juan Quintanadueñas, Spaniard,[3] was given a letter to John Stowell, Vice-Admiral of Devon, ordering him to deliver 22 fardels of linen cloth to the bearer or else appear immediately before the council.[4] On 16th of the same month Antonio de Mazuelos and Antonio Guarras had letters to the mayor of Dartmouth for the restitution of three 'cofres' of linen cloth and to three men of Totnes for a further 36 pieces of cloth.[5] Sometimes the council addressed its mandates to the Lord High Admiral. A letter of 6 January 1546 is typical. It contained the supplication of Pedro de Alleban, Spaniard, for the restitution of goods taken out of his ship by certain Englishmen at Newport in the Isle of Wight. The Ad-

[1] *A.P.C., 1542–47, passim.*   [2] ibid., p. 242.
[3] Juan Quintanadueñas was plaintiff in the case against William Hawkins. *Vide supra,* p. 136.
[4] *A.P.C., 1542–47,* p. 243.   [5] ibid., p. 244.

miral was requested to give him speedy justice in the Court of Admiralty.[1] A letter written on 1 August 1546 to the mayor and fellow officials of Rye, Hastings, Winchelsea and other neighbouring ports, concerned the complaint of Antonio Bonvisi,[2] Antonio de Mazuelos and Antonio Guarras that a galleon named the *Trinity*, master Juan del Campo, laden at Southampton with their merchandise, had been despoiled off the coast of England on her voyage to Spain. Part of the cargo had been recovered and now one of the adventurers who attacked the *Trinity* near Fowey was identified as a captain of Rye who had returned to the Sussex port with 'a good somme of redy money' made from the robbery.[3]

The names of Antonio Guarras, Antonio de Mazuelos, Diego de Astudillo and other leading Spanish merchants residing in England occur frequently in these records. Sometimes they were acting on their own behalf and often for Spanish merchants dwelling outside the country like Juan Quintanadueñas. The name of Pedro de Villanueva, the agent of these merchants, is often mentioned.[4] Villanueva travelled from port to port, armed with letters to the local officials, identifying and claiming the goods of Spanish merchants in the hands of English privateers or others to whom they had been sold. He seems to have been fully occupied in this task until he died in the summer of 1546.[5]

The diplomatic correspondence and the records of the Privy Council in the months following Reneger's successful capture of the Spanish treasure contain ample evidence of the increase in the number and scope of the depredations committed by the English seamen upon Spanish shipping. There can also be discerned quite plainly from these sources a marked coolness towards their old ally on the part of Henry VIII and his councillors. There was growing up at the same time, for more personal considerations, a new hostility and contempt for the Spaniards among English seamen. Abundant evidence of this is to be found in the contemporary records of the High Court of Admiralty. These files throw new light also upon the methods of the pirates and privateers during the last French war of Henry VIII's reign.

[1] *A.P.C., 1542–47*, p. 306.   [2] A prominent Italian merchant.
[3] *A.P.C., 1542–47*, p. 503.
[4] ibid., pp. 434–7, 445–6, etc.
[5] ibid., p. 529.

Despite the constant protests by the Spaniards that their cases were referred to the Admiralty Court, this was, in fact, the correct judicial body to deal with them. The High Court of Admiralty had been instituted in the fourteenth century to meet the difficulty experienced in dealing with piracy and claims of despoliation made by foreign sovereigns or against them.[1] The complaint of the Spaniards was chiefly concerned with the delay in obtaining justice. This was of particular importance, since the loss of the services of their ships and the deterioration of their goods while their cases were being dealt with often cost them large sums of money—even when the English privateers were not disposing of their property in the meantime. This grievance was not confined to the Spaniards, however, for the English merchants experienced the same difficulty. It arose from the fact that the court administered the lengthy civil procedure of the time and not the summary procedure of courts such as the Star Chamber, Chancery and Court of Requests. Merchants used to the commercial courts of the continent would find the procedure of the Admiralty Court particularly tedious.[2]

Almost all the Spanish complaints of despoliation eventually found their way into the Admiralty Court. The records of the court are far from complete and it is extremely difficult to find all the documents of any one case. But ample evidence remains of the activities of the English privateers against the Spaniards, and of the growing hostility between the seamen of the two countries. From the depositions of ordinary mariners who took part in raids on Spanish shipping, the plausible stories of the impudent sea-captains who led them and the tales of woe of the Spaniards who were their victims, a great deal can be learned about the trends of English maritime enterprise during this French war. This evidence shows clearly that the defiance of Spanish maritime authority shown by the Elizabethan seamen had already been aroused among English captains and mariners by the end of Henry VIII's reign.

One of the most interesting cases in the records of the Admiralty Court following Reneger's exploit is one brought by Diego Ortega de Carrion and other Spanish and Portuguese

---

[1] R. G. Marsden, *Select Pleas in the Court of Admiralty*, vol. 1, Introduction, p. xiv.

[2] Sir Wm. Holdsworth, *A History of English Law*, vol. v, pp. 138, 152.

merchants against Robert Collins of Dartmouth. This case illustrates several interesting aspects of the piracy and privateering of the forerunners of the Elizabethan seamen. It tells of the spoliation of Spanish and Portuguese ships in Spanish harbours by a syndicate of West Country captains. It reveals, too, the contempt aroused among the bolder spirits by the reluctance of one of the company who wished to keep strictly to the orders given him by the owners of his vessel to molest none of the king's friends. It describes the usual form of attack, with the small heavily armed pinnace, and the subsequent voyage to Ireland to dispose of the booty in a remote haven. Finally, the familiar figure of Pedro de Villanueva appears with his commission to take the goods into custody.

At the beginning of June 1546 Villanueva laid a complaint before the Privy Council. He was acting on behalf of a number of merchants who had shipped merchandise in some Portuguese ships for a voyage to Flanders earlier in the year. These ships and at least one Spanish vessel had been attacked by English adventurers in the previous March while lying at anchor in the north Spanish port of Munguia. The privateers not only robbed three of the Portuguese ships of some 450 chests of sugar, but captured the *Santa María de la Victoria* laden with cotton wool, oil, elephants' teeth and other valuable goods.[1] The greater part of these goods belonged to Diego Ortega de Carrión and it was while travelling in search of them that Pedro de Villanueva died.[2]

One of the English ships taking part in this enterprise, the *John of Kingswear*, was arrested at Mount's Bay in Cornwall shortly after Easter 1546 on the orders of Sir William Godolphin, the Vice-Admiral of Cornwall, at the suit of Villanueva. Robert Collins of Dartmouth was principal owner of this ship. He had not himself been in the *John* during her privateering expedition, and declared in the High Court of Admiralty that the goods found in her, claimed by the Spaniards, were taken on board without his knowledge or consent. He personally had received no part of them and had given strict instructions at the outset that the privateers were under no circumstances to meddle with the Emperor's subjects. He admitted that certain of the *John*'s company had joined in the attack on shipping in Munguia harbour, but without the permission of her master,

[1] *A.P.C., 1542–47*, pp. 446, 529.   [2] *Vide supra*, p. 156.

who had demanded their return to the ship.[1] The master and
a number of the mariners of the *John* gave evidence supporting
Collins' statement of the original agreement for the hire of the
ship, and, naturally enough, of their own innocence.

William Bery, the master, with the captain, Thomas Mougham,
had made a bargain with the owners, Robert Collins and Thomas
Gale, in the latter's house at Kingswear at the end of November
1545. The owners adventured the *John*, fully equipped with
victuals, ordnance, and ammunition for war against the king's
enemies, the French and the Scots, while Bery, Mougham and
their company agreed to risk their persons in the same cause.
All prizes captured should be divided equally, the owners
receiving one half and Bery, Mougham and the ship's company
the other. Before they departed, according to Bery, the owners
gave them all strict orders that under no circumstances were
they to interfere with any of the king's friends, allies or subjects. Thereupon Bery was appointed by the company to be
master and Thomas Mougham captain of the expedition.[2] The
master's evidence was corroborated by John Cutte, a Dartmouth merchant, who said he was in Gale's house at the time
with several others, drinking and making merry.[3]

The *John* had been at sea some four weeks, according to
Bery, when they fell in with two other English ships off the
coast of Galicia, the *Flying Ghost*, master James Logan, and the
Trinity Gilbert, master James Alday. At the invitation of the
latter, Mougham visited the *Trinity* one night, and when he
returned to the *John* the next morning he told Bery that Alday
had asked him for the services of eight mariners. After he had
transferred these men into the *Trinity* Mougham admitted that
Alday and Logan were planning to enter Munguia haven nearby
and 'fette owte' a Spanish ship or two laden with Frenchmen's
goods. All three then tried to persuade Bery to go with them
into the haven, but he refused, saying that 'he was not wery of
Ingland and wold not leve England to do suche a dede'. He
demanded that Mougham should recall the eight mariners who
were in the *Trinity*, but the latter, infected by the hope of booty

[1] P.R.O., H.C.A., Examinations, 5, 23 April 1548; 5 May 1548.
[2] ibid., 22 January 1547 (*sic*). Actually 1548. The Old Style dating on the
document and not the actual dating is given in all these footnotes for purposes
of reference in the High Court of Admiralty records.
[3] ibid., 1 March 1547.

held out by Alday, refused to return to their ship, so Bery put
out to sea without them, 'the cumpanye callying hym coward
and . . . metter to kepe shepe than to goe to warre'. Shortly
afterwards, when he had been forced to alter his course to avoid
some armed French ships, Bery fell in with Logan and Alday
again, who now had with them a Spanish ship which they had
brought out of the harbour. They sailed to Baltimore in Ireland
and Bery followed them 'for socour'. There, by ill luck, Alday's
men ran the Spaniard, the *Santa María de la Victoria*[1], upon a
rock and she perished. Logan and Alday urged Bery to help
salvage her goods and, although he did not agree, the captain
and some of the crew of the *John* took out of the Spaniard some
elephants' teeth, oil and cotton, declaring that it would be
better to save the goods than see them cast away. The pursers
of the *Trinity* and the *Flying Ghost* made an inventory of this
merchandise. Then they all went into Baltimore haven where
Logan and Alday tried to persuade Bery to take the goods to
Limerick and Galway and sell them there. He refused and finally
parted company with them. About a fortnight later the *John*
arrived at Mount's Bay in Cornwall where the ship was arrested
on the orders of Sir William Godolphin and the goods handed
over to Pedro de Villanueva.[2]

Brought before the Admiralty Court, Robert Cunningham, a
mariner on board Logan's ship, corroborated much of Bery's
evidence. He had been present at the interview with Alday and
Logan in which Bery's virtuous attitude was met with such
scorn. When Mougham came aboard the *Flying Ghost*, according
to Cunningham:

Loggan askyd whether the same John of Kyngeswere shuld goe
with ther shippes into Mungia havon and helpe fett owte a certen
Spanyshe shippe lyeng there where vppon William Bere master of
the sayd John havyng knowledge thereof sayd that he wold not
agree to the same for that he had suche commission of his owner that
he had rather rone his shippe vppon the rockes than he wold accorde
to take any of the kynges frendes shippes or goodes and so dyd not
agree with the sayd Loggyd and Aldeye. . . . Loggyn and Aldaye
perceavyng that the sayd Bere wold not agree to them sayd vnto
hym a venchense takyn suche a coward and sayd that were more

---

[1] It is described as Portuguese in Villanueva's complaint as recorded in the
business of the Privy Council. *Vide A.P.C., 1542–47*, p. 446.

[2] P.R.O., H.C.A., Examinations, 93, 22 January 1547.

meter for hym to kepe shepe than to be master of any shippe of
warre and so bad hym to departe owte of ther cumpanye . . . the sayd
Loggyn and Aldaye (leavyng the sayd John of Kyngeswere at the
see /) dyd enter into the sayd havon of Mungia and there bordyd a
greate Spanyshe shippe beyng ladon with oyle ollyfauntes tethe /
sugar and cotten which shippe the sayd Loggyn and Aldaye brought
fourthe of the sayd havon and caryed her vnto Balettymore an havon
in Ireland where the same Spanyshe shippe beyng sette on grounde
by one of the sayd Aldes men pylote there was was (sic) vtterly
destroyed and peryshyd . . . the sayd John of Kyngeswere for lacke of
men not daryng tabbyde at the see followyd the sayd Aldey and
Loggyn into Balletymore where and whan the sayd Spanyshe shippe
beyng perishyd the sayd Loggyn and Aldey dyd take an accounte
of certen goodes which was laden into the sayd John to thentente to
save the same . . .[1]

Bery's story, corroborated by Cunningham and a number of his
crew, reveals one of the old school of law-abiding seamen to
whom an attack on one of the Emperor's harbours was still an
enormity. His refusal on the grounds that he 'was not wery of
Ingland' accentuates the boldness displayed by Reneger, while
the contempt of Alday and Logan reflects the new spirit which
the Southampton man's feat encouraged.

James Alday of Dartmouth, the leading spirit of the raid on
Munguia harbour, gave a very different version of events, although he did not deny his own share in the action.[2] Alday was
a well known West Country captain of dubious reputation who
figures in numerous enterprises during this period. Many years
later, when applying for employment in Martin Frobisher's
search for the North-West Passage, he claimed that he was the
initiator of the regular Barbary trade in 1551.[3] He appears on
several other occasions in the Admiralty records, sometimes
laying information against his fellow privateers.[4] Alday asserted
that there had been a definite agreement between the masters
and captains of the *Trinity*, the *Flying Ghost*, and the *John* to
act in consort for a period of forty days. It was during this
period that the *Santa María* was taken. When the bargain was
made Mougham and Bery both declared they had the authority

[1] P.R.O., H.C.A., Examinations, 93, 21 January 1547.
[2] ibid., 26 May 1548.
[3] J. A. Williamson, *Sir John Hawkins*, pp. 36–37; Blake, *Europeans in West Africa, 1450–1560*, vol. 2, p. 272.
[4] P.R.O., H.C.A., Examinations, 5, 93 *passim*.

of the owners to enter into such agreements. According to Alday, the *John* did not accompany the *Trinity* and the *Flying Ghost* when they entered Munguia harbour, because she was smaller than them and somewhat 'pesteryd ready with wares', so she waited outside. The captain and a number of her crew took part in the spoliation of the *Santa María*, however, and helped bring her out of the harbour. They rejoined the *John* at sea as arranged and sailed to the coast of Ireland where the Spanish ship perished. All three ships took in as much of the merchandise of the sinking vessel as they could, making careful inventories so that if she was subsequently deemed a good prize the ships' companies could have their share. By general agreement the captains attempted, without success, to sell some of the goods on land.

Most of the existing evidence of the case comes from the depositions of the privateers in the Admiralty Court. But it so happened that there was an Englishman on board the *Santa María*, Christopher Newcombe, a London tailor, having with him goods of his own and some belonging to Sir William Roche, the important London draper,[1] who filed a petition in the Admiralty Court when the case was referred there.[2] Newcombe was robbed of his own and Roche's property to a total value of about £100. His examination is therefore of particular interest. Newcombe said that at the end of March 1546, while on a voyage to Flanders, the ship had been driven by contrary winds into Munguia haven. Some eight or ten days after her arrival there one William Skinner, master of an English 'bote of warre', forcibly boarded the *Santa María* and mariners of his ship 'dyd with ther nakyd swordes and ther bowes bente' drive her company under the hatches and plundered her. Then a number of other English armed vessels came into the harbour whose companies boarded the *Santa María*, including Collins' ship and those of Alday and Logan. These 'dyd ryfell the sayd shippe of all that they mought cum at above the hatches' before they were joined by yet another English privateer, William Cooke.

Newcombe said he told Cooke he was an Englishman and 'desieryd Coke to be good unto hym'. Whereupon the pirate summoned him on to the upper deck of the *Santa María* and commanded him in the king's name to declare whose goods the

---

[1] *Vide supra*, pp. 63, etc.   [2] P.R.O., H.C.A., Libels, etc., 13. no. 9.

ship was carrying. Newcombe said he did not know as she was laden before he boarded her, and Cooke left him to join the other privateers, who 'never lefte ther spoyling by the space of di a daye and a night'. At the end of that time Alday and Logan obtained a certificate from the officials of the town of Munguia that they had not plundered the ship, and departed from the haven. The following evening, however, they entered the harbour again with their ships 'disgysyd havyng Scottyshe flagges' and carried off the *Santa María*. At this time Newcombe was in Logan's ship and was present at the re-assembling of the English vessels outside the harbour the next morning and during the subsequent voyage with the *Santa María* to Ireland. When the Spanish ship was lost off the Irish coast he saw Logan, Alday and a boat from the *John of Kingswear* go to her and save packages of cotton, sugar, cork and elephants' teeth which they carried to their own ships. Newcombe alleged further that Alday and his company had also seized another ship laden with wines in the Spanish harbour.[1]

The affair in Munguia haven and the conduct of the English captains well illustrate the new attitude towards Spain growing up among English seamen. The former friendly relations and the respect felt by the English seamen and merchants for their ally were fast breaking down and being replaced by new feelings of hostility and contempt. This prolonged spoliation of Spanish and Portuguese shipping in a Spanish harbour, disclosing the utter helplessness of the officials in the port and the complete disregard by the English seamen of Spanish authority, already displays the spirit later shown in the attacks on shipping in Cadiz and other Spanish harbours by the Elizabethan sea-dogs. In this case the Englishmen were prepared to justify themselves with the well worn excuse that the Spanish vessels were carrying Frenchmen's goods, whose presence they usually divined whenever a suitable victim offered itself.

An even more flagrant case of piracy was perpetrated by William Cooke of Exmouth when he seized the *Santa María de Camina* before joining the other adventurers at Munguia. Cooke could not even thinly veil the outrage, for this ship, engaged in coastal traffic between two Spanish ports could hardly be accused of carrying Frenchmen's goods. According to

[1] P.R.O., H.C.A., Examinations, 93, 1 March 1546; 6 May 1547.

her owner, Juan Pérez Serrano, the *Santa María de Camina* was taken at the isles of Bayona while on her way from Seville to Plasencia and carried off with all her lading, consisting of oil, wine, fruits and other merchandise, to Topsham in Devon.[1] There were other adventures in the meantime, however, and Cooke had her with him when he joined the others at Munguia. Ochoa de Plasencia, a Biscayan mariner giving evidence on behalf of Serrano, described the capture in some detail.[2] The *Santa María de Camina* had been a night and a day at anchor at the isles of Bayona, he said, when Cooke entered the harbour. The latter was in a pinnace with some twenty armed Englishmen and they had with them eight or nine pieces of ordnance. After firing several times upon the Spaniard, they boarded her with swords drawn, took possession of her and carried her off. Ochoa, who was the pilot, and two other Spanish mariners were taken by the Englishmen to Newport, where he and one of the others were put ashore. He alleged that Cooke offered to take him on as pilot and pay him well if he would say the *Santa María* was French. Ochoa refused to do so.

In the interim Cooke apparently put in to Pontevedra and attempted to sell the *Santa María* there. Unfortunately for him, however, she was recognised as Juan Pérez Serrano's ship and he had to sail away.[3] The next that is heard of him is after he fell in with the Dartmouth captain at Munguia. James Alday, true to his reputation, gave evidence against Cooke in the suit brought against the latter in the Admiralty Court. About the end of February 1545,[4] Alday said, he was at Muros in Galicia when the customer of the port came to him and said that one of his neighbours had been robbed of his ship at the isles of Bayona. The Spanish official described the vessel as of about 60 tons burden, 'a gallion with ij toppes viz one toppe and a spydell vppon the foremaste'. He asked Alday to keep a look out for her or any news of her. On 5 or 6 March, while at sea off Cape Finisterre, Alday chanced to meet with William Cooke in a ship of war. Cooke had with him a vessel which exactly corresponded with the description given to him by the customer of Muros.[5]

---

[1] P.R.O., H.C.A., Libels, etc., 15, f. 34.
[2] ibid., Examinations, 93, 8 June 1547.
[3] ibid., 8 March 1547; 17 March 1547.
[4] Actually 1546.   [5] P.R.O., H.C.A., Examinations, 93, 6 May 1547

Further light upon the character of William Cooke, who seems to have been one of the boldest of these adventurers, is thrown by another suit brought against him in the Admiralty Court. Here he is described as master of the *Anne Sely* of Exmouth. Having satisfied himself that goods he had taken from a ship off the French coast belonged to Frenchmen, Cooke had 'requested' one Peers, the factor travelling with them, to write a confession to that effect. Defending himself in the High Court of Admiralty, Cooke asserted that Peers was willing to do so, but required a pair of spectacles in order to execute the deed. Whereupon the Exmouth pirate, having put in to Falmouth harbour and spent the night at a village nearby, called upon the local parson the following morning and borrowed his spectacles. Then he returned to his ship, where Peers put on the parson's glasses in the presence of certain local dignitaries called in by Cooke for the occasion, and wrote that the goods were indeed the property of Frenchmen.[1]

What threats or bribes were used by Cooke in this particular case are not known, but the suit of Asencio Pérez and others against Michael James and Leonard Sumpter illustrates the great fear in which the Spanish seamen were coming to regard the English privateers. Pérez, according to his own statement,[2] was sailing with his ship, the *Santa María de Guadalupe*, towards Chester in the summer of 1546 when he was attacked by an English vessel captained by Michael James. James was another West Country adventurer who during the same year captained the *Mary Figge* of Plymouth in enterprises upon the Emperor's subjects.[3] After firing upon the Spaniard with guns and arrows, James and members of his company boarded her, according to Pérez:

and put hyme and all his cumpenye in prison vnder hatches by the space of two dayes and one nyght or thereabowtes in the whiche tyme the said pirote and his cumpeny whose names is Michaell James the principall dyd robe the shippe of a greate number of balletes of woad and other wares and marchandizes and when the said pirottes had taken ther pleasure they departyd leavyng the said Censio Perez and his cumpenye faste shytte uppe in the breadehowse of the said shippe wher they had noo space to stande nor sytte but

[1] P.R.O., H.C.A., Libels, etc., 14, no. 6.
[2] ibid., 13, no. 14.
[3] *A.P.C., 1542-47*, pp. 543-4.

dyd lye one apon an other lyke hogges faste bounde in ropes and cordes vnder the hatches . . .[1]

Before departing, however, James told Pérez and his company that since they had begged for mercy he would show it to them. Otherwise he would have sunk them 'for causes which ther cuntrymen had done to the same Mighelles father before tyme'. James finally warned the Spaniards to 'beware for they shuld mete with many shippes which wolde syncke them'.[2] Thoroughly cowed by their treatment at the hands of James, the Spaniards proceeded on their journey. According to the master's statement:

Censio Perez and his cumpanye when they dyd perceve that the said pirottes wer departyd from ther shyppe they dyd begyn to crepe owte of the said prison under the hatches and wolde have takynge there right course towardes Chester accordyng to ther covenante withe ther shippe and goodes that was lefte.[3]

When they were within half a league of Waterford harbour they saw another English vessel coming towards them, 'whiche thynge the said Censio and his cumpanye perceyvyng and knowyng them to be men of warre and dyd knowe of late by experyence of Michaell James and his cumpanye what crueltye was in them'.[4] Therefore, when the English ship, which they subsequently found was under the command of Leonard Sumpter, was within gunshot the Spanish mariners took fright and the whole company, including Pérez, abandoned ship, taking with them only a small quantity of iron. Whereupon, Sumpter boarded the Santa María and made off with her and the remaining cargo. Another Spanish witness, Martín de Larrea, said that Asencio Pérez and his crew abandoned ship only through fear of Leonard Sumpter then coming 'a mayne' towards them, thinking that he would rob them as Michael James had done 'and haue orderyd them as as (sic) yll as the sayd Mighell James dyd'. When Sumpter came within gunshot of the Santa María the Spaniards 'dyd clene for sake the sayd shippe for feare of ther lyves', so that he was able to take the ship without any resistance or firing.[5]

The mariners of Sumpter's ship told a somewhat different

---

[1] P.R.O., H.C.A., Libels, etc., 13, no. 6.
[2] ibid., Examinations, 5, 6 October 1546.
[3] ibid., Libels, etc., 13, no. 6.
[4] ibid.
[5] ibid., Examinations, 5, 14 October 1546.

story in which they emphasised the innocence of their action and their eagerness to act in a legal manner. They described the *Santa Maria* as an abandoned ship which, had they not taken her, would assuredly have perished in the storm that arose shortly afterwards. Thomas Richards described the capture, or discovery, of the Spanish ship as follows:

Leonard Sumpter beyng capitayne of Thantony Sumpter wente vnto the see with the sayd shippe abowte fortenight or iij wekes before Tryinitie Sondaye laste / furnysshyd and preparyd for the warres this deponent then beyng hyryd for a maryner saylyd in the same shippe with the sayd Leonard vntyll the sayd Trynitie Sondaye at what tyme they harde that peas was proclaymyd betwene the kynges grace of England and the Frenche kynge / they came from the see with the sayd shippe and in the same ther comyng from the see abowte none of the sayd Trynitie Sondaye they eskryed a certen shippe abowte iiij leages towardes the shore from them / and imediatly vppon sight thereof gaue chase to the same shippe (she beyng at Tramore baye) betwene Dungarvord and Waterford havon and abowte iiij of the clocke in thafter none of the same daye the sayd Leonard Sumpter came harde to the same shippe / and callyd with a lowde voyce therevnto at what tyme they harde none aunswere bourdyd the sayd shippe / and the sayd Leonard / this deponent and Thomas Norrys ... with certen other of ther cumpanye enteryd into her withowte any manner of gon shotte or other busynes, where they founde nor man ne chylde but evyn the shippe with aboute xx tonnys of yron and xxij bagges of wodde and ij or iij C rosyn her sayles lieng flatte vppon the stayes all abrode and no leauyng creature therein nor thereabowtes that coulde then be seen ... they toke and carryed her with the goodes therein to Pennarte nere the towne of Cardyf in Wales as a thing founde flotyng vppon the see.[1]

Upon arrival at Penarth Leonard Sumpter journeyed up to London 'tenfourme my lorde Admyrall of the fynding of the sayd barke as thorder of the see in suche cases requyrythe'.[2] According to Richards, Sumpter 'was desieryd by his maryners to goe vnto London to instructe my lorde Admyrall of the fyndyng of the same pryse that they mought have then haulf for ther labors accordyng to thuse of the see'[3] Martin de Larrea said in his evidence, however, that it was not until the justices had imprisoned two of his men in Cardiff and seven in Bristol

[1] P.R.O., H.C.A., Examinations, 93, 7 February 1546.
[2] ibid., 6 February 1546.
[3] ibid., 7 February 1546.

that Sumpter had hurried up to London to register the *Santa Maria* in the Admiralty Court as a 'wayfe'.[1]

It was in the environs of Cardiff and Bristol that Sumpter and James had disposed of the woad and iron taken from the Spanish vessel. Miguel de Poza, a Spaniard whose brother in Flanders had an interest in the cargo of the *Santa Maria*, identified some of the woad on the quayside at Bristol by its markings and enlisted the aid of one of the sheriffs of the city to arrest it, and some iron.[2] It transpired that various Bristol merchants had bought it from Michael James, paying much less than its market value. James also disposed of woad and iron to 'dyvers . . . honeste men of Kardyf'[3] who subsequently found themselves in the Admiralty Court. The evidence of Miguel de Poza contains some interesting details of his efforts to obtain these goods and the co-operation he received from certain merchants of the 'old school'. He was apparently standing on the quayside at Bristol one day about St. James' tide when he saw set on land from a small balinger some eighty ballets of woad and six or seven tons of iron. The woad, he noticed, was marked with the sign of Juan de Tola, a merchant of Bilbao, who had laden it at Bermeo for transportation to Chester and Flanders. De Poza's brother had written to Miguel from Flanders in the previous June to inform him of the Chester consignment so that he could identify it when it arrived.

De Poza at once appealed to Francis Codrington, a prominent Bristol merchant, who reported the matter to William Carre, one of the sheriffs of the city. The latter gave orders for the arrest of the woad and iron on behalf of Juan de Tola. The ready assistance given to the Spaniard by Codrington and Carre is of interest because these two Bristol merchants traded a great deal to Spain, often in partnership.[4] They must consequently have lost much money from the recent difficulties of the Anglo-Spanish trade, but there is no record of their taking revenge on the Spaniards as many did. The woad and iron were placed in the 'Backe howse' of Bristol where they remained about twelve or fourteen days. Afterwards, because Miguel de Poza had no commission to sue for them, they were all delivered to one Robert

[1] P.R.O., H.C.A., Examinations, 5, 14 October 1546.
[2] ibid., 93, 6 March 1546.
[3] ibid., 5, 21 January 1546.
[4] P.R.O., K.R. Customs, 21/7 *seq*.

Taylor and other Bristol merchants who had bought them from Michael James. These merchants confessed to the mayor and sheriffs of the city that they had paid only a fraction of their worth to James. They were allowed to retain the goods on providing sureties that they would restore them if at any time they should be proved to belong to Juan de Tola.

The English reputation for cruelty, so prominent in the case of Asencio Pérez, was often mentioned in evidence in the Admiralty Court at this time, although there are not many specific complaints of really cruel treatment. One such instance of English privateers being accused of torturing the Spaniards whom they despoiled is contained in a petition submitted by Martín Pérez Ubilla in August 1546. He stated:

that where your orator dyd ffreight and lade yn Vermew and in Burdex a certeyn Spanysshe shipp called the Barbara of Lequetia in Spayne *with* wynes and other wares to be conveyed vnto the porte of Galvye and Cheragoye in the king his ma*jesties* roy*me* of Irelond the same shipp in followyng her viage beyng at a place called Ballynskellyl in the same yo*r* ma*jesties* roy*me* of Irelond the fourthe day of May last past a certeyn Inglisshe shipp of to toppes whereof was capytayn as he was called Thomas Rose of Yarthmouthe and Rychard Mougham of Adsanne besydes Derthmouth maister of the same together *with* an other pynk wherof was owner as he was called Ellyestete of Plymouth was burded the said Spanysshe ship and toke from her xxx[ti] tons of wynes and spoyled more too tons and besydes that toke also dyverse pec*es* of artyllary and meny other wares and thing*es* to the vtter vndoyng of yo*r* orato*r* and yet not therwi*th* content most cruelly dyd turment yo*r* orator and his company *with* bowstring*es* wrysted about their handes and about theyr prevy members.[1]

An interesting account of the treatment they received from Scottish privateers before falling foul of the English is given by some Spaniards in a suit brought by Juan de Arestiqueta of San Sebastian against men of Totnes in the autumn of 1545.[2] The notarial certificate of Nicolás de Plazaola, public notary of San Sebastian, was produced in evidence in the Admiralty Court and possesses the additional interest of being endorsed by three Englishmen residing in the Spanish port. These men, Robert Tyndall,[3] Lawrence Boureman and Nicholas Woseley,

---

[1] P.R.O., H.C.A., Libels, etc., 13, no. 15.   [2] ibid., no. 57.
[3] Tyndall is described in John Smith's ledger (f. 55) as 'my p*rentis* resydent at S.S. (San Sebastian) in Spayne.'

factor of Nicholas Thorne, confirmed that Arestiqueta's ship, the *San Juan*, was of San Sebastian and that her cargo was shipped by merchants of the same town.[1]

The *San Juan* was on her way to Flanders by way of Bordeaux when she was taken at sea by Scots who carried her off to Brest. There they released her when they discovered she was Spanish, but not before robbing the mariners of their clothes and the ship of part of her lading, according to some witnesses.[2] While in Brest the Spaniards learned there were great numbers of English armed vessels in the vicinity, whose captains took all the Spanish and Flemish ships they could lay their hands upon and treated their crews cruelly. According to these reports the English privateers:

tomavan todas las naos espanolas y flamencos y . . . tratavan muy mal . . . y a los vnos echavan a la mar e a otros quitavan las orejas e narizes y a otros atormentavan por diversos generos de tormentos deziendoles *que* tenian guerra con espanoles.[3]

Having learned all this the Spaniards of the *San Juan* left Brest in company with a ship of Bilbao. On 1 June they were met by three armed English vessels which opened fire on them. They protested that they were Spaniards of San Sebastian, but the English did not cease firing. The master and crew of the *San Juan*, realising that they could not defend themselves and fearing to be ill-treated, mutilated and thrown into the sea, surrendered. The English privateers took all her goods and carried them off to an English port.

The ship of Bilbao was also taken by the same adventurers. She was the *Trinity*, master Juan de Larrea. According to the statement of Francisco de Ugarte, Spaniard, acting on behalf of Pedro de Ugarte, his brother, the *Trinity* had previously been despoiled and carried off by Frenchmen. There were, in fact, Frenchmen on board her when she was taken by men of Totnes and Winchelsea. Part of her lading of wines and salt belonged to some Irish merchants and the rest to Pedro de Ugarte, the ship's owner. The *Trinity* and the goods were still in the possession

---

[1] P.R.O., H.C.A., Libels, etc., 14, no. 22.

[2] ibid., no. 8; also ff. 8–11 (not numbered), etc.

[3] ibid., no. 22, f. 36v. i.e. 'took all the Spanish and Flemish ships and . . . treated (the crews) very badly . . . and some they threw into the sea and others they cut off their ears and noses and others they tormented with various kinds of tortures, telling them that they were making war on Spaniards'.

of the Englishmen, and the Spaniards were demanding their restitution and the freight charges for the merchandise shipped by the Irishmen.[1]

Among the files of the Admiralty Court are scattered references to the West Country syndicate in which Thomas Wyndham was one of the leading figures.[2] The partners seem to have been involved in lawsuits with Spaniards and others of the Emperor's subjects throughout most of this last stage of the French war, and their ships, under different masters, were active all the time. There were constant complaints of their activities, of which the following, made in March 1547, is typical:

Allunso Sanbitoris Anthony Sanbitoris and John Baptista de Sanbitores marchantes of . . . Spayn, dyd in somer was a twelve monthe beyng in the yere of owr lord God a thowsande fyve hundrethe fortie and fyve ladyd by them their factours and frindes a Portingales shipp withe sugar amber grese and other marchandizes to be transportid frome the partes of Portingale to the towne of Anwerp in Braband, whiche shipp beyng so ladenid did take hir right cowrse towardes the place to hir apoyntid, and comyng on hir voyage was apphendid and taken by certeyn shippis of warr callid the Mary Winter the Fawcon the Fygge *and* withe the said shippis being certeyn barkes *and* a pynowce in consert whiche shippis *and* barkes dyd apperteyn and belong to John Ellyot Thomas Winter John Espert Thomas Crowner Rychard Saunder Richard Howper Thomas Windham *with* other and was browght frome hir right coursse towardes Kassubey besides Plymowthe in the west cuntrie *and* ther was spoylid by the owners victualers capytaynes pursers masters quartermasters sowlgiers *and* maryners of the fore namid shippis of warr or by their deputes of fowre score chestis of sugar and fourescore ounces of amber grese to the valew of cccccli.[3]

The change in the attitude of the English merchants and seamen towards the Spaniards is perhaps nowhere better illustrated than in the case brought by Diego and Juan de Aranda, Spanish merchants dwelling in the Low Countries, against some men of Bristol. The latter, including William Aphowell, John Cappes and William Aplom, had long been trading to Spain[4] and it was doubtless their bitterness at the decay of their trade

[1] P.R.O., H.C.A., Exemplifications, 1, f. 149.
[2] *Vide supra*, pp. 134 *seq.*
[3] P.R.O., H.C.A., Exemplifications, 2, f. 68.
[4] *Vide supra*, p. 152.

—if there were no more personal considerations—that led them to have a share in this enterprise and even to adopt an attitude of defiance when ordered by the council to compensate the Spaniards. According to the latter, they had been robbed of 1,028 bags of rice, 25 pipes of molasses and 41 bales of almonds laden in the *Saint Peter*, Pedro Yáñez master, at Denia in Alicante. The ship was first taken by Frenchmen, who declared the goods in her were English. While she was being carried off to Scotland she was taken from the Frenchmen by two English ships of the West Country. The captain of one of these, John Hill, and his company had subsequently 'don*e* their plea*sure* *w*ith the for*s*aid m*a*rchaundizes all this tyme in dystrybuting and selling them in Irelonde and other places'.[1]

The case went against the two English captains, John Hill and John Dowding of Minehead, and the Bristol merchants who had financed them. On 29 May 1546 the mayor and his brethren of Bristol and the king's officers at Minehead were instructed to see that full restitution was made to the Spaniards, including payment for goods which had been disposed of in the meantime.[2] Nearly five months later, however, John Dowding, John Hill, William Aphowell and John Cappes had not carried out the terms of the award against them and paid the money to Antonio de Mazuelos acting on behalf of the Spaniards. On 9 October they were ordered to do so at once or appear before the council within twelve days.[3] At the end of December they had still failed to comply with the order and the council expressed its amazement at their contemptuous attitude.[4] This episode is of special interest because these Bristol merchants were no mere adventurers like William Cooke of Exmouth and James Alday of Dartmouth, taking advantage of difficult times to make quick profits, but men who had plied an honest trade to Spain for a great number of years. Anglo-Spanish commercial relations had indeed reached a bad state when merchants like these took to piracy.

It has not yet been possible to trace the conclusion of these suits owing to the nature of the records. Sometimes the Spaniards had to invoke the aid of the Privy Council in recovering their

[1] P.R.O., H.C.A., Exemplifications, 1, f. 151.
[2] *A.P.C., 1542–47*, p. 435.
[3] ibid., p. 540.   [4] ibid., p. 558.

goods when judgement had been given in their favour in the Admiralty Court. In these instances copies of the letters sent by the council on their behalf are often found among its records. In outstanding cases, such as those of Wyndham and Hawkins, where the Imperial ambassador was constantly bringing the matter before the council and mentioning it in his despatches, it is possible to follow the progress of the suits in some detail and to ascertain the outcome.[1]

The 'Reneger Incident' itself was obviously too important and delicate a matter to be handled by the Admiralty Court and there are no traces of it in its records. It seems to have been conducted throughout at the highest diplomatic level and was an important factor in Anglo-Spanish relations during the last years of Henry VIII and the beginning of Edward VI's reign. State papers and diplomatic correspondence passing between England, Flanders and Spain reveal the details of a diplomatic struggle lasting over three years and rapidly transforming the friendly atmosphere of the earlier Tudor period into one often resembling the hostility of the Elizabethan era.

[1] *Vide infra*, pp. 181 *seq.*

CHAPTER VIII

THE DIPLOMATIC STRUGGLE

RENEGER's capture of the Spanish gold gave rise to a diplomatic struggle forming an important landmark in Anglo-Spanish relations in the sixteenth century. Events during the latter years of Henry VIII's reign must have shown more far-seeing Englishmen how incompatible the interests of England and Spain had become, and in the dispute over the 'Reneger Incident' a new attitude towards their former ally found its expression. This diplomatic struggle also provided a valuable lesson to Tudor statesmen of the later period, not only in dealing with similar situations, which by then had grown more common, but in the whole field of Anglo-Spanish relations. It is more than probable, too, that the memory of his own part in the matter influenced Philip II's later policy towards England.

The frequent references to the 'Reneger Incident' in the diplomatic correspondence reveal the importance which the two governments attached to it and their consciousness that vital issues were at stake. For Henry VIII and his councillors, the justification of the Southampton captain was a vindication of their own policy. Reneger's emphasis on the legality of his actions and his frequent demands for a lawsuit to establish it are echoed in the appeal to the strict letter of the treaties by the English government. Similar legal arguments were to be a feature of Elizabeth's approach to such questions. The Spaniards saw quite clearly, too, that precedents were being set which were fraught with grave danger to their interests. Yet, although they were convinced that Reneger's act was the most flagrant piracy and their ships were being despoiled daily, they could get little redress. The English seemed always to produce a plausible argument to put them in the wrong. The Spanish diplomats matching their wits against Elizabeth could scarcely have been more baffled and frustrated.

The diplomatic struggle over Reneger's treasure has three main features, each having an important bearing on future Anglo-Spanish relations. The first is the astuteness of English diplomacy which more often than not put the Spaniards, who were the aggrieved party, in the wrong. The English, throughout, paid lip service to the treaties, which the Spaniards, not without extreme provocation, had broken. It is reasonable to suppose that if the latter had abided by the agreements they would have gained nothing, for Reneger's exploit showed clearly how dead the spirit of the treaties had become by this time. The fact remains, however, that the Spaniards played into the hands of the English by breaking them. In contrast to English diplomacy the Spanish was pitifully weak. The inefficiency of Spanish officials is evident, not only from the diplomatic correspondence, but also from letters to the *Casa de la Contratación* dealing with the incident.[1] The bewilderment of Van der Delft,[2] so plain from his despatches, arose because for a long time he was not sent the detailed information he needed to overcome the arguments of Henry VIII and his councillors. The Emperor himself was ignorant of the true facts of the matter and was easily misled by Reneger's story to believe that the Spanish merchants had been defrauding him.[3] Even the Andalusian merchants were divided among themselves, and this division of interests greatly weakened the Spanish case.[4] The third and most important feature of this struggle is the growing realisation among English statesmen of the inability of the Spaniards to back their diplomacy with force. Here the English seamen gave a lead to the government, for they had first-hand knowledge of Spanish maritime weakness.[5]

The struggle falls into two phases. Up to the death of Henry VIII English policy was uncompromising, for it insisted that the arrest in Andalusia was a breach of the treaties and that until it was released there could be no restitution of Reneger's plunder. There was the implication, too, that the Spaniards could look forward in the meantime to no respite from the privateering raids of the other English adventurers, to whose activities Reneger's feat had given great encouragement. After the death of Henry VIII, who had been determined to have no compromise over Reneger, there grew up a feeling among the

[1] *Vide infra*, p. 187.
[2] Van der Delft succeeded Chapuys as Imperial ambassador in 1545, but the latter remained in England a while before departing for the Diet of Bourbourg.
[3] *Vide supra*, p. 145. [4] *Vide infra*, p. 185.
[5] *Vide supra*, Introduction, pp. xxi–xxii.

councillors that the incident should be settled. Even so there were sufficient sympathisers with Reneger to ensure that the settlement when it came was very much in his favour—and theirs.

It was not until the middle of April 1545 that the English envoy with Charles received a protest against Reneger's action. Wotton was told that two Spanish ships had been despoiled on their way back from the Indies and their men cruelly handled.[1] The Imperialists, who had recently learned of Wyndham's capture of a ship of San Sebastian,[2] were confusing him with Reneger and the charge of cruelty was not again levelled against the Southampton captain. Shortly afterwards Charles sent Chapuys an account of the incident and gave him instructions for presenting his case to Henry VIII. It was a difficult situation. Only recently it had been re-iterated that disputes at sea should be settled not by reprisals but by special arbitration.[3] Charles was therefore acutely conscious of Philip's error in authorising reprisals and told the ambassador that, if they were mentioned when he demanded restitution of the Spanish property, he was to make the best excuses he could, saying that they were made without the Emperor's knowledge. He was to promise that as soon as Reneger's plunder was restored Charles would take reciprocal action.[4]

Before these instructions arrived, however, Chapuys and Van der Delft had already visited the Privy Council. The councillors tried to justify Reneger's action on the grounds that some of his ships had been seized and detained in Spain. The ambassadors afterwards reported, however, that all his property had been sequestrated and he himself summoned to appear before the council.[5] By 9 May Chapuys was very optimistic about the result of his representations. He had been assured there would be complete restitution of the goods and ships taken by both Reneger and Wyndham on the understanding that like measures would be taken in Spain. Moreover, the reprisals authorised by Philip had not been mentioned.[6]

His optimism was misplaced, however, and it must have been badly shaken by a sinister incident reported to him very shortly

[1] *State Papers, Henry VIII*, x, p. 399.
[2] *Spanish Calendar, 1545–46*, no. 35, p. 76.
[3] ibid., nos. 21, 22. [4] ibid., no. 46.
[5] ibid., no. 48. [6] ibid., no. 51, p. 105.

afterwards. It is recorded among the business of the Privy Council on 12 May 1545 that a complaint was made by the Imperial ambassador that in the matter 'betwene Reneger and a certeyne master and other Spanisshe mariners', one of the mariners coming to the council for justice was 'by meane of the sayde Reneger trapped and convayed per force in to a veassell upon the see'.[1] No more is heard of this charge or of the mariner, but the small episode throws interesting light upon Reneger's character and exploits. Perhaps the patriotic captain, not content with furnishing his sovereign with gold of the ally who had deserted him, pressed one of the Emperor's subjects into the king's service. At all events we do not know who these Spanish sailors were or any details of their complaint against Reneger. It is quite certain that the master was not Francisco Gallego of the *San Salvador*, for at this time he was with his ship in the river at Seville preparing for another voyage to San Domingo.[2] It is most unlikely that the mariners came from the treasure ship either, because no mention is made of Reneger abducting members of her crew either in the report of the officials of the *Casa* or in any other document concerning the incident. The Spanish master and mariners must, therefore, have belonged to another ship despoiled by Reneger.

The Imperial ambassador, who regarded Reneger as 'the notorious pirate', accused him later of committing many outrages upon the Emperor's subjects. According to Van der Delft, the Englishman had preyed upon Spanish shipping on the coast of Andalusia, violated its harbours and despoiled everything he came across at sea.[3] This was, of course, gross exaggeration, but in the same letter the ambassador described Reneger as the Englishman against whom Antonio Guarras[4] was making certain claims. It does not seem possible that Van der Delft was confusing Reneger with someone else because he had interviewed the Southampton man, and in this despatch he said that Charles would undoubtedly know of him as the despoiler of the treasure ship. The possibility that Guarras was acting on behalf of the merchants of the *San Salvador*, as suggested by Hume,[5] is somewhat remote.

---

[1] *A.P.C., 1542–47*, p. 159.
[2] Archivo General de Indias, Contratación, *Legajo* 1079, *no. 7, Ramo* 1.
[3] *Spanish Calendar, 1545–46*, no. 62.
[4] *Vide supra*, p. 17.
[5] *Españoles é Ingleses en el Siglo XVI*, p. 100.

If this had been so, Van der Delft would surely have mentioned it
and not have referred to Reneger's capture of the treasure as to
another matter. Moreover, a year later he admitted that until
then there had been no representative of the Spanish merchants
in England to press their claim.[1] Guarras was not one of the
merchants listed as shipping gold in the *San Salvador*.

The absence of further reference to this episode of the abduc-
tion of the mariner and Reneger's employment with the Fleet
during the ensuing months, show that the Southampton captain
and his vessels were too important for the council to sequestrate
his property and keep him in London in attendance upon its
meetings, as the Imperial ambassador had optimistically reported. It is unfortunate that more details of the case, which
is discussed at such length in the diplomatic correspondence of
the time, are not to be found among the records of the business
of the Privy Council where it must obviously have been a
frequent topic of conversation. The register for the period between 1 March and 10 May 1545 is missing,[2] and after that it
would almost seem that it was purposely kept 'off the record'
as in the case of Drake's celebrated exploit, for on both occasions certain influential members of the council were undoubtedly interested parties.[3]

Meanwhile Chapuys had departed for the Diet of Bourbourg,
which was meeting to discuss commercial disputes between the
Emperor's dominions and England, leaving Van der Delft in
London to deal with the Reneger affair. The diet was concerned
chiefly with the trade between England and the Low Countries,
but a considerable number of complaints were lodged by the
English commissioners on behalf of their merchants in Spain.
It does not appear that any satisfaction was obtained and most
of them were ruled out as concerning incidents which had taken
place prior to the treaty of closer amity between Charles and
Henry.[4] Such protests were against the wrongful exaction of
33,000 ducats from the English merchants in Andalusia between
the years 1528 and 1535, the imposition levied at Cadiz upon

---

[1] *Spanish Calendar, 1545–46*, no. 364, p. 524.
[2] *A.P.C., 1542–47*. p. 157.
[3] This was often done, of course, for the clerk who recorded the business of
the council did so under its instructions. It does not appear that he was neces-
sarily present at each meeting and minutes must therefore have been dictated
to him. *Vide A.P.C., 1542–47*, Preface, pp. vii–viii.
[4] *Letters and Papers*, xx (1), no. 1202.

ships which merely called in passing, and the arrest of English ships in Andalusia to serve the Emperor. In June 1545 the English commissioners reported that English merchants were complaining that they had been persecuted by the Inquisition in Spain and expelled from Spanish courts as heretics and ex-communicates.[1]

Early in June, Reneger was sent by the council to give an account of himself to the ambassador, doubtless in full confidence that he would acquit himself well. Van der Delft, of course, claimed that at this interview he completely refuted the Englishman's case. He relates that he censured Reneger's conduct towards the Emperor's subjects as particularly disgraceful in view of the close friendship between the two sovereigns. Apparently he went so far as to advise the Southampton captain that it would be better for everyone, including himself, if he forsook the sea for some other trade, as he was rendering no good service either to his king or to himself by his present course of action.[2] Henry apparently did not share the ambassador's opinion of one of his leading sea-captains, for at least three of Reneger's ships were with the Fleet at that time ready for service against France.[3]

When Van der Delft next approached them, Henry's councillors made much of the arrest in Spain, saying it was a violation of international intercourse and of the treaty of friendship between the two countries. The ambassador met this with a criticism of the council's defence of Reneger, who, he said, had violated all treaties and rights. If the councillors were so zealous for what was right they should set an example by dealing with Reneger as a pirate instead of making a hero of him.[4] Chapuys claimed that the English argument about Philip's decree was weak. It could not be considered a reprisal, since the Regent had ordered only the seizure of English goods in Spain to the value of Reneger's depredations.[5] Chapuys declared that the English ought in any case to be ashamed of pressing the point as it seemed they were willing to give more licence to Reneger, a

[1] *Letters and Papers*, xx (I), no. 981.
[2] *Spanish Calendar, 1545–46*, no. 62, p. 118.
[3] *Vide supra*, p. 151.
[4] *Spanish Calendar, 1545–46*, no. 62, p. 120.
[5] The English merchants declared that this seizure was to the value of 26,000 ducats. *Vide Letters and Papers*, xx (i), no. 590. This sum is approximately equal to 19,315 ducats plus one third. *Vide supra*, pp. 141, n. 2 and 148.

mere private individual, than to the Prince of Spain, who had, moreover, acted much more moderately.[1] As for letters of reprisal, Chapuys thought Philip had granted them because Reneger went unpunished.[2] It is difficult not to sympathise with the Spanish point of view, but the arguments of Chapuys were quite invalid. There was no question of the English favouring Reneger as a private individual. It was the treaties themselves that stated they should not be invalidated because of infractions of their terms by private individuals and that reprisals should not be authorised by either government without reference to the other.[3] Morally strong, the Spanish case was legally weak.

Meanwhile Granvelle, Charles' principal secretary, complained to Wotton that Reneger went free while Spanish merchants who had been despoiled could neither have the offenders punished nor recover their goods, but had their cases transferred to the Admiralty Court where the delay was interminable. Wotton replied that Reneger's action was clearly not piracy or he would not have given a receipt for what he had taken, and the fact that he was going openly about the Court was itself an indication that he could justify what he had done. As for the complaint about the Admiralty Court, that was the proper court for such causes.[4] The English always met Spanish complaints on this matter by claiming that the Emperor's subjects were given more expeditious justice in England than their own merchants in Spain. There the English were either refused the right to make a claim on the grounds that they were heretics and excommunicates, or, if they managed to obtain a sentence in their favour, its execution was delayed by constant appeals. Yet the Spaniards insisted on being heard by the Privy Council as if all other business could be forsaken to attend to their affairs.[5]

Van der Delft in England was having no more success. He was also trying to obtain a satisfactory settlement of the cases involving Wyndham and Hawkins,[6] whose captures, the Emperor

---

[1] *Spanish Calendar, 1545–46*, no. 80.
[2] *Letters and Papers*, xx (1), no. 1044.
[3] Treaty of Medina del Campo, clauses 13, 14, etc. *Spanish Calendar, 1485–1509*, no. 34.
[4] *Letters and Papers*, xx (1), no. 1132.
[5] ibid., no. 989.
[6] *Vide supra*, pp. 134–136.

claimed, were worth more than all the English goods arrested in Spain.[1] According to Charles, Wotton had declared that these ships were held as a reprisal for the arrest in Spain, but justified the English action on the grounds that the Spaniards had broken the treaties first.[2] Although these two important captures were undoubtedly used for a while as a diplomatic weapon, such an acknowledgement would have been contrary to English policy. In fact, unlike the 'Reneger Incident', both cases were referred to the Admiralty Court where, much to the gratification of Van der Delft, decisions were eventually given against the English captains.

Wyndham's case is of particular interest because there are details of the division of the plunder among the members of syndicate. It also provides an excellent example of the difficulty encountered by the Spaniards in recovering their merchandise when a sentence was eventually given in their favour. The story of the capture of the *Santa María de Guadalupe* told by the mayor of Plymouth[3] was proved in the Admiralty Court to be false. Martín de Miranda was the owner of the goods, as he claimed, and the ship had not sailed away with a contented crew but was held by Wyndham.[4] Called before the council, the latter admitted that damages amounting to £500 were due to Miranda. Of this sum, the owners of the *Mary Figge* had received £130 as a third share; Lord Russell, the owner of the *Mawdelyn Russell*, and Wyndham, her captain, £78 each; the mariners of the *Mawdelyn* £104, and £110 had been paid for freight charges. In October 1545 Wyndham was ordered by the council to pay his share of the money and it was also decided that he should be held responsible for obtaining the rest. Several months passed, during which time it appears that Wyndham was absent on further privateering expeditions. On 12 May 1546 the council addressed a letter to the mayor of Bristol, instructing him to seize a prize recently brought into the port by Wyndham. The mayor was ordered to inform the council of the sale of the prize, as it was intended to compensate Miranda from the proceeds. At the end of the same month Wyndham was in further trouble over a quantity of pepper taken from a Portuguese ship.

[1] *Letters and Papers*, xx (1), no. 1203.
[2] *Spanish Calendar, 1545–46*, no. 97, p. 176.
[3] *Vide supra*, p. 135.
[4] *A.P.C., 1542–47*, p. 158.

Not until the following July was a final decision made of the sums to be paid to Miranda by the different members of the syndicate. Wyndham was to pay £85 9s. 5d.; the Lord Privy Seal (Russell) £85 9s. 5d.; the mariners of the ship the same amount and the owners of the *Mary Figge*, namely John Elliott, Richard Hoper, John Broken, Richard Saunders and Thomas Crotone, £130. Wyndham appeared before the council and agreed that the money from the sale of his prize at Bristol should also be delivered to Miranda. He was given a fortnight to raise the rest, being liable for a total of £248 17s. 5d. of which he might get what he could from the mariners. A few days later the council sent the mayor of Bristol a copy of an agreement made between Miranda and Wyndham for the compensation of the Spaniard. The mayor was instructed to hand over to Miranda the sum of £244 obtained from the sale of Wyndham's prize of wines. On 18 August a letter was sent to the mayor of Plymouth and his fellow officials. They were to assist the owners of the *Mary Figge* in recovering from their mariners the money they had received as their share of the prize, but on no account were they to deal rigorously with those who refused to refund their portion.[1]

Van der Delft had speedier success in his handling of the case of William Hawkins. This suit was remitted to the Admiralty Court in May 1545 and Hawkins was also sent along with Wyndham to be interviewed by the Imperial ambassador.[2] It has been suggested that these two captains were associated in this enterprise,[3] but there appears to be no evidence to substantiate this theory. Hawkins claimed he could prove that the goods in question were French falsely 'coloured' as Spanish and that the factor travelling with them had letters instructing him to alter the title of their ownership as circumstances demanded. Evidence was given in another case in the High Court of Admiralty that Quintanadueñas was a subject of the French king,[4] but Hawkins was unable to prove that the goods in his case were French. In the meantime, perhaps emboldened by Reneger's success, Hawkins and the mayor of Plymouth had been selling the goods while the case was still being heard. They were

[1] *A.P.C., 1542–47*, pp. 265, 415, 435, 486, 493, 520.
[2] ibid., p. 176.
[3] *Vide supra* p. 136.
[4] P.R.O., H.C.A., Libels, etc., 14, nos. 23, etc.

not the first to do so, but the council decided to make an example of them and they were sent to prison.[1]

J. A. Williamson has said of this incident that Hawkins was thrown as a 'sop to the Emperor' because of the precarious situation arising from the formidable French preparations against England.[2] This may well be so, but there was no weakening of the English resolve to have no compromise over Reneger. They further justified his action by supporting the contention that he had been illegally deprived of his French prize in a Spanish port. The English claimed that by the custom of navigation a foreign ship in a friendly port was not subject to local jurisdiction, but the Emperor denied this.[3] It is clear that the parties were at cross-purposes. The English statement referred to Reneger's story that he took his prize voluntarily into a Spanish port to restore some goods to their rightful owners and was deprived of it by the local authorities. The Spaniards, however, had in mind Reneger's seizure of a neutral ship in a Spanish harbour. The legal point depended upon the circumstances to which it referred and if, as is most likely, the Spanish version of the capture of the French prize was true, the English claim was untenable. Had Reneger done as he said, which is much less likely, it would have been a different matter.

Meanwhile Van der Delft was still trying to get satisfaction from the council. He was able to report success in other cases, including the imprisonment of William Hawkins and the mayor of Plymouth. He continued to press for an early conclusion of the Reneger affair and to request that the gold should be handed over to him. The council asked him to have a little patience as Reneger was at sea and the property was doubtless still intact.[4] There are several references in the diplomatic correspondence to Reneger's absence at sea, and it is apparent from various lists and orders of battle that he took a prominent part with his ships in the naval campaign of 1545–46 against the French. In April 1545, soon after his return to England, three of his ships were in the Fleet lying off Portsmouth and in Southampton Water. They were the *Trenyte Renygare,* of 160 tons and 130

[1] *A.P.C., 1542–47,* p. 220.   [2] *Sir John Hawkins,* p. 29.
[3] *Spanish Calendar, 1545–46,* no. 97, p. 177.
[4] ibid., no. 106, p. 203. The council's assurance would be necessary after the Quintanadueñas case when Hawkins had been selling the goods while the suit was still *sub judice! Vide supra.*

men; the *Jamys Runygare*, of 100 tons and 80 men and the *Gallyone Runygare* of equal tonnage and the same number of men.[1] The order of battle of the ships in service with the Navy four months later shows the *Trinitie Renneger*, captained by Robert himself, this time described as of 200 tons and a complement of 120 men, 'For the vanwarde'; the *Galigoe Renneger*,[2] captained by John Reneger, his brother, 'For the battaill' and *Renneger's Pynnes*, captained by Christopher Stockton, 'For the wyng'.[3]

An undated order of battle, which includes an interesting instruction for the effective firing of broadsides, shows the *Trinitie Renneger*, probably captained by Robert himself, in the first rank of the battle.[4] A list of ships with the Navy in March 1546 includes the *Shallop Renneger*.[5] The *Marlyne*, listed as a 'prize in the Narrow Seas',[6] was captained by Reneger at some time during the war and we have a detailed account of her complement and armament.[7] A list purporting to be of ships mustering for the Scottish enterprise of the late summer of 1547 includes the *Trinitie Renneger*, the *Galligoe Rennegre* and *Rennegers Pynnes*.[8] These lists show that Robert Reneger, besides being the most daring of the privateers of this last French war of Henry VIII's reign, also made the biggest contribution of them all to the defence of the country. It is not surprising that the English government was not disposed to discourage a man of such calibre.

The Spanish case against Reneger was greatly prejudiced by the fact that the interests of the merchants who had been despoiled were opposed to those of the Emperor, who claimed the gold as legally confiscated.[9] The former, who foresaw that they would derive no advantage from the efforts of the Imperial ambassador, would have preferred a lawsuit as the lesser of two evils, or even a settlement with Reneger out of court. Charles

---

[1] P.R.O., State Papers, Henry VIII, vol 200, f. 27v.
[2] This may have been an old ship renamed after the unhappy Francisco Gallego or a new one bought from the profits of the exploit. At all events it displays the same sort of humour as the *Trego–Ronnyger. Vide supra*, p. 137.
[3] P.R.O., State Papers, Henry VIII, vol. 205, ff. 160–162.
[4] P.R.O., H.C.A., Exemplifications, 3, f. 195.
[5] *Letters and Papers*, xxi (1), no. 498.
[6] *Vide supra*, p. 151.
[7] Salisbury MS. 137, f. 79.
[8] P.R.O., State Papers, Scotland, Edward VI, vol. 1, ff. 68–69v.
[9] *Vide supra*, p. 145.

himself was especially anxious that this should not happen. He wanted the matter conducted through diplomatic channels so that the gold should be handed over to Van der Delft.[1] A despatch of Bernardino de Mendoza, Philip II's ambassador to Elizabeth at the time of Drake's similar exploit, throws interesting light upon this aspect of the Reneger case.Mendoza advised Philip not to allow the merchants of Seville to make separate claims for their property because each would strive to make the best bargain for himself to the detriment of the king and the others. Events in the Reneger case, he went on, strengthened this opinion, for when the owners sent attorneys to England restitution was long delayed and incomplete, being made only on the intervention of the ambassador.[2]

A further division of Spanish interests is revealed by a letter written to Prince Philip by officials of the *Casa de la Contratación* on 1 October 1545. They said they had carried out the arrest of the English property as ordered by him[3] and it had caused great losses to the merchants of Andalusia. The trade in oil and wine, in particular, had suffered since the embargo because the English had been the largest buyers of these commodities, but the general situation was bad. Not only was the population suffering but the royal revenues were being adversely affected. The officials believed it would be better to relax the embargo so that the English could trade freely again. They said the Marqués de Cortés[4] was writing to the Regent in the same strain.[5]

The embargo was not raised, however, and during the autumn of 1545 Van der Delft in England and Granvelle in the Low Countries continued, without success, to demand the return of the gold. Claiming it for the Emperor, they emphasised his personal interest in the question. On Christmas Eve, home from sea, Reneger paid the Imperial ambassador a second visit. Van der Delft received him coldly and refused to entertain his explanations. Reneger said that everything he had taken was still intact and offered to submit the whole matter to the abitra-

---

[1] ibid.
[2] *Documentos Inéditos para la Historia de España* (ed. M. F. Navarette, etc.) Tomo xci, p. 560.
[3] *Vide supra*, p. 148.   [4] ibid.
[5] Archivo General de Indias, Contratación, *Legajo* 5103. *Vide infra*, Appendix D, p. 244.

tion of the chancellor and the Imperial ambassador. Van der Delft approached Wriothesley with this suggestion but thought that the chancellor appeared unwilling to have anything to do with the case because Reneger was, he said, in his service. The ambassador was assured, however, that justice would be done.[1] Although the exact relationship between Thomas Wriothesley, Earl of Southampton, and Robert Reneger is not clear, there are several indications that the chancellor was Reneger's chief supporter in the council. It is possible they were acquainted before Wriothesley's rise to power and that the Southampton merchant traded on behalf of his patron.[2] Perhaps Wriothesley assisted Reneger in fitting out his original privateering expedition against the French and received some of the Spanish gold as his share of the profits. If this was so it would explain the chancellor's reluctance to arbitrate in the matter between the Imperial ambassador and his 'servitor'. But perhaps Wriothesley's excuse was merely prompted by a desire to avoid a settlement. Reneger's nomination of the chancellor as arbitrator in his case shows his astuteness and hints at their relationship. His purchase of the manor of Broughton from Wriothesley a few months after his case had been settled is another link of significance between them.[3]

Early in the following January the council sent to Van der Delft some English merchants who had complained of their illtreatment by the Inquisition in Spain. One of them said that he had seen an English captain committed to prison at San Sebastian because a New Testament and other books in English had been found in his ship. The captain had been asked if he thought Henry VIII a good Christian and had replied that he did. This may be the Bristol captain who, according to Nicholas Thorne's report in the previous November, had been imprisoned with three more English merchants by the Inquisition when his ship with several French prizes had been driven by bad weather into San Sebastian.[4] This and other complaints the Imperial ambassador forwarded to Granvelle.[5] Perhaps to speed up an

[1] *Spanish Calendar, 1545–46*, no. 182, pp. 290–1.
[2] Wriothesley traded from Southampton (*Vide* Southampton Municipal MSS., Local Port Books, *temp.* Hen. VIII) but the name of his agent is not known. It may well have been Reneger.
[3] *Cal. Pat. Rolls, 1547–48*, p. 268. [4] *A.P.C., 1542–47*, p. 275.
[5] *Spanish Calendar, 1545–46*, no. 182, p. 291.

amicable settlement of the Reneger affair, Charles dealt promptly with these new complaints and directed that no injury should be done to English subjects so long as they made no remarks derogatory to the Pope.[1]

Meanwhile the Imperial ambassador was no nearer laying his hands upon the gold. He was quite unable to get satisfaction from the English while their ships remained under arrest in Spain, but the Emperor was not willing to raise the embargo until those of his subjects arrested in England had been released and the gold handed over. At the end of January Van der Delft reported that he had promised the king and council that the Emperor would release the English property when these conditions were fulfilled. Accordingly, they had released the Spanish ships and assured him that when Reneger returned from sea his plunder would be restored. Reneger was said to have offered to give an account of all he had taken and to place the Emperor's property into the ambassador's hands, so Van der Delft expected that the English council would demand the fulfilment of his promise that the embargo in Spain should be lifted. As he was ignorant of the state of affairs in Spain and of the Emperor's intentions, however, Van der Delft decided not to hasten matters too urgently. He was in a dilemma also because Reneger's assessment of what was due to the Emperor seemed inordinately small and he himself had not been told the amount of the gold he was to demand.[2]

Charles had been unable to send Van der Delft the information he needed because he himself had not received it from Spain. Two letters from Madrid to the officials of the *Casa de la Contratación* at Seville, showing that Philip was demanding this information in May 1546, reveal the incredible inefficiency of the Spanish officials. The first of these letters, dated 29 March 1546, told the officials that the report which they had already sent to the Prince's secretary, Samano, was not adequate and ordered them to send an attested copy of the ship's register as soon as possible.[3] This is of further interest because there is also among the records of the *Archivo General de Indias* a document purporting to be a list of the gold, silver and other goods taken

---

[1] *Spanish Calendar, 1545–46*, no. 185.
[2] ibid., no. 189.
[3] Archivo General de Indias, Contratación, *Legajo* 5010. *Vide infra*, Appendix D, p. 246.

by Reneger but which only specifies bullion and pearls.[1] This may be the list which Philip's ministers considered inadequate. The second letter, dated 12 May, was a reminder to the officials that they had not sent the document demanded in the first letter and pointed out that it had to be sent to the Emperor in Flanders. They were told to despatch it by the first courier.[2] It is little wonder that the wretched Van der Delft did not know what to do next.

The ambassador continued during the spring to request further instructions. An impasse had been reached. The English would restore nothing until the embargo on their property in Spain had been lifted and the Emperor would not sanction this until the gold was restored. It was not until the summer that the Emperor sent the ambassador a detailed report of the property taken by Reneger.[3] Even armed with this Van der Delft got no satisfaction from the English. The latter argued that Henry had freely released the Spanish ships taken by other English captains on the understanding that the arrest in Spain should be ended. Paget also stated that Reneger had offered to restore everything that could be proved to have been captured illegally.[4]

The Emperor then ordered his ambassador to approach the King once more and to tell him that Charles, entirely out of his friendship for Henry, was issuing instructions that the embargo placed on English property in Spain should be lifted against security, although Reneger had not yet restored what he had unjustly taken.[5] If Van der Delft and his master expected a favourable reception for this gesture they were swiftly disillusioned. Henry indignantly demanded to know why security was required and when the ambassador replied that it was to ensure that justice was obtained in the Reneger affair, the king asserted that he denied justice to no one. No legal claim had been made for Reneger's seizures and in any case the arrests in Spain were a violation of the treaties. The interview shows Henry's deep interest in the case and his clear appreciation of the weakness of the Spanish position. He must have realised, too, the significance of the gold in the Tower in the steadily

---

[1] Archivo General de Indias, Patronato, *Legajo 265, Ramo 3. Vide infra,* Appendix D, p. 241.
[2] ibid., Contratación, *Legajo 5010. Vide infra,* Appendix D, p. 246.
[3] *Spanish Calendar, 1545–46,* no. 287.
[4] ibid., no. 331.   [5] ibid., no. 342.

deteriorating Anglo-Spanish relations. Van der Delft replied that a special representative of the merchants despoiled by Reneger, who were supported by a letter from Prince Philip, had arrived with powers to recover the property. He omitted to tell the king, however, that this man had only recently come and that until his arrival no legal claim could be made. In fact, the Emperor had wanted if possible to avoid such procedure. Henry declared impatiently that his relations with Charles were not dependent upon merchants, who could prosecute their claims before his council. The wretched ambassador finally promised not to mention the matter to the king again until the English property in Spain had been released.[1]

Van der Delft then approached Paget who, as a strong advocate of friendship with Spain, was also anxious to get the case settled. In a letter to Petre on the subject Paget reveals his own attitude towards the Reneger affair and hints significantly that other important people were less disinterested. Deprecating all the fuss about a private case, he said that if 'som other men' had been as ready to give up their share of the booty as the king had been to deliver his, the whole matter would have been settled much earlier.[2] The councillors with the king told Paget Henry was willing that Reneger should restore what he had taken, provided that the English goods and ships in Spain should be released upon security and the Southampton captain received justice against those 'which iniustly stayed his prise'.[3] But the embargo was not raised and when Henry died in the following January the position remained a stalemate. Meanwhile, according to Van der Delft, the difficulties of the Spanish merchants in England were growing daily. Privateering and piracy against the Emperor's subjects were increasing and no redress was forthcoming, for until English property in Spain was released upon security all suits were held in abeyance.[4] The death of Henry VIII, however, increased the influence of some of those councillors who favoured a settlement of the case; their influence can indeed be seen in the last weeks of his reign.

At all events, early in April 1547 Van der Delft was informed

---

[1] *Spanish Calendar, 1545–46*, no. 364.
[2] P.R.O., State Papers, Henry VIII, vol. 227, f. 17v.
[3] ibid., f. 26v.
[4] *Spanish Calendar, 1547–49*, pp. 58–9.

that a commissioner had been appointed to hear the evidence on both sides and to give a full report of the case.[1] In June he told the Emperor he had been compelled to defer a visit to Princess Mary as developments in the case made it desirable for him to remain in London just then, so evidently the commissioner was making progress.[2] Things were not going well for the Spaniards, however, for when Van der Delft denounced Reneger yet again before the council the Southampton captain declared the gold was not in his possession. Moreover he retaliated by producing a statement in which he claimed more than twenty thousand ducats from the Emperor.[3] On 18 August Van der Delft sent a further report to Prince Philip, saying Reneger denied he had taken as much gold as the merchants asserted they had lost. Therefore the council decreed that he should restore what he admitted he had seized and be handed over to the Spanish authorities for justice concerning the rest. The acting Lord Chancellor, Lord St. John, however, seems to have persuaded the Imperial ambassador to allow him to arrange an amicable settlement of the whole business to everyone's satisfaction, pointing out that it would be more profitable for the claimants to be recompensed than to have Reneger in prison.[4] Van der Delft apparently accepted Lord St. John's proposal, but there can be little doubt that the only people likely to be satisfied were those interested parties who had no intention of surrendering either Reneger or their share of the spoils. Early in September the ambassador reported that Lord St. John had gone to London from Hampton Court to bring about the proposed settlement.[5] It was reached in the New Year.

Writing to the Emperor on 22 January 1548[6] Van der Delft announced that the representatives of the merchants had come to terms with Reneger. The Englishman agreed to surrender what he admitted he had taken, a part to be handed over in England and the rest in the form of money in Spain. The total value of this would be six thousand ducats, some fourteen thousand less than the merchants claimed. Reneger persisted in

---

[1] *Spanish Calendar, 1547–49*, p. 70. The commissioner is not named, but subsequent events indicate that it was almost certainly Lord St. John. Paget also assisted in reaching the settlement. ibid., p. 105.

[2] ibid., p. 101. [3] ibid., p. 105.

[4] ibid., pp. 135–6.

[5] ibid., p. 148. [6] ibid., pp. 243 *seq.*

his assertion that he had only captured goods to the value of the six thousands ducats he offered and continued to demand a lawsuit in which, he declared, the evidence of his opponents themselves would prove his case. He further asserted that he could bring forward at least two hundred witnesses to prove that the chest he took contained no more than the property he offered to restore. Eager to avoid such a lawsuit, the representatives of the merchants made another compromise with Reneger. The Southampton man agreed to pay a further sum of five thousand eight hundred ducats at the expiration of eight years under security. Van der Delft advised the acceptance of Reneger's offer in view of his poverty. It appears he was unable to find even the first six thousand ducats except by subscriptions from the other English merchants who were anxious to secure the release of their property in Spain. Nor would he have been able to provide sufficient security for the second amount without the assistance of the king. Edward's council granted Reneger a large quantity of lead, the spoils of dissolved monasteries, at a reasonable price and on easy terms of credit.

The Protector and other members of the council told the ambassador that they would never have agreed to all this had it not been for the sake of friendship with the Emperor. For this reason also they were making Reneger pay the five thousand eight hundred ducats which the Southampton man still said were demanded unjustly. Members of the council assured Van der Delft that they would have handed over Reneger and all his possessions to be proceeded against as he wished, had his goods been sufficient to meet the Spanish claims. The ambassador believed this was true, for he reported that Somerset was not well disposed towards Reneger because he had always been Wriothesley's 'servitor'. This reflection of the well-known rivalry between Wriothesley and the Protector gives added interest to the Reneger affair. Reneger is typical of the pushing, ambitious new type of men appearing in Henry's reign who would be appreciated by a man of Wriothesley's calibre, but who would be out of harmony with the Lord Protector.

The settlement was conditional upon the free release of the English property in Spain. Van der Delft thought the Emperor should agree to this, for until it was done Spaniards in England would have great difficulty in getting satisfaction of their claims.

Again he emphasised the need to avoid a lawsuit, in which, he said, the master of the Spanish ship would not escape suspicion.[1] The attorneys of the Spanish merchants, who were going to the Spanish Court to petition for the release of the English property, would inform Prince Philip of these developments. In the meantime, the property surrendered by Reneger was in the custody of an Italian. Even at this stage Van der Delft was still uncertain of what was to be done with the gold and silver claimed by the Emperor, for the Spanish merchants emphatically denied that Charles had any right to it. On 15 June the ambassador informed Prince Philip that one Gonzalo de Hinojosa was leaving London for Spain in connection with the Reneger business.[2] Some months later, when he was begging the Emperor to fulfil his part of the arrangement, Van der Delft expressed complete satisfaction with the English terms and commended the way in which the Spanish claims had been met.[3] Then the case fades out of the diplomatic correspondence until another Spanish ambassador a generation later recalled it in relation to Drake's similar exploit.

The account of the settlement of the 'Reneger Incident' contained in the diplomatic correspondence of Van der Delft can be checked at various points from scattered entries in the English records. A warrant from the Privy Council to the Chancellor of the Court of Augmentations, reveals that the ambassador's information about the lead was correct.[4] Similar warrants were issued to the Master of the Mint and the Clerk of the Wardrobe to hand back to Reneger a certain quantity of gold, silver and pearls which the Southampton man had originally delivered to them 'to the Kinges Majestes use'.[5] They disclose further, that Reneger received £250 towards his expenses.[6] The purchase of Broughton manor a few months after the settlement was made perhaps gives us a clue to how Reneger employed this money.[7] It cannot be doubted that certain persons still retained a considerable part of Reneger's plunder in England. We know that the gold, silver and pearls handed back by Reneger to the Spaniards were only part of the 6,000 ducats the

---

[1] *Vide supra*, pp. 144–146.   [2] *Spanish Calendar, 1547–49*, p. 272.
[3] ibid., p. 339.   [4] *A.P.C., 1547–50*, p. 155.
[5] *A.P.C., 1547–50*, p. 155. Reneger was handed back 13 lb. 3 oz.. of gold, 131 lb. 5 oz. of silver and pearls weighing 103 lb. 9 oz. (*sic*).
[6] ibid.   [7] *Vide supra*, p. 186.

Imperial ambassador said he had agreed to restore. The residue was to be paid back in the form of money in Spain, perhaps from assets of the Southampton man there.[1] Perhaps the Spaniards were able to recoup part of their losses from the English ships and goods in Spain, although the terms of the settlement stipulated their free release. At all events Reneger's 6,000 ducats was less than a third of the sum claimed.

It is significant that the bullion was to be handed over to Reneger to make the actual restitution and that Van der Delft never suggests the plunder was anywhere but in the English captain's possession. Perhaps he did not know that much of it was elsewhere, though this fact was known later to Bernardino de Mendoza. Van der Delft's despatches at times are those of a bewildered man, unsure of his facts and at a grave disadvantage when arguing his case with Henry and his council. This was due to a large extent to the failure of the Spanish government to keep him fully informed of the details of the case. His account of the agreement cannot be taken to represent the real state of affairs. It is true that Somerset was ill-disposed towards the Earl of Southampton and might on that account have entertained no good feeling for Reneger. Possibly the fall of Wriothesley weakened Reneger's position. It is most unlikely, however, that the council had any desire or intention of handing Reneger over to the Spaniards since, according to Paget, some of them had a share of his booty. On the contrary, they appear to have done their best to make it easy for him to reach a settlement. There is more than a slight suspicion, too, that they used the threat of a lawsuit to persuade the Imperial ambassador to agree to a settlement on their terms. Nor could Reneger, who was now appointed controller of the port of Southampton,[2] have been a poor man as Van der Delft believed, for he had ships and property and was soon, in fact, to give signs of renewed prosperity. Everything points to the conclusion that the incident made rather than broke the Southampton man.[3]

An unofficial but illuminating commentary on this very question and the only reference to the incident to be found in

---

[1] It is of interest to note that no mention is made in the settlement of Reneger's alleged losses in Spain.

[2] *Cal. Pat. Rolls, 1553*, Appendix, p. 321.

[3] Chapuys had asserted in June 1545 that Reneger was a poor man until he took the treasure. *Letters and Papers*, xx (1), no. 1044.

the proceedings of any of the English law courts is contained in a petition to the Lord Chancellor made by one Thomas Hervest of Salisbury.[1] Suing Robert Reneger and his brother John in the Court of Chancery for a debt of £20 19s., Hervest said that when payment was due the Southampton merchant was being 'trowblyd for a shipe taken apon the seas' but had promised that when this trouble was over he would discharge the debt. But now 'althoughe the said Robert Reneger haithe past hys said trowble, and ys nowe verey welthey and purchasyd lande*s*' he still did not pay.[2] The outcome of the suit is neither known nor important, but the information it gives about Reneger is useful evidence in support of the contention that the Imperial ambassador's belief that he was a poor man was mistaken. The lay subsidy rolls show that his wealth had more than doubled between the year of the seizure of the Spanish treasure[3] and the return of 1550 when he was assessed as one of the wealthiest men in Southampton.[4]

In the *Archivo de Protocolos de Sevilla* there is evidence of the eventual distribution of the plunder handed back by Reneger. The papers of Alonso de Cazalla, public notary of Seville, contain more than thirty entries during the year 1551 concerned with the 'Reneger Incident'. These are mostly receipts of merchants and their representatives for sums of money paid to them by Fernando de la Fuente and Juan Núñez who were appointed attorneys for the purpose of recovering the plunder in March 1545.[5] It is stated that each received compensation '*que le cupieron de lo que para el venia desde Santo Domingo en la nao San Salvador robada el año 1545 por el ingles Roberto Reneguer cerca del cabo San Vicente*'.[6] In some cases it specifies the merchandise for which the compensation is being paid; in others it states only '*lo qu*&*para el venia desde Santo Domingo*';[7] in one case it specifies gold.[8] It is possible, by referring to the ship's register,

---

[1] P.R.O., Early Chancery Proceedings, Bundle 1438, no. 26.

[2] A reference to the purchase of Broughton manor and other lands from Wriothesley.

[3] P.R.O., Lay Subsidy Rolls, 239/163.

[4] ibid., 174/314.

[5] *Vide supra*, p. 142.

[6] i.e. 'due to him for what was coming for him from San Domingo in the ship *San Salvador* robbed in the year 1545 by the Englishman Robert Reneger near Cape St. Vincent'. Archivo de Protocolos de Sevilla, *Oficio* XV, 1551, *Libro* I, ff. 45v, 120rv, 123rv, etc.

[7] ibid., ff. 232, etc.   [8] ibid., f. 643.

to discover what the consignments were. The total recorded sum paid out by the attorneys was over 1,200,000 *maravedís*, just about a half of the sum Reneger agreed to restore in the first place. There is also among these papers the record of an English merchant receiving back a sum of money for goods seized in the arrest of English property made '*por la toma de Roberto Reneguer y por mandamiento de los jueces y oficiales de la Casa de la Contratación*'.[1] It is unfortunate that the register of Alonso de Cazalla for the first six months of the year 1545 is missing because it must have contained many entries of the arrest of English property in Seville. It is from his office that all the notarial documents we have concerning Reneger were issued. There is also an entry made in 1549 by one George Florey, whose goods had been sequestrated on account of Reneger's exploit, empowering Richard Darrell, a fellow English merchant, to claim his property when the embargo should be raised.[2]

The arrest of English property in Andalusia and the widespread privateering and piracy in Henry's last French war greatly diminished Anglo-Spanish trade in the last years of the reign. Certain long established traders in Spain, such as John Sweeting, continued to prosper during these years, but for the majority of Englishmen conditions were very precarious. The fortunes of the English merchants in Spain had fallen so low that the colony in Port St. Mary had to petition the Emperor against the appointment of a Spanish mat-maker as their consul early in 1547.[3] The English struggled on to retain a trade which had been so profitable to them in the past, but political and religious differences made it increasingly difficult for them to succeed. When the treaties had been made in the time of Henry VII and the Catholic Kings, England and Spain had important common interests. During the following reign these had steadily diverged until the cleavage was almost complete by the death of Henry VIII. The brief interlude of friendship under Mary served only to show how incompatible the interests of the two countries had become. By the time of Elizabeth, Spain was replacing France as England's great rival in Europe. Yet

---

[1] Archivo de Protocolos de Sevilla, *Oficio* XV, 1551, *Libro* II, f. 2031. i.e. 'because of Robert Reneger's seizure and by order of the judges and officials of the House of Trade'.
[2] ibid., 1549, *Libro* I, f. 123v.
[3] P.R.O., State Papers, Miscellaneous, vol. 107, p. 9.

the persistent efforts of the Elizabethans to trade with Spain and her dominions, in themselves a determining factor of the later conflict, bear testimony to the importance of the Anglo-Spanish trade which they had built up and striven to retain under such difficult conditions in the early Tudor period.

THE FORERUNNERS OF DRAKE

SIR JULIAN CORBETT has traced the causes of the rupture of England's old friendship with Spain from Drake's early years until the final outbreak of war. He affirmed that there were three main causes of the Anglo-Spanish struggle, political, religious and commercial, each having its special influence on a particular class in the State. It was the aggressive policy of English commerce, he declared, which finally made war inevitable, and it was that, too, which furnished the men and the means for carrying it on.[1] Corbett believed it was the disaster at San Juan de Ulua that first marked the rupture between England and Spain in the Tudor period. Of this event he wrote:

It may fairly be said to mark the opening of a new book in the great epic of the Reformation. For the first time the long commercial intimacy between England and Spain received a rude shock, and from that shock it pined and died.[2]

A study of Anglo-Spanish relations in the early Tudor period reveals, however, that the causes of the rupture can be traced further back than the early years of Francis Drake, and in fact, are plainly to be seen in the probable year of his birth.[3] It was, indeed, the commercial and sea-faring classes who gave the lead to the rest of the country and among them the three causes of the struggle were already combining by the end of Henry VIII's reign to engender a hatred and contempt for the Spaniard.

It has already been shown that an aggressive English commercial policy against Spain dates from the earliest years of Henry VII's reign. A flourishing Anglo-Spanish trade, which swiftly became dominated by the English merchants, for a long time absorbed the energies of some of the most enterprising elements of this realm. They even gained a footing in the New World. It was with the break-down of this lucrative trade that these men turned to privateering and piracy and took revenge

---

[1] *Drake and the Tudor Navy*, vol. I, p. 73.
[2] *Sir Francis Drake*, p. 16.
[3] 1545. *Vide, Drake and the Tudor Navy*, vol. I, p. 56.

on those who had deprived them of the source of their wealth. The men of the West Country were prominent in the commerce with Spain, and it is therefore not surprising to find that they were also the foremost despoilers of the Spaniards when the old amity gave way to hostility, a development which began many years before the incident at San Juan de Ulua. It is of great significance that the Anglo-Spanish trade during the reigns of the first two Tudors attracted some of the leading English merchants and sea-captains and brought them into close contact with Spanish maritime power. It is no matter of mere speculation to suggest that Englishmen frequenting the Spanish ports and seeing the great ships sailing in and out on their voyages to the New World must have been filled with patriotic envy and even resentment at their own country's lack of similar rich sources of wealth. Men like Robert Thorne and Roger Barlow, who themselves had participated in the trade to the Spanish Indies, made great efforts to arouse interest among their fellow countrymen at home in projects of discovery which they believed would bring great benefits to England. Barlow and another Englishman, Henry Patmer, took part in Sebastian Cabot's voyage to La Plata in 1526 in order to obtain information bearing upon a possible English route to the Spice Islands. Thorne and his partner had invested a large sum of money in this enterprise to ensure that these two were allowed to take part in it.[1] Close contact with the Spaniards led such men to feel quite sure that they could at least equal their feats although, in fact, in the science of navigation England lagged far behind Spain.

The patriotism of the English merchants in Spain was fiercely aroused and at the same time identified with religious hatred by their persecution at the hands of the Inquisition in the years following the Reformation. The religious quarrel at this stage was political rather than doctrinal since it arose from Henry VIII's Supremacy over the English Church and the loyalty of the merchants to him. His subjects in Spain were almost the only Englishmen who found themselves in this predicament[2] and thus tended eventually to become the most fiercely Pro-

---

[1] *Vide supra*, p. 72.
[2] Religious persecution of Englishmen in the Low Countries at this time was negligible by comparison.

testant section of the community. The activities of the Inquisition dealt a severe blow to the trade of the English merchants in Spain from which it never fully recovered. The link between the political and religious differences between the two countries is also shown by the fact that the persecution of the English in Spain was severest when political relations were most strained. This was during the period between the Truce of Nice and the renewal of the Hapsburg-Valois struggle in 1542. The negotiations for a new alliance against France led to a resumption of friendly relations between England and Spain and a mitigation of the troubles of the English merchants. It did not last long. The final French war of Henry VIII's reign served to emphasise how hollow the old friendship had become. Wars fought by the allies against France had never ended satisfactorily and had always strained the friendly relations between the two countries. Their persecution at the hands of the Inquisition and great loss of trade caused by its activities had embittered many English seamen against the Spaniards. It was not long before clashes between the allies on the high seas had reached proportions far exceeding anything taking place during the earlier conflicts. The Peace of Crépy, regarded by Englishmen as an act of treachery, extended the feeling of resentment towards the Spaniards to the country as a whole, while it furnished an excuse to the adventurers to engage in bolder enterprises against them.

Then, in 1545, which Corbett saw as the crucial year marking a turning point in English naval history and believed to be the probable year of Drake's birth, there occurred the most daring English maritime enterprise against Spain of the earlier period when Robert Reneger despoiled the *San Salvador* off Cape St. Vincent. The French had long been active against the ships from the Indies, and this act of Reneger's, if condoned by the English government, would mean that it, too, had flung down the gauntlet to Spanish maritime power. It is of the deepest significance that the Spanish government did not wait to see if Reneger would be disowned and his plunder returned to its rightful owners. It at once ordered the arrest of English ships and property in Andalusia as a reprisal, without making the representations to Henry VIII enjoined by the treaties. This reveals clearly that to all intents and purposes the spirit of those treaties was dead. At all events Philip and his ministers were

not disposed to take the risk of assuming that it was still alive·
The ensuing diplomatic struggle, lasting over three years, confirmed the fears of the Spaniards. Henry, angered by the Peace
of Crépy, had Reneger at Court and justified his conduct as
firmly as ever Elizabeth supported her great seamen. There is
every indication that the English king took a strong personal
interest in the affair and was in full sympathy with Reneger's
attitude. Nor were the majority of Henry's councillors more
encouraging to the Spaniards. The English stood by the letter
of the treaties and until the death of the old king there was no
serious attempt to compromise over Reneger, although some
of the lesser captains were made to surrender part of their
plunder. It was becoming clear to the English that Spain could
not back her diplomacy with effective force to protect her
shipping.[1] Charles and Philip were only too aware of the same
weakness.

Reneger's exploit is therefore of great importance as showing
quite clearly the changing relations between England and Spain
during the latter years of Henry VIII's reign. More far-seeing
Englishmen could already perceive both the disadvantages of
the Spanish alliance and the diminishing need for pursuing it.
The lesson could not have been lost upon the Spaniards. The
effect upon Philip of Spain of his unfortunate experience with
Reneger is a matter of speculation, but it can hardly be doubted
that the memory of the episode influenced in some measure his
later policy towards England· The contrast between his rash-
ness in 1545 and his later extreme caution suggests that the two
were perhaps not entirely unconnected. We know that Philip
was reminded of Reneger's exploit by his ambassador more than
thirty years later—as an example of how such situations should
not be handled. It is doubtful, too, whether Juan Martínez de
Recalde, his great sea-captain, who had experience later of
Drake's prowess, ever forgot Spanish ineffectiveness against
Reneger and his fellow adventurers in the earlier period.

Reneger is also an outstanding example of the 'New Man',
whose rôle in Tudor history is so important. His career up to
the outbreak of the last of Henry VIII's French wars was like
that of many English merchants who were growing wealthy in
the Spanish trade until it was prejudiced by religious and politi-

[1] *Vide supra*, p. 153.

cal differences between England and Spain. It was the boldness and far-reaching consequences of his revenge that made him a figure of national importance. The remainder of his life, spent in the continued enjoyment of his ill-gotten gains, in a royal appointment, may be seen as a symbol of the triumph of the new order against which Mary's desire to revert to the spirit of the old alliance with Spain was fore-doomed to failure.

The significance of the despoliation of the *San Salvador* has not hitherto been fully realised by later generations, but it was fully appreciated by Reneger's contemporaries. It is unfortunate that the discussions of the exploit and speculation over its outcome which undoubtedly took place among English sea-captains and mariners have not been recorded after the fashion of the long arguments of the statesmen. Its effect upon Reneger's fellow privateers can be seen very clearly, however, not only in the accounts of their depredations in the official language of the council records and the ambassadors' despatches, but in the vivid and picturesque phrases of the adventurers themselves in the files of the High Court of Admiralty. The exploits following Reneger's success demonstrate clearly a new boldness which grew with the knowledge of the inability of the Spaniards to take strong counter-action. The contempt with which they flaunted the Spanish authorities was exceeded only by the wholesome fear they obviously inspired among the Spanish mariners. Of special interest is Michael James' reference during his spoliation of the ship of Asencio Pérez to wrongs which his father had suffered at the hands of the Spaniards.[1] It is the only occasion on which mention is made of revenge for personal injury, but it displays a spirit which could not have been uncommon. The prolonged raid on Munguia harbour is perhaps the best example of the new temper of the English seamen.

The Emperor was concerned most of all with the dangerous precedent which would be created if Reneger went unchecked. Even in a period already characterized by extreme lawlessness at sea, the spoliation of a treasure ship from the Indies by English seamen was a new departure. If it remained unpunished it would be an example to others of a form of privateering far more lucrative than the usual depredations in the Narrow Seas. Another important feature of the affair was the attitude of Charles'

[1] *Vide supra*, p. 166.

own subjects. Where the Spanish merchants and their ruler were not in complete agreement against the increasingly adventurous Englishmen there was a danger that the merchants would come to terms with them to the detriment of their master, as indeed they eventually did with Reneger. The discord fostered between Charles and the merchants of the *San Salvador* by the Southampton captain foreshadows an important aspect of the activities of John Hawkins in the New World.

Charles' fears were realized, however, for Reneger's exploit created a precedent which a generation later must have strengthened the hand of the party supporting Drake when he brought back his treasure in 1580. We know from the correspondence of Bernardino de Mendoza that the precedent was consciously followed on the later occasion. There is, moreover, a striking similarity between the situation created by Reneger's arrival with his gold and the circumstances attending Drake's return to England in 1580. Both exploits were undoubtedly viewed with mixed feelings, and it was ordered that the treasure should be consigned to the Tower while the government made up its mind what was to be done with it. In each case the captain doubtless extracted a portion before handing over the remainder to the authorities. The principals themselves, leading captains of their day and far too valuable in perilous times to be sacrificed to the Spaniards, were both received at Court, where, much to the disgust of the Spanish envoys, they were treated as heroes. In both cases the council itself was divided between those members who wanted to restore the treasure in order to maintain good relations with Spain and those who held the opposite view, often because they had a share of the booty. There is an ominous absence of reference to their deliberations from the records of the Privy Council on both occasions, and there is the same technique of fobbing off the Spanish ambassador with fair promises of justice and finding a dozen excuses and legal quibbles for not punishing the offenders.

Thus Robert Reneger is clearly to be regarded as the greatest of the forerunners of Drake. If his treasure was less valuable the circumstances of the time made the consequences of his action as hazardous. It must be borne in mind, too, that Reneger had been specifically ordered not to molest the Emperor's subjects. Moreover he must be given all the credit due to the pioneer in this new form of maritime enterprise. Reneger's blow against the Spaniards, like the feats of the great Elizabethans, was struck in protest against the efforts of Spanish maritime authority to thwart his activities at sea.

A new spirit of animosity towards the Spaniards had been growing among the English seamen, many of whom had personal scores to settle over the loss of their goods or persecution at the hands of the Spanish Inquisition. It was only a matter of time before one of them, more daring than the rest, risked the wrath of the king, still nominally allied with the Emperor, and threw down to the Spaniards the most serious challenge it was possible for a private individual to make. The Spanish economy was becoming increasingly dependent upon the flow of treasure from America; any interference with that by the English as well as the French would be a serious blow at all the Emperor's schemes. What would the outcome of such an exploit be and what the fate of the bold adventurer who accomplished it? Had the Anglo-Spanish alliance been a firm one at this stage, as it has been generally supposed, there could be little doubt that he would have received short shrift from the English king and his council. Robert Reneger of Hampton, swaggering about Henry's Court, treated as a hero for what he had done, provided the true answer a generation before the exploits of the famous Elizabethan sea-captains. This above all entitles him to be considered in history the great forerunner of Drake.

APPENDIX A

APPENDIX A

SOME STATISTICAL EVIDENCE OF THE ANGLO-SPANISH TRADE OF BRISTOL

1. *An Indication of the Trade of Bristol with Spain in the Early Tudor Period from an analysis of available Particulars of Customs*[1]

Date	Exports to Spain			Wine (tuns)	Imports from Spain
	Ungrained Cloths	Tanned Hides[2]	Value of other Merchandise £ s. d.		Value of other Merchandise £ s. d.
1485–1486	1,977 (E. 1,903 S. 74)	7 (E. 3 S. 4)	236 11 8 (E. 149 10 0 S. 87 1 8)	253 (E. 240 S. 13)	1,577 10 10 (E. 1,362 15 10 S. 214 15 0)
1492–1493	3,283 (E. 3,240 S. 43)	—	284 17 1 (E. 212 15 10 S. 72 1 3)	746 (E. 653 S. 93)	6,495 11 0 (E. 6,361 4 4 S. 134 6 8)
1503–1504	975 (E. 974 S. 1)	14½ (E. — S. 14½)	235 3 4 (E. 189 18 4 S. 45 5 0)	580 (E. 550 S. 30)	1,148 15 2 (E. 1,112 18 6 S. 35 16 8)
1512–1513	1,681 (E. 1,663 S. 18)	218 (E. 139 S. 79)	346 18 1 (E. 256 3 5 S. 90 14 8)	593 (E. 504 S. 89)	2,986 5 2 (E. 2,909 6 10 S. 76 18 4)
1517–1518	1,988 (E. 1,986 S. 2)	117 (E. 75 S. 42)	528 19 7 (E. 476 8 4 S. 52 11 3)	561 (E. 546 S. 15)	2,767 6 6 (E. 2,743 2 11 S. 24 3 7)

[1] These are the only years for which sufficient information is given in the particulars of customs for such an analysis to be made.
[2] In dickers.

E = English Merchants.   S = Spanish Merchants.

2. *Details of the Trade of Bristol with Spain from the Particulars of Customs analysed.*

I. *Mich. 1485–Mich. 1486*

(i) VALUE OF EXPORTS[1]

	English			Spanish			Total		
	£	s.	d.	£	s.	d.	£	s.	d.
Welsh 'Straits' ..	106	5	0	87	1	8	193	6	8
Welsh Cloths ..	20	0	0	—			20	0	0
Beans	20	0	0	—			20	0	0
Alabaster	2	0	0	—			2	0	0
Tanned Calfskins..	1	5	0	—			1	5	0
	149	10	0	87	1	8	236	11	8

(ii) VALUE OF IMPORTS[2]

Woad	582	2	6	—			582	2	6
Iron	392	0	0	106	15	0	498	15	0
Oil	277	0	0	—			277	0	0
Fruit	24	0	0	108	0	0	132	0	0
Sugar	46	0	0	—			46	0	0
Salt	25	16	8	—			25	16	8
Wax	8	0	0	—			8	0	0
Vinegar	6	0	0	—			6	0	0
Combs	1	6	8	—			1	6	8
Soap		10	0	—				10	0
	1,362	15	10	214	15	0	1,577	10	10

[1] Other than ungrained cloths and tanned hides given in table on p. 207.
[2] Other than wine given in table on p. 207.

2. *Mich. 1492–Mich. 1493*

(i) VALUE OF EXPORTS

	English £	s.	d.	Spanish £	s.	d.	Total £	s.	d.
Welsh 'Straits' ..	162	18	4	51	11	3	214	9	7
Welsh Cloths ..	39	10	0	4	0	0	43	10	0
Wrought Tin ..	—			12	15	0	12	15	0
Tanned Calfskins	4	7	6	1	15	0	6	2	6
Herrings	3	10	0	—			3	10	0
Alabaster	—			2	0	0	2	0	0
White Herrings ..	1	10	0	—			1	10	0
Hake	1	0	0	—			1	0	0
	212	15	10	72	1	3	284	17	1

(ii) VALUE OF IMPORTS

	£	s.	d.	£	s.	d.	£	s.	d.
Woad	3,012	3	1	30	0	0	3,042	3	1
Iron	1,551	6	0	90	0	0	1,641	6	0
Oil	1,278	0	0	4	0	0	1,282	0	0
Pepper	110	12	0	—			110	12	0
Wax	105	0	0	—			105	0	0
Almonds	65	13	4	—			65	13	4
Salt	62	18	8	—			62	18	8
Fruit	42	18	4	3	0	0	45	18	4
Honey	30	0	0	—			30	0	0
Sugar	26	0	0	2	0	0	28	0	0
White Herrings ..	23	12	6	—			23	12	6
Hake	14	5	0	—			14	5	0
Dates	5	15	4	—			5	15	4
Combs	5	10	0	—			5	10	0
Resin	2	13	4	2	13	4	5	6	8
Gunpowder ..	4	14	8	—			4	14	8
Salt Fish	4	6	8	—			4	6	8
Bowstaves ..	4	0	0	—			4	0	0
Saffron	3	6	8	—			3	6	8
Vinegar	3	0	0	—			3	0	0
White Cork ..	2	10	0	—			2	10	0
Prunes	—			2	0	0	2	0	0
Carpets	1	10	0	—			1	10	0
Aniseed	1	8	9	—			1	8	9
Fish	—				13	4		13	4
	6,361	4	4	134	6	8	6,495	11	0

3. *Mich. 1503–Mich. 1504*

(i) VALUE OF EXPORTS

	English			Spanish			Total		
	£	s.	d.	£	s.	d.	£	s.	d.
Welsh 'Straits' ..	32	14	2	7	3	9	39	17	11
Welsh Cloths ..	81	10	0	15	0	0	96	10	0
Tanned Calfskins	25	2	6	7	16	3	32	18	9
Bacon	6	13	4	15	5	0	21	18	4
Wrought Tin ..	13	10	0	—			13	10	0
Wrought Lead ..	10	15	0	—			10	15	0
Beans	9	6	8	—			9	6	8
Breton Linen ..	8	0	0	—			8	0	0
Coverlets ..	2	0	0	—			2	0	0
Mantles		6	8	—				6	8
	189	18	4	45	5	0	235	3	4

(ii) VALUE OF IMPORTS

	English			Spanish			Total		
Iron	546	17	6	—			546	17	6
Oil	249	0	0	23	0	0	272	0	0
Fruit	102	15	6	2	0	0	104	15	6
Smigmates ..	54	6	8	10	10	0	64	16	8
Wax	46	0	0	—			46	0	0
Orchil	34	5	0	—			34	5	0
Almonds	25	3	4	—			25	3	4
Salt	16	5	0	—			16	5	0
Bowstaves ..	9	6	8	—			9	6	8
Sugar	9	0	0	—			9	0	0
Pepper	6	5	0	—			6	5	0
Black Cork ..	2	18	4	—			2	18	4
Woad	2	10	0	—			2	10	0
Hops	2	0	0	—			2	0	0
Salmon	1	10	0	—			1	10	0
Dates	1	0	0	—			1	0	0
Tar	1	0	0	—			1	0	0
Cinnamon ..		17	6	—				17	6
Mantles		16	8	—				16	8
Conserves ..		13	4	—				13	4
Cloves		8	0	—				8	0
Marmalade ..	—				6	8		6	8
	1,112	18	6	35	16	8	1,148	15	2

4. *Mich. 1512–Mich. 1513*

(i) VALUE OF EXPORTS

	English			Spanish			Total		
	£	s.	d.	£	s.	d.	£	s.	d.
Tanned Calfskins	56	5	0	65	0	0	121	5	0
Beans	95	8	4	6	13	4	102	1	8
Welsh Cloths ..	35	0	0	10	0	0	45	0	0
Welsh 'Straits' ..	35	8	4	4	3	4	39	11	8
Wrought Lead ..	25	0	0	1	8	0	26	8	0
Bacon	5	18	9	—			5	18	9
Tin	2	10	0	—			2	10	0
Candles	—			1	13	4	1	13	4
Chequered Cloths		13	0	—				13	0
'Groc' Cutt'' ..	—			1	16	8	1	16	8
	256	3	5	90	14	8	346	18	1

(ii) VALUE OF IMPORTS

	English			Spanish			Total		
Iron	1,562	1	8	3	15	0	1,565	16	8
Woad	882	5	0	—			882	5	0
Oil	128	0	0	29	0	0	157	0	0
Orchil	88	13	4	—			88	13	4
Fruit	52	10	0	—			52	10	0
Sugar	49	0	0	—			49	0	0
Lokeram	30	13	4	—			30	13	4
Canvas	4	10	0	24	10	0	29	0	0
Soap	25	17	6	—			25	17	6
Aniseed	25	0	0	—			25	0	0
Ginger	24	6	0	—			24	6	0
Brazil	—			10	0	0	10	0	0
Smigmates ..	8	10	0	.			8	10	0
Alum	8	0	0	—			8	0	0
Pitch	6	0	0	—			6	0	0
Oranges ..	—			5	0	0	5	0	0
Wax	5	0	0	—			5	0	0
Raisins	3	10	0	—			3	10	0
Spanish Lambskins	—			2	0	0	2	0	0
Pepper	2	0	0	—			2	0	0
Rolls of Bever ..	—			2	0	0	2	0	0
Black Cork ..	1	6	8	—			1	6	8
Marmalade ..		16	8	—				16	8
Liquorice	—				13	4		13	4
Serches	1	6	8	—			1	6	8
	2,909	6	10	76	18	4	2,986	5	2

5. *Mich. 1517–Mich. 1518*

(i) VALUE OF EXPORTS

	English			Spanish			Total		
	£	s.	d.	£	s.	d.	£	s.	d.
Welsh Cloths ..	316	10	0	22	0	0	338	10	0
Tanned Calfskins	97	16	8	14	10	0	112	6	8
Wrought Lead ..	35	0	0	2	17	6	37	17	6
Welsh 'Straits' ..	20	12	6	9	3	9	29	16	3
Friezes ..	1	10	0	4	0	0	5	10	0
Beans	3	6	8	—			3	6	8
Hake		15	0	—				15	0
Goat Skins ..		15	0	—				15	0
'Pell' Edor'' ..		2	6	—				2	6
	476	8	4	52	11	3	528	19	7

(ii) VALUE OF IMPORTS

	English			Spanish			Total		
Iron	1,820	16	8		15	3	1,821	11	11
Oil	454	0	0	—			454	0	0
Woad	110	6	3	—			110	6	3
Soap	108	17	6	—			108	17	6
Alum	77	2	6	—			77	2	6
Sugar	64	16	8	3	0	0	67	16	8
Fruit	59	0	0	4	10	0	63	10	0
Orchil	40	0	0	—			40	0	0
Oranges ..	—			4	0	0	4	0	0
Wax	4	0	0	—			4	0	0
Canvas ..	—			4	0	0	4	0	0
Vinegar	1	10	0	—			1	10	0
Marmalade ..	1	6	8	—			1	6	8
Liquorice	—			1	1	8	1	1	8
Resin	—			1	0	0	1	0	0
Almonds		13	4	—				13	4
Pomegranates ..	—				13	4		13	4
Conserves ..	—				10	0		10	0
Fish	—				3	4		3	4
Serches		13	4	4	10	0	5	3	4
	2,743	2	11	24	3	7	2,767	6	6

APPENDIX B

APPENDIX B

DOCUMENTS FROM THE HIGH COURT OF ADMIRALTY RECORDS
ILLUSTRATING THE TECHNIQUE OF ANGLO-SPANISH TRADE

1. *The Charter Party made between James Castelyn and Philip Barnes in the office of Luis Vivían, Public Notary of Cadiz, on 5 January 1538.*[1]

(f. 19) En el nonbre de Dios Amen sepan quantos esta carta de fletamento vieren como yo Jacome Castelin capitan que soy de la nao nonbrada Sant Jorje surta al presente en el rrio de la villa del Puerto de Santa Maria / otorgo e conosco por esta carta que afleto a vos Felipe Barns mercader yngles estante en esta çiudad de Cadiz que soys presente conbiene a sauer la dicha nao en la forma e manera siguiente—

Primeramente que de / oy en diez e / ocho dias primeros siguientes tienpo aviendo e aquel no perdiendo vos el dicho mercader seays / obligado a me dar e yo a rresçeuir a bordo de la dicha nao en el dicho rrio dozientas botas de vinos encaxcados—

Yten que rresçeuido que aya los dichos vinos aviendo tienpo me / obligo de partir con la dicha nao del dicho rrio e venir a esta vayya de Cadiz donde faziendo bueno pueda rresçeuir en la dicha vayya el rresto de la carga de la dicha nao de vos el dicho mercader de las mercaderias que me quisierdes dar—

Yten que si al tienpo que saliere con la dicha nao del dicho rrio no fiziere buen tienpo para poder estar en la dicha vayya e rresçeuir carga en la dicha nao vaya con ella derechamente en paraje de la villa de Puerto Real donde este con ella rresceuiendo la carga que a bordo se me diere—

(f. 19v) Yten tengo de tener de demora para tomar la carga en esta vayya / o en paraje del dicho Puerto Real e que este presto para partir en seguimiento del viaje para Ynglaterra quarenta e doss dias contados desde el dia que saliere del dicho rrio digo que se entiende que los dichos quarenta e doss dias corren y se cuentan desde seys dias deste presente / mes de henero en que estamos en el qual dicho termino tengo de rresçeuir la carga de la dicha nao en el dicho rrio y en esta vayya / o paraje de

Puerto Real y estar presto para mi viaje tienpo aviendo e aquel no perdiendo—

Yten que rresçeuida la carga de la dicha nao sea / obligado e me / obligo de partir con ella aviendo tienpo como dicho es e yr en seguimiento de mi viaje para la çiudad de Londres que es en el rreyno de Ynglaterra donde ha de ser su derecha descarga de la dicha nao donde de y entregue las mercaderias della a quien fueren dirigidas por los conosçimientos de cargazon

Yten he de aver de flete por cada vna tonelada que son doss botas seys ducados de / oro y de peso y vn sueldo de moneda de Ynglaterra pagados los dichos fletes despues de aver entregado la carga en Ynglaterra en / ocho dias luego siguientes y mas me aveys de pagar por averias de cada vna tonelada doss rreales y medio las quales dichas averias se me han de (f. 20) pagar al tienpo que firmare los conosçimientos de cargazon—

Yten me / obligo de llebar en la dicha nao treynta e doss personas que puedan governar la nao e mas quatro lonbarderos para serviçio della—

E desta manera sobre dicha e con las dichas condiçiones e con cada vna dellas yo el dicho capitan me / obligo e prometo de dar la dicha nao estanca de quilla e costados e cubiertas e bien aparejada e amarinada e con piloto sufiçiente e con las cosas nesçesarias como conbiene a nao que tal viaje ha de fazer e si trova / o buena ventura Dios nos diere aver / o ganar en este dicho viaje se parta entre nos segund costunbre de España—

E yo el dicho Felipe Barnes seyendo presente / otorgo e conosco por esta carta que rresçibo en mi afletada la dicha nao de vos el dicho maestre segund e de la forma e manera que por vos esta dicho e rrecontado e en esta carta se contiene a que me rrefiero y me / obligo e prometo de vos dar la dicha carga e pagar los dichos fletes e averias en el plazo e termino e segund dicho es y no vos dando la dicha carga de vos pagar el flete della de vasio—

E anbas partes para cunplir lo que a cada vno toca / obligamos de asi lo aver por bueno e firme e de no nos salir a fuera e si asy no lo fizieremos e cunplieremos / o a fuera nos salieremos que nos no vala y de mas de no valer que pague la parte de nos yn / obidiente a la (f. 20v) parte / obidiente dozientos ducados de / oro y de peso por su dano e ynterese e pagada la dicha pena / o no que todavia vala lo contenido en este fletamento e para lo asy tener e pagar e guardar e cunplir / obligamos / nuestras

personas e bienes avidos e por aver e espeçialmente yo el dicho
capitan / obligo e ypoteco la dicha nao e sus fletes e aparejos
e yo el dicho mercader la mercaderia que en el fuere cargada—
E para lo mejor cunplir damos e / otorgamos todo poder cunplido libre e llenero [sic] bastante a qualesquier justiçias e
juezes que nos apremien a lo asy cunplir por todo rremedio e
rrigor del derecho asy por execuçion como en / otra qualquier
manera fasta tanto que lo contenido en esta carta aya su cunplido e devido efetto bien asy como si esto que dicho es asy
fuese juzgado e sentençiado por sentençia de juez conpetente
por nos e cada vno de nos pedida e consentida e no apelada e
pasada en cosa juzgada en testimonio de lo qual / otorgamos
esta escritura ante y en presençia de Luys Viuian escriuano
publico de Cadiz e de sus magestades e los testigos de yuso
escritos la qual firmamos de / nuestros nonbres en su rregistro
que es fecha la carta en la dicha çiudad de Cadiz en el poyo e
avdiençia (f. 21) publica della sabado / çinco dias del mes de
henero año del nasçimiento de / nuestro Saluador Jhesucristo
de mill e quinientos e treynta e / ocho años testigos que fueron
presentes Diego de Padilla escriuano de su magestad e Juan
Ginete e Martin Perez de Ariçabalo Vizcayno vezino y estantes
en Cadiz Jacome Castelin Felipe Barnes / enmendado çino/ [1].

I Phellype Barnyes knoleg I ham govntente for to layde in thes chepe
afore rersyd a (   )[2] of laydyng in kuske or elyes in watt I
wyll layde yt—per Phellype Barnyes

I Nycolas Lawford am content to layd in good shipe / callyd the
Geore Doffeld to the summ of xv tons / I saye ffeften ton and to paye
acordyng to the charter party—per me Nycolas Lawford
(f. 21v.)

I John Swetynge ham contynt to lade xx ton ladynge acordynge as
I wos bownd affor Lewys de Avyban and to pay acordynge as by yt
shawll apyr—weche es xxxijˢ starlynge ffor evary ton and avaryges
acostomyd

I Mathewe Hulkott hame content to lade in the George Doffell—
aleuen ton for London—ande to paye for the frayght of euery—ton

---

[1] This appears to refer to an alteration to the document made at the foot of
f. 19v which I have been unable to decipher. The contemporary translation
given in this appendix, however, corresponds with the unaltered original. *Vide
infra*, p. 220. There follows the notary's declaration and 'mark' and underneath, in their own handwriting, the merchants' agreements given above.

[2] Obscured by ink in the manuscript.

acordynge vnto the chartar party ande averege acostomyde—per me Mathewe Hulkott—

I Georg Thornton promysyth for x ton per me Georg Thornton

I Thomas Wall do promes to layd in the sayd good schip / x / ton ladyng per me / Thomas Wall

I George Mason promes to lay yn the good schyp v ton I say fyue ton—per me George Mason

I Mathew Kent promes *and* bynd me bie this my firme to lade abowrde the good ship xv ton of reasons of Malaga conformyng as I am bownde yn a band to Thomas Wilson—per me Mathew Kent

(N.B. – In this and all transcriptions of documents in the book capitals have been given to sacred and proper names whether in the originals or not, but the punctuation has not been modernised. Contracted forms of undoubted meaning have been written out in full, but varied spellings of the same word and errors of the writers are as in the originals.)

2. *A Contemporary English Translation of the Charter Party made between James Castelyn and Philip Barnes.*[1]

(f. 17)   In the name of God amen. / Be yt knowen vnto all men to whome this present charterpartye shall see. / howe that I Jamis Castlyn captayne that ame of the shyppe named Sainct George beinge at this presint at an anker in the ryver of the towne of Porte Sainct Mary I graunte *and* knowlege that by this byll that I doo frayght to yo*u* Phillype Barnis marchant ynglyshman beinge in the citie of Cadyz wher nowe yo*u* beinge present that ys to saye the sayd shippe in the forme and man*er* followinge First that frome this day vnto xviij days fyrst next cum*m*ynge hauynge wynde *and* wether not to be lost. / yo*u* the sayd m*ar*chant ys bounde to gyve me *and* I to receyue aborde of the sayd shyppe in the sayd ryu*er* two hundrythe butt*es* of wynes in casked. / /—

Item that whan the sayd wynes be receyuyd hauynge wynd and wether I bynde me to dep*art* w*ith* the said shippe from the said ryu*er and* cu*m* in to this baye of Cadyz wher then beinge good wether that I may receyue in the sayd baye the rest of the lodynge of the sayd shipe / of yo*u* the said m*ar*chant of marchandyzes what so ever you wyll gyue me.

Item yf that in the tyme of the com*m*ynge owt w*ith* the sayd shippe frome the sayd ryu*er* / were not good wether that she myght abyde (f. 17v) in the said baye to receyue the ladynge in to the said shippe that then I may go w*ith* her strayght ways for socore before the towne of Port Ryall wher as I may tarye w*ith* her receyuynge ther the ladynge that aborde shalbe broght or delyuerd me / /—

Item I ame bound to kepe the taryinge / for to take the lodinge in this baye / or ell*es* wher in the soco*r* in the sayd Port Ryall *and* that I be redy to dep*art* w*ith* her in p*ro*cedinge of the viage for Ynglond w*ith*in xlij days to be reconyd from the daye that she shall cu*m* owt of the sayd ryu*er* I say that ys to be vnderstoud that the sayd xlij days shall rine *and* to be reconyd from the vj day of this presint monthe of Januarii that we be in nowe /. in the w*hich* said terme I ame bound *and* mvst receyue the lodynge

---

[1] P.R.O., H.C.A., Libels, etc., 6, ff. 17–18v.

of the sayd shipe in the said riuer *and* in the sayd baye / or socor
of Port Ryall and to be redy for my viage hauynge wether *and*
that not to be lost / /—

Item that whan I haue receyuyd the ladynge of the sayd shippe
she ys bownd *and* I bynd me for to dep*art* w*ith* her hauynge
wether as ys sayd. / to go in procydinge of my viage for the citye
of Londo*n* w*hich* ys in the realme of Ynglond wher owght to be
her ryght dyscharge of the sayd shippe / wher mvst be delyverd the marchandyzes so laden in here / vnto whom they be
consyned by knowelege of the byll*es* of ladinge—

(f. 18) Item I mvst haue for frayght for every tone w*hich* ys ij
butt*es* for a tonne vj ducatt*es* of gold *and* wayght *and* one
shyllynge st*er*lynge monnye of Ynglond to be payd the sayd
fraight aft*er* the ladynge ys delyverd in Ynglond at viij days
then next followinge / *and* more over yo*u* shall pay me for
averag*es* of eu*er*y ton ij ryall*es* *and* a halffe the w*hich* sayd averag*es*
shalbe payd me at the time that I shall affyrme the byll*es* of
ladynge.

Item I bynd me to have in the sayd shippe / xxxij p*er*sons that
may governe the shippe / *and* more iiij gounn*er*s to serve in her
in the maner above said / *and* w*ith* the said condicyons *and* eu*er*y
one of *them* *and* I the sayd capitane bynd me *and* p*ro*mes to gyue
the said shipp*e* stanche of kele *and* rybb*es* *and* overloft*es* and
well aparellid *and* furnished for the se *and* w*ith* a pilote sufficient
and w*ith* thyng*es* necesarye as owght to be for a shippe that hathe
suche a viage to make /.

And yf other chaunce then good wether or fortune that God
shall giue vs or wyne in the said viage / be dep*art*yd among*es*
vs after the custome of Spayne. / /. and I the said Phillype Barnis
being present graunt *and* knowelege by this p*re*sint wrytynge
that I res [*sic*] *and* take vppone me to frayght the said shippe
of you the said captayne or m*aster* aft*er* the forme *and* man*er*
as by you ys sayd and declaryd in *this* byll *and* conteyned to
w*hich* I refer me *and* bynde me. / *and* p*ro*mese to gyue yo*u* the
said ladynge *and* pay the sayd frayght *and* averig*es* / in the
place *and* terme as aboue ys declaryd. / *and* nott gevynge you
the said lodynge to pay you the frayght offe here as emptye and
bothe p*art*es for to fulfyll that to euery of vs dothe towche we
do bynd vs so for to holde for good and sufficient / (f. 18v) and
not to go owt of yt and yf so we do not kepe. / hold *and* obserue

the same./ and he that of vs shall dysobey *and* go owt the same
so doynge *witho*wt delaye shall pay vnto the p*a*rty of vs obedyent
too hundrythe ducatt*es* of gold *and* wayght for hys domage *and*
interesses and the sayd paynes payd / or not / all way to be in
strenght *and* valore the contentt*es* of this charturp*a*rtye / *and*
so for to hold *and* pay *and* kepe and cu*m*plye. / we bynd vs ow*r*
p*er*sons *and* good*es* that we haue or shall haue./ *and* especially
I the said captayne bynd *and* deposyte the said shipe *and* her
frayght*es* and aparrellyng*es* / and I the said m*a*rchante the
said m*a*rchandyzes that in here shalbe laden./ /—
And for the bett*er* to cu*m*ply we gyve *and* graunte all the hole
pow*er* cu*m*plyed ffre ffull *and* suffyciente to all man*er* of justicys
judg*es* that we shall cu*m* before to cu*m*plye yt for all remedy
and strengthe for the ryght:/ and so to be executyd as in anny
other what so ever man*er* wyse myght be / vnto the co*n*tent*es*
of this present be ffully co*m*plyed of due *and* good effecte / and
yf that be as this ys sayd as yt were judgyde and sentensyd / by
sentence of a judge copetente of auctorite / by vs *and* every of vs
required *and* co*n*sentyd *witho*wt apelacione and as a thynge past
and judgyd. In wytnes of the w*hich* we graunte this wrytynge./
bcfore *and* in presence of Lewys Vivian notary publyque of
Cadyz *and* of themprors maieste and *the* wyttnessys that ware
present *and* sawe thys wrytinge./ w*hich* we do afyrme./ off ow*r*
names in hys regest*er* that ys made by this letter in the said
citye of Cadyz in the howse of awdience publique of yt./ vpon
Saterday the vth day of Januarii / in the yere of ow*r* Lord God
1538./ wytnesys that were present Diego de Padylya a scryvner
of thempo*res* maieste./ *and* John Gynete./ *and* Martyn Perys of
Arysaballo/. Byskayne *and* neghbore abydynge in Cadyz.//

JAMIS CASTLEN
PHILLYPE BARNIS

3. *A Copy of the Bill of Exchange issued by James Castelyn to Thomas Chamber on 27 March 1538.*[1]

This byll wytnessythe that I Jamys Castelyn mercer of London owe vnto Wyllyam Ashley grocer of the same cety / thyrty and one / powndes and fyve shyllynges starlyng monney off Ynglond / whiche ys for so mooche I the sayd Jamys Castelyn have receyvyd in Calyz in Andolozia of Thomas Chamber servantt vnto the sayd Wyllyam Ashley / / for which thyrty and one powndes and fyve shyllynges I promyse shall be well and truly payd vnto the sayd Wyllyam Ashley or hys assyngnes in London / by Wyllyam Castelyn my brother / mercer of the sayd cety / or by hys assyners wythe in ten days afftter the arryvynge of a good shype namyd the George Dowffyld / wher in ys master vnder God for the presentt vyage Chrystofer Sargen / wythe in the ryver of Teamys or in anny other portt where she shall make here dyscharge / and for the true paymentt off the sayd thyrty and one powndes and fyve shyllynges / I the sayd Jamys bynd me / the sayd Wyllyam Castelyn my brother /—and the sayd good shype wythe all here aparell and frayght by vertue of a letter of aturney that my sayd brother gave me in London the sevynthe day of Aprell in the yere of owere Lorde God 1536 by Edwarde Barbare notary / / and more I bynd vs that the sayd Wyllyam Ashley shall stand in sewarte of his monney or the sayd shype shall dyscharge anny off here ladynge owtt of here after here arryvynge / / and also for lake off paymentt at the sayd day yt shall be lawfull for the sayd Wyllyam Ashley or hys assyngnes to take vp the sayd 31 li. 5s be exchange re-change or other wyse at the costes and lossys of vs the sayd Wyllyam Castelyn and Jamys / / and for wyttnes of truthe I the sayd Jamys Castelyn hathe cawsyd 3 bylles to be made of thys tennor where of one beynge complyed / the other to stand to none effecte whyche bylles I have / ffyrmyd wythe my owne hande the 27/day of Marche in ano 1538 / and thus Jhesus send the good shype in saffete / /—

[1] P.R.O., H.C.A., Libels, etc., 6, f. 27. *Vide supra*, p. 27.

I Phellype Bayrnes knovythe
thatt thes a bovfe sayde ys fo /
trovthe /—

          / by me Jamys Castlyn

for wyttnes   Jamys Hall /   / Walter Jobson for wytnys

APPENDIX C

APPENDIX C

DOCUMENTS IN THE ARCHIVO DE PROTOCOLOS DE SEVILLA
ILLUSTRATING THE COMMERCIAL ACTIVITIES OF THE ENGLISH
MERCHANTS IN SPAIN

1. *A Receipt given by Thomas Howell to two Spanish merchants for part payment of a quantity of Olive Oil they owed him.*[1]

Sepan quantos esta ca*rta* vieren como yo Tomas Hoel mercad*er* yngles estante en est*a* çibdad *de* Seuilla oto*rg*o e conosco q*ue* he rreçibido e rreçibi de vos Bartolome de Xeres e Fernan P*er*es ve*zino*s *de*st*a* d*i*cha çibdad q*ue* estades absentes bien asi como sy fuesedes presentes cinq*uent*a q*ui*nt*al*es de azeyte de olivas claros e linpios e *de*spachados del diezmo e alcavala[2] los q*u*al*e*s son q*ue* herad*es* obligados a me dar e pagar de plazo pasado p*art*e en quent*a* de dozientos q*ui*nt*al*es de azeyte que me deveys p*o*r vn contr*at*o de d*e*bdo [*sic*] q*ue* paso ante Franc*isc*o de Cast*ellan*os escriv*ano* pu*b*lico *de* Seuilla en el mes de oc*tubr*e deste año en q*ue* estamos d*e* la fecha d*e*sta ca*rt*a por man*er*a que del d*i*cho d*e*bdo me rrestays deviendo çiento e cinq*ue*nt*a* q*ui*nt*al*es de azeyte e d*e* los d*i*chos çinq*uent*a q*ui*nt*al*es de azeyte me do e oto*rg*o de vos por bien contento e p*a*gado e *en*tregado a toda mi voluntad e rren*uncio* q*ue* no pueda d*e*s*ir* ni alegar q*ue* los no rreçibi de vos como d*i*cho es e si lo dixere o alegare q*ue* me no vala en f*i*rmeza d*e* lo q*u*al otorgue est*a* ca*rt*a de pago ante *e*l escriv*ano* pu*b*lico e t*e*stig*o*s yuso escr*i*ptos q*ue* *e*s fecha en Seuilla *en e*l oficio del escriv*ano* pu*b*lico yuso escr*i*pto martes ocho dias del mes de Novie*n*bre año del nasçimi*ento* de n*uest*r*o* Salua*dor* Jh*e*su*cristo* de mill e quini*ento*s e veynte e q*u*atro años e el d*i*cho Tomas Hoel f*i*rmo su no*n*bre t*e*stig*o*s q*ue* fuero*n* pr*e*sent*e*s Alo*n*so de Caçalla e Melchior de P*o*rt*e*s escriv*ano*s d*e* Seuilla.
Es ca*rt*a de p*a*go a B*a*rtolom*e* de Xeres e Fern*a*n*d* P*er*es de çincuenta qui*n*tal*e*s de az*e*yte.[3]

---

[1] Archivo de Protocolos de Sevilla, *Oficio* V, 1524, *Libro* II, f. 399v.
[2] Spanish taxes. *Vide supra*, p. 46, n. 1.
[3] Underneath are the signatures of Howell and the notaries.

(Howell acknowledges that he has received 50 quintals of olive oil in part payment of 200 quintals owing to him by Bartolome de Xeres and Fernando Peres. It is of interest that reference is made to the *alcabala* (sales tax) and *diezmo* (tenth) of which the oil has already been cleared.)

2. *A Notarial Instrument whereby Robert Thorne made over to Thomas Tison, Powers of Attorney given him by Paul Withypoll.*[1]

Sabado quinze dias del mes de octubre año del nasçimiento del nuestro Saluador Jhesucristo de mill e quinientos e veynte e quatro años.

Sepan quantos esta carta vieren como yo Roberto Torne mercader yngles estante en esta çibdad de Seuilla en nonbre y en boz de Polo Videpolo mercader yngles vezino de la çibdad de Londres del rreyno de Yngalaterra estante que fue en la çibdad de Cadiz por vertud del poder que del tengo que paso ante Fernan Sanches escrivano publico de la dicha çibdad de Cadiz otorgo e conosco que sostituyo en mi lugar e en el dicho nonbre e do e otorgo todo mi poder conplido segund que yo lo tengo del dicho Polo Videpolo e de derecho mas deve valer a Tomas Tizon yngles estante en la dicha çibdad de Cadiz que esta absente asy como sy fuese presente para todas las cosas e casos en el dicho poder que tengo contenidos et quand conplido e bastante poder yo he e tengo del dicho Polo Videpolo para todo lo en el contenido tal e tan conplido e bastante lo otorgo e do e sostituyo en mi lugar e en el dicho nonbre al dicho Tomas Tizon con todas sus ynçidençias e dependençias anexidades e conexidades e lo rrelievo [sic] en el dicho nonbre segund que yo soy rrelevado por el dicho poder e otorgo en el dicho nonbre de lo aver por firme agora e para en todo tienpo e para lo conplir obligo la persona e bienes del dicho Polo Videpolo en cuyo nonbre lo yo otorgo segund que los el obligo por el dicho poder que del tengo fecha la carta en Seuilla en el oficio del escrivano publico yuso escrito sabado quinze dias del mes de octubre año del nasçimiento de nuestro Saluador Jhesucristo de mill e quinientos e veynte e quatro años e el dicho Roberto Torne firmo su nonbre testigos que fueron presentes Alonso de Caçalla e Melchior de Portes escrivanos de Seuilla.[2]

(While in Cadiz on business Paul Withypoll, Robert Thorne's old master, gave the Bristol merchant power of attorney to act on his behalf in those parts. By the above instrument Thorne makes over that power to Thomas Tison.)

[1] Archivo de Protocolos de Sevilla, *Oficio* V, 1524, *Libro* II, f. 293.
[2] Underneath are the signatures of Thorne and the notaries.

3. An Acknowledgement of Debt by Thomas Harrison.[1]

Sepan quantos esta carta vieren como yo Tomas Aresun yngles
vezino desta çibdad de Seuilla en la collacion de Santa Maria
otorgo e conosco que deuo dar e pagar a vos Leon de Haro Bur-
gales vezino desta dicha çibdad en la dicha collacion que estades
absente asy como si fuesedes presente e a quien vn poder ouiere
treynta e quatro mill e cincuenta e seys maravedis desta moneda
los quales son de rresto de dos mill arrouas de azeyte que de vos
rrecibi cunpradas e son en un poder de que so e me otorgo de
vos por bien contento e pagado y entregado a toda mi voluntad
y rrenunçio que no pueda dezir ni alegar que los non rresçebimos
de vos y si lo dixere o alegare que me non vala e a esto en
espeçial rrenunçio la sevsion [sic] de los dos años que ponen las
leyes en derecho de la pecunia non vista ni contada ni rresçebida
ni pagada e a estos dichos treynta e quatro mill e cincuenta e
seys maravedis deste dicho devdo otorgo e prometo e me obligo
de vos los dar e pagar aqui en Sevilla en pas y en salvo sin pleyto
e sin contienda alguna desde nueve dias del mes de febrero que
paso deste año en que estamos de la fecha desta carta dende
fasta quatro meses cunplidos primeros siguientes so pena del
doblo e demas desto si lo ansi no pagare e cunpliere como
dicho es por esta carta doy poder cunplido a qualesquier juezes
e justiçias ansi desta dicha çibdad de Sevilla como de fuera
della doquier y ante quien esta carta fuere mostrada para que
sin yo ni otro por mi so (sic) llamado a juyzio ni rrequerido ni oydo
ni vençido sobre esta dicha rrazon me puedan prender e prendar
e fagan e manden fazer entrega execuçion en mi y en todos mis
bienes muebles e rrayzes doquier que los fallaren e los yo aya e
los vendan e los rrematen luego sin plazo alguno que sea de
alongamiento por que de los maravedis que valieren vos en-
tregen e fagan pago destos dichos maravedis deste dicho devdo
al dicho plaso e de la dicha pena e costas que sobre ello se vos
rrecreçieren sobre lo qual rrenunçio toda apelaçion e suplicaçion
agravio e nulidad bien ansi como si lo suso dicho fuese conten-
dido en juyzio e fuese sobre ello dada sentencia difinitiva e la
sentencia fuese consentidas [sic] de las partes en juyzio e para lo

[1] Archivo de Protocolos de Sevilla, Oficio XV, 1542, Libro I, f. 217v.

ansi tener e guardar e cunplir como dicho es obligo mi persona
e bienes muebles e rrayzes avidos e por aver fecha la carta en
Seuilla *en el* oficio de mi el escriuano yuso escrito sabado quatro
dias del mes de março año del nasçimiento del nuestro Saluador
Jhesucristo de mill e quinientos e quarenta e dos años e lo firmo
de su (   )[1] Fernando de Cacalla e Rodrigo de Mayorga
escriuanos de Seuilla.

Es que de (uo a Leon)[1] de Haro treynta e quatro mill e cinquenta
e seys maravedís de oy en quatro mezes /.[2]

(Thomas Harrison acknowledges a debt of 34,056 *maravedís* to Leon
de Haro a Seville merchant for oil and undertakes to settle within
four months.)

[1] Obscured by ink in the manuscript.
[2] Underneath are the signatures of Harrison and the notaries.

APPENDIX D

APPENDIX D

1. *The Report of the Inspection of the* San Salvador *by officials of
the* Casa de la Contratación *on her return from San Domingo
in March 1545.*[1]

(f. 1) *En el* rrio d*e* Se*ui*lla veynte e ocho de março de mill e
qui*nientos* e q*u*arenta e çinco a*ño*s se visyto esta nao de venida
de S*anto* Domingo de q*ue es* m*aestre* Fra*n*cisco Gallego el moço
el q*u*al d*i*cho m*aestre* y los m*a*rineros y p*a*sag*e*ros declaron q*ue*
sobre el cabo de San Vic*ente* diez leg*u*as *en* la mar salier*on* tres
navios los dos de yngleses y el ot*ro* q*ue* lo abian tom*ado* de
franceses los d*i*chos yngleses y q*ue* rrobar*on* a esta nao todo el
oro y plata q*ue* traya y las p*e*rlas y çiento e veynte e q*u*atro
caxas de aç*u*car*es* y çiento e çinquenta cueros poco m*as* o menos/
la q*u*al d*i*cha nao se visyto po*r* nos el jur*ado* Ju*an* de Almanssa
theni*ente* de fator y P*edro* Mexia[2] theni*ente* de *contado*r *en* la
forma sig*uiente*—

Pasage*r*os

Sancho de Cevallos vez*ino* de Seui*lla*[3]
P*edro* de la Fuente v*ezino* de Tenerife
Luis de Baeça v*ezino* de Baeça
Luis Her*nande*z de Sala*manca*
Antonia Hernandez morisca libre
Alo*nso* de Sepulveda v*ezino* de San M*a*rtin de V*a*ldeyglesyas no
se hallo a la b*i*syt*acion*
Alo*nso* de Ovalle v*ezino* de Sa*n* M*a*rtin no se hallo a la bisyt*acion*
Fray Miguel de la ho*r*den de Santo Domingo salio syn lic*encia*
de la nao y no estubo a la bisyt*acion*

Yndios

no ay ningu*n*d yndio

---

[1] This report was entered at the back of the ship's register. Archivo General
de Indias, Contratación, *Legajo* 2439, *Ramo* 6, *no.* 2.

[2] The famous Spanish humanist. *Vide supra*, p. 149, n.2.

[3] The list of passengers, etc., contains a mark prefixed to each name or
item indicating it as such.

Difuntos

Juan de Bermeo vezino de Bermeo el qual murio en Santo Domingo y alli saco sus bienes y que el maestre dara quenta dello (f. iv) nao / Santo Saluador / maestre Francisco Gallegos— jUDXLV / de Santo Domingo /

Juraron el maestre y marineros y pasageros que no ha venido en esta nao oro ni plata ni perlas ni otra cosa por rregistrar salvo dos partidas vna de doze marcos de perlas que le dio Juan Garcia para Gonsalo y Gaspar Jorge y otra de hasta trezientos pesos poco mas o menos que le dio Juan de Salamanca para Alonso de Leon y que se las tomaron los yngleses y que trae al vale dellas

Declaro Francisco Hernandez que diz que viene por contador y que le nombro el maestre porque el otro que se llamava Juan Valla lo prendieron en la rredondela al tiempo de la partida y declaro que Antonia Hernandez morisca pasagera trae en vna fee aparte çiento e çinquenta pesos de oro y que dize que los escapo de los yngleses en vnos chapuces y que el mismo traya vn marco de perlas por rregistrar que le tomaron los yngleses—

Esto se dio a la dicha y esta asentado en vna fee que presento en el legajo de 545 y no heran sino 115 pesos

Tanbien declaro Juan Diaz despues que la dicha Antonia Hernandez trae por rregistrar çiento e çinquenta pesos—

Juraron los dichos maestre y marineros y pasageros que no vino mas oro ni plata ni perlas ni piedras ni otra cosa y que no saben quien lo trayga ni a havido mas pasageros ni yndios ni difuntos de los de suso conienidos y se cataron las calas y se hizieron las otras diligencias conforme a las hordenanças desta cassa—

(f. 2)

Que en el rregistro dicho estan escritas y asentadas las partidas de cueros y açucares y otras cosas que se traeeron [sic] de las

Yndias de 1545 años *en* la nao no*n*brada San
Saluad*o*r de q*ue* vino por m*aestre* Fran*cisco*
Gallego el moço le q*ual* diz q*ue* çiertos navios
de yngleses le tomaron *en* *el* camino el oro
y plata y çiertos cueros y otr*as* cosas de las
q*ue* venian *en* la d*i*cha nao / esta escri*to* y
asentado lo syguiente—[1]

Re*gistro* de la nao q*ue* Dios salue no*n*brada
San*to* Salvador de q*ue* es *governador* e
m*aestre* Fran*cisco* Gallegos que va cargada
desta muy noble e muy leal çibdad de San*to*
D*omin*go de la Ysla Española de las Yndias
del mar oçeano para la çibdad de Sevilla de
los rreynos de Castilla con buen viaje.[2]

En xxviii de março de jUDXLV *años* en-
trego el d*i*cho m*aest*re Fran*cisco* Gallego a
los of*iciales* d*e*sta cassa los despachos sig*uien*-
tes q*ue* diz q*ue* se los dio el s*eñor* lic*e*nci*ado*
çerrado [*sic*] p*r*esydente de S*anto* Domingo

Vn p*r*oceso grande de dos mill y tantas
hojas q*ue* *e*s la rresyd*enc*ia del p*r*esydente e
oydores de l*a* abdi*enc*ia rreal de la Espa*ñ*ola
y de otr*os* of*iciales* de la d*i*cha abdi*enc*ia q*ue*
la tomo el lic*e*nci*ado* Vadillo diola abierta
q*ue* diz q*ue* la abrieron los yngl*es*es qu*ando*.
la rrobaro*n*

Vn p*r*ocy*s*o cerr*ado* y sellado q*ue* *e*s çierta
ynform*acion* q*ue* se hizo *contra* don Alo*n*so
de Lugo *governado*r de Santa Marta p*o*r
m*andado* del p*r*esyd*ente* e oydores de la
Espa*ñ*ola

Vn libro de pliego horadado q*ue* p*a*resçe
q*uenta*s de la hazi*enda* d*e* su m*agestad* del
c*a*rgo de Alo*n*so de la Torre the*sorero* q*ue*
fue de Santo Domingo

Vn testim*oni*o de las demand*as* y q*ue*rellas
q*ue* se pusyero*n* al p*r*esydente e oydores y

---

[1] This must refer to a separate list or a page of the register which is now
missing.
[2] This is the main heading of the register and no part of the report.

otros oficiales del abdiencia de la Española
Otros pliegos horadados que son las quentas
que se tomaron al thesorero Alonso de la
Torre de las personas de camara de su magestad—

(This document, comprising the last two folios of the register of the *San Salvador*, is an entry made by two officials of the *Casa de la Contratación* after they had inspected the ship on 28 March 1545. It contains a list of the passengers, including one dead body brought back to Spain for burial (f. 1). The questioning of the passengers and crew is mentioned and the result (f. 1v). It is evident that there was a list of goods taken by Reneger made either on a separate sheet or on a part of the register now missing, for reference is made to it (f. 2). Finally, there is a list of documents brought by Gallego from San Domingo, one of which, he said, had been opened by the English-men (f. 2v).)

2. *A Petition submitted by the merchants despoiled by Reneger to the officials of the* Casa de la Contratación *demanding the immediate arrest of English Property in Andalusia.*[1]

Muy magníficos señores

Los mercaderes que aqui abaxo firmamos nuestros nonbres por nos y en nonbre de todos los otros mercaderes e tratantes en las Yndias dezimos que como a vuestras mercedes e a todos es notorio que çiertas naos de yngleses an tomado todo el oro e plata e perlas y çierta cantidad de açucar e cueros que venia en la nao de Francisco Gallego de Santo Domingo lo qual se a fecho contra el amistad que ay entre los rreynos de su magestad e los rreynos de Yngalaterra e por que en lo suso dicho conviene poner algun rremedio y el que mas de presente conviene es enbargar todos los bienes e hazienda de yngleses que se hallaren ansi en esta çibdad como en Cadiz e Sanlucar y en el Condado e otras partes para que podamos ser satisfechos del daño que nos an fecho lo qual a lugar de se hazer luego con brevedad syn esperar mas ynformaçion pues basta la que agora ay y de aver dilaçion daria cabsa que los bienes de los dichos yngleses fuesen trasportados e pues consta de lo suso dicho a vuestras mercedes pedimos y con el acatamiento devido rrequerimos manden luego hazer el enbargo en esta çibdad y en las otras partes que arriba dezimos en los bienes de los dichos yngleses y si ansi lo hizieren faran lo que deven fasta que su magestad mande proveer sobre ello lo que se deva de hazer e proseguir en el negocio donde no les protestamos todos los daños fechos hasta agora por los dichos yngleses e todos los mas que hizieren y de como lo pedimos e rrequerimos a vuestras mercedes dezimos al presente escriuano e testigos nos lo den por testimonio e de todo lo que los yngleses ovieren traspuesto o traspusieren dende que vino esta nueva si vuestras mercedes no lo provean luego como pedimos protestamos sea a cargo de vuestras mercedes e de coballo de sus bienes e hazienda e sobre todo pedimos justicia—Hernando de Avila Hernando de Xerez Luys de Armenta Diego de Medina Juan de Alfaro Gonçalo Jorje Alonso de Leon Rodrigo Perez /

[1] Archivo General de Indias, Patronato, *Legajo* 265, *Ramo* 59.

(This petition is undated but must have been made before 27 March 1545 when the order for the arrest of English property was issued from the *Casa de la Contratación*. The Spanish merchants insist upon the immediate seizure of the goods of Englishmen before they can be carried away. Reference is made to other recent English outrages and it is emphasized that swift action must be taken on this occasion.)

3. *A Report of the Spanish Treasure taken from the* San Salvador *by Robert Reneger.*[1]

(f. 1)   1545

Relaçion del oro / y plata y otras cosas que venieron por el mes de março deste presente año de mill y quinientos y quarenta y çinco años en la nao nonbrada Saluador que viene de Santo Domingo de que vino por maestre Françisco Gallegos—la qual tomaron los yngleses—

	para Francisco Hernandes de Vtrera cccij pesos	cccij pesos
	para Juan de Mendoça cc pesos	cc pesos
	para el jurado Alonso Banegas	cccxvj pesos
	para Anton Manuel ccxxxiiij pesos	ccxxxiiij pesos
perlas	para Juan Rodriguez de Baeça xij	
xij marcos	marcos de perlas comunes	
	para Ysauel Aryas xxv pesos	xxv pesos
	para Catalina Rodriguez e Leonor Claros cc pesos	cc pesos
	para el jurado Alonso Vanegas	cxxjx pesos
	para Alonso de Xerez liij pesos	liij pesos
	para Hernando Tellez c pesos	c pesos
xxv marcos	para Geronimo de Herrera / xxv marcos perlas	
xij marcos	para Juan de Castro xij marcos de perlas	
xxxviij marcos	para Francisco de Castro xxxviij marcos de perlas comunes	
	para Luysa de Alfaro cxcij pesos	cxcij pesos
	para Gregorio de Ayala cl pesos	cl pesos
	para Tomas de Aryson[2] xxxviij pesos	xxxviij pesos
	para Juan de Alfaro ccxxxiiij pesos	ccxxxiiij pesos
	para Melchior de Carrion cclxviij pesos	cclxviij pesos
	para Alonso de Aravx cxvj pesos	xcvj pesos [*sic*]

---

[1] Archivo General de Indias, Patronato, *Legajo* 265, *Ramo* 3.
[2] Thomas Harrison.

perlas (f. 1v)

	para Teresa de Muñoz vj marcos de	
vj marcos	perlas / y mas xxxj pesos	xxxj pesos
	para Luys Hernandez Vizcochero	cclxvij pesos
	para Hernando de Xerez de Baeça	ccxxv pesos
	para el jurado Luys Hernandez	ccccv pesos
	para Pedro Cauallero lxxxj pesos	lxxxj pesos
	para Luys Hernandez Coronado	l pesos
	para Hernan Veltran ccxjx pesos	ccxjx pesos
	para Diego y Albaro Veltran l mar-	
l marcos	cos de perlas comunes	
	para Baltasar de Caçalla vj marcos	
vj marcos /	de perlas comunes y xxxvij pesos	xxxvij pesos
	para Juan Sanchez cxcviij pesos	cxcviij pesos
	para Rodrigo de Yllescas clxjx pesos	clxjx pesos
	para Hernan Perez de Jaen	cccclxx pesos
	para Galceran del Selergue lxxxiiij	
	pesos	lxxxiiij pesos
	para Rodrigo Franco cxxxv pesos	cxxxv pesos
	para el dicho ccl pesos	ccl pesos
	para Hernando de la Fuente	jUcccxxxvij pesos
	para Hernando de Xerez y Juan	
	Nuñez	jU pesos
	para el mariscal Diego Cauallero	cciiij pesos
	para Hernando Davilla cxjx pesos	cxjx pesos
	para el dicho Hernando Davilla ciiij	
	pesos	ciiij pesos
	para Francisco de Molina el moço	cc pesos
xxvij marcos	para Melchior de Carrion xxvij marcos de perlas comunes	

(f. 2)

perlas	para Hernan Sanchez de la Barrera	D pesos
	para Hernando Guillen cccjx pesos	cccjx pesos
	para Alonso Sanchez / o Martin San-	
	chez de la Barrera x marcos de	
x marcos	perlas comunes	
xxv marcos	para el jurado Juan de la Barrera xxv marcos de perlas comunes	
	para Geronimo de Herrera Dcxxviij	Dcxxviij pesos
	pesos para el jurado Gaspar de Torres	cj pesos

para Geronimo de Herrera cxiiij
     pesos   cxiiij pesos
para Pedro de la Fuente pasajero   Dcccxlj pesos

(This list is incomplete. It makes no mention of the hides and sugar taken by Reneger and does not specify the gold. In fact it may well be the list which Philip's ministers rejected as unsatisfactory. *Vide infra*, p. 246.)

4. *A Letter to Prince Philip from officials of the* Casa de la Contratación *recounting the difficulties arising from the arrest of English Property in Andalusia.*[1]

(f. 1)   Muy alto y muy poderoso señor

Vuestra alteza nos enbio a mandar que juntamente con el marques de Cortes entendiesemos en enbargar y secrestar de bienes de yngleses otra tanta cantidad como paresçiese que montava lo que tomaron los dichos yngleses y mas la tercera parte dello y en cunplimiento de lo que vuestra alteza enbio a mandar hezimos enbargar todos los bienes de yngleses que hasta agora se an podido / aver como vuestra alteza lo mandara ver por los testimonios que alla se enbian / y agora visto que en la contratacion de los azeytes y vinos asy desta çibdad como de la çibdad de Xeres y todos los puertos y partes destas comarcas rreçiben mucho daño en que como se enbargan los bienes de los dichos yngleses no vienen a contratar como solian y el marques de Cortes escribe a vuestra alteza dandole rrelaçion dello y parescio nos hazer lo mismo y avisar a vuestra alteza que con esto que se haze y con estar rretirados los yngleses de la contratacion que solian hazer / con la carestia del pan que al presente ay se espera que padeceran mucha necessidad porque ellos (f. 1v) principalmente conpraban todos los mas de los vinos y azeytes de todos estos pueblos y al no hazerse el mucho daño que se rrecibe asy en las rrentas rreales de su magestad como sus subditos y los destos pueblos que biben y se valen de sus cosechas y si vuestra alteza fuese seruido podria mandar suspender el enbargo que se haze a los yngleses y que pudiesen tratar libremente y que no se les enbargare mas pues es poco lo que falta de la cantidad que esta mandado por vuestra alteza que se enbargue y tornando al trato que solian thener en esto seria muy grand beneficio el que rreçibirian los vezinos destos pueblos y no seria perjuyzio de las rrentas rreales de su magestad y porque por los testimonios que se enbian y por lo que el marques de Cortes escribe a vuestra alteza mandara ver lo demas que sobre esto se

[1] Archivo General de Indias, Contratación, *Legajo* 5103.

puede dezir a ello nos remitimos nuestro señor escrito en primero de octubre de 1545 /

(This document is of particular interest for the light it throws upon Anglo-Spanish trade at this time. The officials report that they have carried out Philip's orders to arrest English property in Andalusia and the result has been disastrous—for the Spaniards! The English merchants were the largest buyers of the wine and oil of those parts, but now, because of the arrest, they did not trade as they used to do. So great was the distress of the people as a result that the officials and the Marqués de Cortés were writing to advise Philip to relax the embargo.)

5. *Two Documents illustrating the difficulty experienced by the Emperor in obtaining from Spain a Detailed Account of Reneger's Plunder.*[1]

(*a*) Extract from a letter written by Ochoa de Luyando[2] to the officials of the *Casa de la Contratación* on 29 March 1546.

Samano mi señor departio para su casa abra doss o tres dias y a esta causa no va carta suya con esta de su alteza por la qual se enbia a mandar a vuestras mercedes que con toda deligencia entiendan en averiguar y saber lo que verdaderamente Renegat cosario yngles tomo en la nao que los dias pasados venia de las Yndias y bien aberiguado enbien rrelaçion dello y el rregistro duplicado si se houiere traydo o vn traslado avtorizado del que a esa casa se traxo porque la rrelaçion que vuestras mercedes enbiaron a Somono [sic] esta avtorizada [sic] no basta / vuestras mercedes deben luego proveer como se enbie el traslado del rregistro avtorizado y la ynformacion que se podiere aver porque todo ello se ha de enbiar a su magestad y conviene que venga con breuedad /

(This letter reveals that over a year after the despoliation of the *San Salvador* Philip was still demanding from Seville details of the plunder. Apparently a list had been sent which had proved inadequate. This may be the one contained in document no. 3 of this appendix. Samano, Philip's secretary, mentioned in this letter, issued the order for the arrest of English property in Andalusia.)

(*b*) A second letter from Ochoa de Luyando to the officials of the *Casa de la Contratación* on the same subject. Dated 12 May 1546.

Muy magnificos señores

Su alteza ha mandado rresponder a la que vuestras mercedes le escrivieron en xij del pasado lo que veran por su carta que va con esta y en ello no tengo yo que dezir mas de que del rreçibo manden dar aviso /

[1] Archivo General de Indias, Contratación, *Legajo* 5010.
[2] Probably at this time secretary of Samano.

los otros dias se escrivio a vuestras mercedes que enbiasen
rrelacion de lo que valio el oro y plata de la nao que tomaron los
yngleses y si huvo rregistro se enbiase vn traslado del avtorizado
porque se avia de enbiar a Flandes a su magestad y hasta agora
no han rrespondido vuestras mercedes en ello cosa alguna / y de
Flandes dan prisa por el / con el primer correo deven vuestras
mercedes mandar a lo enbiar o avisar de lo que en ello hay.
Nuestro Salvador guarde y acreça las muy magnificas personas y
casas de vuestras mercedes como dessean de Madrid a xij de
Mayo de 1546

besa las manos a vuestras mercedes

su servidor

OCHOA DE LUYANDO *secretario*

(This letter was sent to remind the officials that they had not replied
to (a) and to tell them to send the required information by the first
courier. It is stressed that the Emperor is demanding it in Flanders.)

APPENDIX E
BIBLIOGRAPHY

APPENDIX E

BIBLIOGRAPHY

(a) *Primary Sources*

I. ENGLISH MANUSCRIPTS.

Public Record Office

Early Chancery Proceedings.
Exchequer K.R. Customs.
Exchequer K.R. Lay Subsidy Rolls.
Exchequer K.R. Memoranda Rolls.
High Court of Admiralty.

i. *Oyer and Terminer.*
  Examinations   Bundles 33, 34.

ii. *Instance and Prize.*
  Examinations   Bundles 2–6, 92, 93.
  Exemplifications   Bundles 1–3.
  Libels, Allegations,
  Decrees and Sentences.   Bundles 6, 13–15.

Star Chamber Proceedings.
State Papers, Henry VIII.
State Papers, Miscellaneous.
State Papers, Scotland, Edward VI.

British Museum

Cotton MSS. Vespasian C III, C IV, C VII.
Harleian MS. 36.
Lansdowne MS. 171.
Add. MS. 28, 420.

Somerset House

Registers of Wills proved in the Prerogative Court of Canterbury.

Drapers' Hall, London

Ledger of Thomas Howell.

Hatfield House

Salisbury MS. 137.

Southampton Civic Centre
  Book of Oaths and Ordinances, 1473–1704.
  Brokage Books, Hen. VIII.
  Local Port Books, Hen. VII–Hen. VIII.

2. SPANISH MANUSCRIPTS.

Archivo Histórico Nacional, Madrid
  Sección Histórica.
  Inquisiciones de la Corona de Aragón y Navarra, Cartas del Con-
  sejo de la General Inquisición a las Inquisiciones de la Corona de
  Aragón y Navarra, Libro VII (9 Enero 1536–8 Enero 1548).

Archivo General de Indias, Sevilla
  Patronato Real, Legajo 265.
  Casa de la Contratación, Legajos 1,079, 2,439, 5,103, 5,010.

Archivo de Protocolos de Cádiz
  Oficio XIX   1545–53.

Archivo de Protocolos de Sevilla
  Oficio I   1513, 1516, 1525.
  Oficio IV   1522.
  Oficio V   1513, 1523–27.
  Oficio XV·   1509, 1516, 1539–40, 1542, 1545,
                                 1549, 1551.

Archivo Histórico de Protocolos de Vizcaya, Bilbao
  Miscellaneous Registers.

3. ENGLISH PRINTED SOURCES.

Public Record Office Publications
  Acts of the Privy Council.
  Calendar of Patent Rolls.
  Calendar of State Papers, Foreign Series, Elizabeth.
  Letters and Papers of the Reign of Henry VIII.
  Proceedings and Ordinances of the Privy Council of England.
  State Papers, Henry VIII.
  Statutes of the Realm.

Blake, J. W. *Europeans in West Africa, 1450–1560.* (Hakluyt Society,
  Second Series, nos. lxxxvi, lxxxvii.) London, 1942. 2 vols.
Campbell, W. (ed.) *Materials for a History of the Reign of Henry VII.*
  (*Rolls Series.*) London, 1873–77. 2 vols.
Ellis, Sir Henry, (ed). *Original Letters illustrative of English History,*
  Second Series. London, 1827. 4 vols.

Gairdner, J. (ed.) *Memorials of King Henry the Seventh.* (*Rolls Series.*) London, 1858.

Hakluyt, Richard. *The Principal Navigations, Voyages, Traffiques and Discoveries of the English Nation.* (Maclehose Edition.) Glasgow, 1903–5. 12 vols.

Hume, M. A. S. *Chronicle of King Henry VIII. of England.* London, 1889.

Marsden, R. G. *Select Pleas in the Court of Admiralty,* vol. i. (Selden Society, vol. vi for 1892.) London, 1894.

Marsden, R. G. 'Voyage of the Barbara to Brazil, Anno 1540', *The Naval Miscellany* (Navy Records Society), vol. ii. London, 1912.

Rymer, Thomas (ed.). *Foedera, conventiones, litterae et cujuscunque generis acta publica inter reges Angliae et alios quosvis imperatores, reges, pontifices, principes vel communitates.* 3rd edition. The Hague, 1739–45. 10 vols.

Tawney, R. H. and Power, E. (ed.) *Tudor Economic Documents.* London, 1924. 3 vols.

4. FOREIGN PRINTED SOURCES.

Calendar of State Papers, Spain.

Calendar of State Papers, Venice.

Colección de Documentos Inéditos para la Historia de España. By M. F. Navarrete, Miguel Salvá, Pedro Sainz de Baranda, el Marques de la Fuensanta del Valle, *et al.* Madrid, 1842–95. 113 vols.

Bermúdez Plata, Don Cristóbal. *Catálogo de Pasajeros a Indias durante los Siglos XVI, XVII y XVIII,* vol. i (1509–1534). Seville, 1940.

Carriazo, Juan de Mata (ed.) *Historia del Emperador Carlos V, escrita por su cronista el magnífico caballero Pedro Mexía.* Madrid, 1945.

Cuevas, Zarco. *Catálogo de los Manuscritos Castellanos de la Real Biblioteca del Escorial,* vol. ii. Madrid, 1911.

Echegaray, D. Carmelo de. *Indices de documentos referentes a la Historia Vasca que se contienen en los Archivos de Brujas.* San Sebastian, 1929.

Gilliodts-van Severen, L. *Cartulaire de l'ancien Consulat d'Espagne d Bruges.* Bruges, 1901.

(b) *Secondary Works*

Barbadillo Delgado, Pedro. *Historia de la Ciudad de Sanlúcar de Barrameda.* Cadiz, 1942.

Boyd, P. *Roll of the Drapers' Company of London.* Croydon, 1934.

Busch, W. *England under the Tudors,* vol. i., *King Henry VII,* London, 1895.

Carande, Ramon. *Carlos V y sus Banqueros. La Hacienda Real de Castilla*. Madrid, 1949.

Carande, Ramon. *Carlos V y sus Banqueros. La Vida Económica de España en una Fase de su Hegemonía, 1516–1556*. Madrid, 1943.

Castro y Bravo, F. *Las naos españolas en la carrera de las Indias*. Madrid, 1927.

Connell-Smith, G. 'English Merchants trading to the New World in the early Sixteenth Century'. (*Bulletin of the Institute of Historical Research*, vol. xxiii, no. 67, May 1950.)

Connell-Smith, G. 'Roberto Reneger, Precursor de Drake'. (*Anuario de Estudios Americanos*, Tomo vii, Seville, 1950.)

Connell-Smith, G. 'The Ledger of Thomas Howell'. (*The Economic History Review*, Second Series, vol. iii, no. 3, 1951.)

Corbett, Sir Julian S. *Drake and the Tudor Navy*. London, 1898. 2 vols.

Corbett, Sir Julian S. *Sir Francis Drake*. London, 1890.

Fernández Alvarez, Manuel. 'Orígenes de la rivalidad naval hispano-inglesa en el siglo XVI'. (*Revista de Indias*, Año viii, Núms 28–29, 1947.)

Finot, J. *Relations commerciales et maritimes entre la Flandre et l'Espagne au Moyen Age*. Lille, 1898.

Froude, J. A. *English Seamen in the Sixteenth Century*. London, 1895.

Goris, J. A. *Etude sur les Colonies Marchandes Méridionales (Portugais, Espagnols, Italiens) à Anvers de 1488 à 1567*. Louvain, 1925.

Gras, N. S. B. *The Early English Customs System*. Cambridge, Mass., 1918.

Hamilton, E. J. *American Treasure and the Price Revolution in Spain, 1501–1650*. Cambridge, Mass., 1934.

Hamilton, E. J. 'The Role of Monopoly in the Overseas Expansion and Colonial Trade of Europe before 1800'. (*The American Economic Review*, vol. xxxviii, no. 2, May 1948.)

Haring, C. H. *Trade and Navigation between Spain and the Indies in the time of the Hapsburgs*. Cambridge, Mass., 1918.

Harrisse, Henry. *John Cabot, the Discoverer of North-America and Sebastian his Son*. London, 1896.

Holdsworth, Sir William S. *A History of English Law*. London, 1922–52. 13 vols.

Hume, M. A. S. *Españoles é Ingleses en el Siglo XVI*. Madrid, 1903.

Johnson, A. H. *The History of the Worshipful Company of the Drapers of London*. Oxford, 1914–22. 5 vols.

Kingsford, C. L. *Prejudice and Promise in XVth Century England*. Oxford, 1925.

Klein, J. *The Mesta. A Study in Spanish Economic History, 1273–1836*. Cambridge, Mass., 1920.

Larraz, José. *La Epoca del Mercantilismo en Castilla* (*1500–1700*). Madrid, 1943.

Mattingly, G. 'The Reputation of Doctor de Puebla'. (*The English Historical Review*, vol. lv, no. 217, January, 1940.)

Power, E. and Postan, M. M. (ed.) *Studies in English Trade in the Fifteenth Century*. London, 1933.

Quinn, D. B. 'Edward IV and Exploration'. (*The Mariner's Mirror*, vol. xxi, no. 3, July 1935.)

Rogers, J. E. T. *A History of Agriculture and Prices in England*. Oxford, 1866–1902, 7 vols.

Ruddock, Alwyn A. *Italian Merchants and Shipping in Southampton, 1270–1600*. University College, Southampton, 1951.

Ruddock, Alwyn A. 'London Capitalists and the Decline of Southampton in the early Tudor Period'. (*The Economic History Review*, Second Series, vol. ii, no. 2, 1949.)

Ruddock, Alwyn A. 'The Earliest Records of the High Court of Admiralty (1515–1558)'. (*Bulletin of the Institute of Historical Research*, vol. xxii, no. 66, November 1949.)

Sayous, A. E. 'Partnerships in the Trade between Spain and America and also in the Spanish Colonies in the Sixteenth Century'. (*Journal of Economic and Business History*, vol. i, no. 2, February 1929.)

Schäfer, E. *El Consejo Real y Supremo de las Indias*, Tomo i. Seville, 1935.

Schanz, G. *Englische Handelspolitik gegen Ende des Mittelalters*. Leipzig, 1881. 2 vols.

Singer, Sir Charles. *The Earliest Chemical Industry*. London, 1948.

Taylor, E. G. R. *Tudor Geography, 1485–1583*. London, 1930.

Temperley, Gladys. *Henry VII*. London, 1917.

Williams, C. H. *The Making of the Tudor Despotism*. London, 1935.

Williamson, J. A. *Hawkins of Plymouth*. London, 1949.

Williamson, J. A. *Maritime Enterprise, 1485–1558*. Oxford, 1913.

Williamson, J. A. *Sir John Hawkins*. Oxford, 1927.

Williamson, J. A. *The Age of Drake*. London, 1946.

Williamson, J. B. *The Foreign Commerce of England under the Tudors*. Oxford, 1883.

Yamey, B. S. 'Scientific Bookkeeping and the Rise of Capitalism' (*The Economic History Review*, Second Series, vol. i, nos. 2 and 3, 1949.)

INDEX